HOW TO DAY TRADE FOR A LIVING

A Beginner's Guide to Tools and
Tactics, Money Management,
Discipline and Trading Psychology

ANDREW AZIZ

©Founder and CEO, Peak Capital Trading
www.PeakCapitalTrading.com

©Founder and Trader, Bear Bull Traders
www.BearBullTraders.com

Published in Vancouver, BC, Canada

andrew@bearbulltraders.com
www.BearBullTraders.com

First published in 2015
Copyright © Andrew Aziz 2020

Aziz, Andrew
How to Day Trade for a Living: A Beginner's Guide to Tools and Tactics, Money Management, Discipline and Trading Psychology

Cover design by Volodymyr Pashchuk
Book typesetting by Nelly Murariu at pixbeedesign.com

Printed by Createspace

DISCLAIMER

The author and *www.BearBullTraders.com* ("the Company"), including its employees, contractors, shareholders and affiliates, is NOT an investment advisory service, a registered investment advisor or a broker-dealer and does not undertake to advise clients on which securities they should buy or sell for themselves. It must be understood that a very high degree of risk is involved in trading securities. The Company, the authors, the publisher and the affiliates of the Company assume no responsibility or liability for trading and investment results. Statements on the Company's website and in its publications are made as of the date stated and are subject to change without notice. It should not be assumed that the methods, techniques or indicators presented in these products will be profitable nor that they will not result in losses. In addition, the indicators, strategies, rules and all other features of the Company's products (collectively, "the Information") are provided for informational and educational purposes only and should not be construed as investment advice. Examples presented are for educational purposes only. Accordingly, readers should not rely solely on the Information in making any trades or investments. Rather, they should use the Information only as a starting point for doing additional independent research in order to allow them to form their own opinions regarding trading and investments. Investors and traders must always consult with their licensed financial advisors and tax advisors to determine the suitability of any investment.

CONTENTS

CHAPTER 10

NEXT STEPS FOR BEGINNER TRADERS   287

FOREWORD

"Individually, we are one drop. Together, we are an ocean."
—Ryunosuke Satoro

T he first time I met Andrew, he taught me an important lesson.

I was sitting in Sarabeth's, my absolute favorite weekend brunch spot in New York City, waiting to meet a new acquaintance in the trading community who I was starting to hear a lot about. For the most part, I keep my head down and spend 85 percent of my time running our proprietary trading desk in NYC. And while my firm also has a separate trader education division (SMB Training), I frequently am made fun of by our staff for not knowing others in the trading education space. Andrew walks in. We meet. We order. We talk shop. He politely indulges me in my complete lack of knowledge of his work and most things outside of the walls of SMB Capital, that prop firm I co-founded in 2005.

Sipping on my fresh brewed iced tea, with extra lemon, I wait for the answer to the question I have just posed to Andrew, *"Hey, how many members are a part of Bear Bulls?"* Andrew matter-of-factly replies, *"Over 600."*

I literally almost spit out my iced tea. I think to myself, *"You are such an idiot. How do you not know this guy?"*

What an impressive number of members to have inspired in such a short period of time. More importantly, he schooled me on the culture of learning he had built for retail and independent traders at his trading community, Bear Bull Traders. Andrew taught me to never again show up to another meeting with a leader in the retail and independent trader space, like him, unprepared and uninformed about the important work they are doing with and for so many.

I greatly appreciated that lesson and I still remember it every day in my work.

Since that conversation, Bear Bull Traders has continued to grow. It is not just the number of members that are impressive, but rather the entire community and learning culture that Andrew has built. Let me share a few anecdotes.

After my clueless brunch, SMB and Bear Bull Traders partnered on an educational webinar for their trading community. Here is where I learned quickly about the goodness of their culture - their learning culture. Normally when asked to present for a webinar, I am also asked what topic I would like to present. Unfortunately, but in reality, no one really cares what it is as long as they are getting that trading author and Co-Founder of SMB to present. Except that is when I was asked to present to the Bear Bull Traders community. With them, I had an entirely different and pleasantly surprising experience. A key member of their community suggested that he present a PlayBook trade to me and receive my critical feedback on his work. Excuse me? That would be something I had never done before and a smashing learning opportunity for webinar attendees. Who were these people (at Bear Bull Traders)?

So we chose the topic: *How to become a consistently profitable trader using the PlayBook.*

Let me provide some context for this webinar topic. The second book I wrote is called *The PlayBook*, and it lays out how a serious trader can build their trading business. In short, you build a PlayBook of very specific trades that you trade best. And you then just trade that PlayBook. Producing a PlayBook trade is an exercise that our homegrown new traders at SMB utilize daily to develop their business. Andrew writes convincingly inside this book about the importance of a business plan to a trader's success. So in its truest context, the ask for this webinar topic was:

"I am a serious retail trader who would like to show you my serious work so that our trading community of serious developing traders will make real and significant progress."

And we had a substantive and high-level teaching session on this member's PlayBook that truly benefited their trading community.

In addition, of course, the webinar was packed and as large as any of the ones I have participated in. This author and trader was sensing a pattern with this Bear Bull Traders community.

And then there was the Q&A. This always unmasks the culture of a trading community. Are the questions about all of the money our trades make or about the process that leads to success? Their questions were about the process. Or said better, the type of questions we would expect our professional developing traders from our own desk to ask of me.

Important communities require great leaders. In my experience, great leaders think about how they can help others before anything else. I found that with Andrew.

So Andrew and I had built a bit of a relationship, but admittedly we were still feeling each other out. Around the same time, I had recently signed on to become a board member for Traders4ACause, and I was assisting with the creation of the agenda of speakers for our in-person Las Vegas event. We were seeking quality speakers, who were real traders, who offered real value to the trading community, and were not the hucksters that all too often permeate trader education. I thought of Andrew.

I reached out to Andrew to see if he might speak and help us promote the charity event. Usually this requires a long presentation of how involvement in the charity would help the presenter and their company. We actually have a lengthy slide deck that says as much. Within a few minutes of the conversation though, Andrew said he was in. And not only that, Bear Bull Traders was in. And not only that, he would be donating, and he would be alerting his mailing list to encourage his community members to attend. He could not have been more generous and gracious, and all without even caring or knowing how it might help him and/or his company.

And I cannot leave out the time that SMB and Bear Bull Traders were partnering to do another webinar for his trading community. This time we settled on: *Collective Learning In A Trading Community / Including An Inside Look At How An NYC Proprietary Trading Firm Mentors Their New Traders.* Andrew suggested SMB promote during the webinar, as a resource to his trading community, our flagship training program, SMB DNA. An avid traveler, he mentioned this while piping into a Zoom call with his team and SMB from the trails of Machu Picchu. He had to climb a bit higher to make the connection. Our marketing team from SMB Training, our education division, responded that we ought to track those who sign up from his community and compensate Bear Bull Traders for any sales. We all agreed. Then, about fifteen minutes later, Andrew shot me an email, directing any cut of sales owed to Bear Bull Traders to be sent to Traders4ACause, as that was a better landing spot for the money. Who does that?

Great leaders of important communities attract the following of serious and quality people. I have found that to be the case with Bear Bull Traders. Recently, Bear Bull Traders was having an event in NYC for its members and asked Steve Spencer, my trading partner, Dr. Brett Steenbarger, who coaches and mentors our traders and some of the most successful hedge fund and institutional traders in the world, and myself to attend. I could not attend because of a prior commitment to my son, but my partner relayed that the event was packed and filled with serious traders. For the next morning, Andrew and I had scheduled an early breakfast in the city to catch up on things. He asked if he could bring along a few key members from the Bear Bull Traders community to meet with me as well. To me, a few are two, maybe three. Eight key members showed up from Bear Bull Traders to chat, with another sending a text message apologizing for not being able to make it. It was a wonderful way to spend a Saturday AM in NYC - talking trading with serious traders.

If there is a seminal lesson I have learned in running a trading firm since 2005 and being a professional trader since the late 90s, it is that no one becomes a great trader alone. On the home page of Bear Bull Traders you can find that lesson: Don't Trade Alone.

SMB is firstly a PnL (profit and loss) proprietary trading desk, located in NYC. We hire traders, train them, pay them, and provide them with all of the resources they need to succeed. We are quite proud that one of our traders just crossed 10 million in trading profits for the year, with two not far behind. And as I write, it is June. When this remarkable trader crossed this PnL milestone, the first thing he did was personally call all of the people at the firm who had helped him achieve this goal. One person in particular he thanked was our floor manager, who had encouraged him to express his best trading ideas also with Options, which had led to a significant increase in profits. In this book, Andrew rightly advocates that retail and independent traders need continuous education.

So what I say next, I hope inspires the next generation of retail and independent traders. All of our traders trade and develop on a Team. They train with the firm and then move to a specific team run by a highly successful senior trader. No junior trader does anything by themselves. They do not spend one day of training and development by themselves. The importance of communities, serious trading communities like Bear Bull Traders, is that you develop with other traders who can significantly help you progress. Andrew teaches this point to you in this book.

Trading is hard. As Andrew counsels in this book, it is not a get-rich-quick scheme. You are not owed the right to succeed. It will challenge you psychologically, even making you doubt whether you will succeed. In this book, Andrew tackles trading psychology, the 800-pound gorilla on the desk of every trader at every level. It is fair to expect that you will have a legitimate opportunity to find out how good you can be as a trader. Quality trading communities give you that chance.

Our trading coach, Dr. Brett Steenbarger, hands clenched in fists, said to a new hires class, *"We are meant to do something great."* Working with serious retail and independent traders, in a terrific community, gives you that opportunity to do "something great".

You are in good hands, with a good person, who has built an important community and culture for serious independent and retail traders. Enjoy Andrew's latest contribution to the trading community.

Mike Bellafiore
New York City, June 2020

Mike Bellafiore is the Co-Founder of SMB Capital, a proprietary trading firm in NYC, and SMB Training, their trader education division. Mike is also the author of the "trading classic" *One Good Trade* and *The PlayBook*.

CHAPTER 1

INTRODUCTION

2020 HINDSIGHT

The first version of this book was published in the summer of 2015 and, as of today, has been an international best seller for five consecutive years. It has also been published thus far in five languages (English, Japanese, Chinese, Vietnamese and Portuguese). The book remains a most "wished-for" on Amazon and various other platforms in several categories related to online trading, strategy, business and finance, as well as trading and investment analysis.

In the early months of 2020, my personal trading was going better than ever, and with the volatility that the global financial markets were experiencing due to the pandemic, I did not sense there was a need to revisit this book. In an earlier edition, I had included my email address at the end of the book and invited readers to be in touch with me if I could help them along in their path to become a profitable trader. I tend to receive a few emails every week from both new and experienced traders, asking questions or requesting more clarification of an example or strategy highlighted in one of my books. Being in touch with readers is exciting for me, as I'm always interested to learn about their trading experiences. But in March and April 2020, during the COVID-19 pandemic, I started receiving an unusual number of emails from new traders. I wondered why suddenly so many novice traders were reaching out to me. What had changed?

The answer is found in Google Trends, as shown in Figure 1.1 below. As the COVID-19 pandemic struck, the stock market began to sell off as the reality of an economic meltdown and global recession set in. The sell off of the stock market, growing unemployment and a looming recession were in the news every single day. After eleven years of a straight "bull market" (since the 2007/2008 financial crisis), the 2020 pandemic recession became the first "bear market" many traders and investors had ever experienced. And that is why I was receiving so many emails and requests for help. People were at home, often locked down, and had more time on their hands. The financial meltdown was in the news and people were curious to know more about it. Many were reading and learning about the markets. Even if one does not work in a bank or have a brokerage account, virtually everyone's life is in some way connected to Wall Street and the other international financial markets.

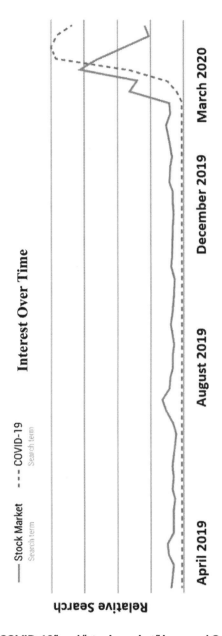

Figure 1.1: "COVID-19" and "stock market" keyword Google search trends between April 2019 and April 2020. As you can see, there is a clear correlation. As the stock market drop hit the news cycles, people started searching more and more about the stock market in Google!

I find the most interesting observation in the above figure to be that as the stock market crashed, and its drop made the news, people wanted to learn more about the stock market. This correlation is in fact visible in almost every previous stock market crash, including the 2007/2008 financial crisis and the 2000 dot-com bubble, the latter being when the excessively exaggerated and mostly overvalued prices of the majority of Internet and tech companies burst.

Figure 1.2: Comparison between the bull market of 2019 and the bear market of 2020, as shown by the change in share value of 500 of the largest American companies. These companies are tracked by the S&P 500 and are traded in an Exchange-traded fund known as the SPDR S&P 500 ETF Trust (ticker: SPY). For your information, S&P refers to Standard & Poor's, one of the companies which used to track this information.

The spring 2020 market volatility of course arose from the COVID-19 pandemic, which resulted in a horribly painful global recession, as shown by Figure 1.2 above, a comparison between the 2019 bull market and the 2020 bear market. It is during bear markets that stock markets usually hit the news headlines.

As I studied the inquiries I was receiving from new traders in March and April 2020, and as I continue to receive emails from readers in the late spring of 2020 as I am writing and editing these very words, some common themes have emerged. Are the tools and brokers you have recommended in your previous books still valid? Have you changed the strategies you are using or, if not, do they still work in these volatile markets? What do you think about some of the new brokers and commission-free apps such as Robinhood that it seems almost everyone has an account with now?

These are all valid, fair and straight-to-the-point questions and concerns, and I knew that I needed to address them in this new edition of my book. The timing of this revisit of *How to Day Trade for a Living* also very nicely complemented my personal life. I am an avid traveler, runner and climber and have spent much of my time in the last few years traveling the world as a trader/explorer, with a laptop and several portable screens always near at hand. In recent years, I have traded from everywhere, ranging from my hometown of Vancouver, Canada to the most remote hills of Papua New Guinea while climbing Mount Giluwe (14,327 ft or 4,367 m), the highest volcano in Oceania. By late 2019,

I was on a mission to climb the highest volcanoes in all seven continents, a challenge known to climbers and alpinists as the *Volcanic Seven Summits*. However, with the pandemic, most borders were closed and I, like everyone else, had to stay close to home.

I had a lot of free time, and although I was working on improving my personal trading as well as writing and finalizing a few new publications, I also had time to review *How to Day Trade for a Living*. Publication of a book involves many back-and-forths between myself, my assistant writer, and my editor. While I am waiting for one or both of them to get back to me with the first edit of a new book, I am able to work on reediting and redrafting the older versions of my books! That led me to look into a new edition of *How to Day Trade for a Living* while my amazing editor was tidying up what I was trying to say in drafts of other material he was working on. He is a genius! He writes what I am trying to say! He receives a mess from me and reworks it to read just as I want it to read.

Some of the material in the earlier editions of this book was now outdated and I therefore deleted it. For example, I used to publish all of my trades and the strategies used in a blog, with screenshots posted to it. I decided to adapt to newer technology and instead of writing blogs, I moved to online tools for journaling and keeping track of my trades. Good journaling and record-keeping is an important element for success in any endeavor, and that is certainly true in trading. How many doctors or surgeons do you know who memorize the names of all of their patients, their prescribed medications, their medical history, and a summary of each appointment they've ever had? None. They all have excellent record-keeping tools, some mandated by their profession and some personally chosen. A successful and consistently profitable trader is the one who keeps excellent records about their trading.

In the last five years, I have mentored many new traders who have become successful. As a way to encourage novice traders, I felt it was important to reach out to some of my students and share their success stories in this new edition.

In this updated version of my book, I explain the fundamentals of day trading and how day trading is different from other styles of trading and investing. In the process, I also describe important trading strategies that many traders use each day. This book is deliberately short so readers will actually finish reading it and not get bored halfway through and put it to one side. We are all distracted by Internet diversions; emails; notifications from *Facebook, Snapchat, Instagram* and *TikTok*; as well as the dozens of other apps that we have on our smartphones and tablets. Therefore, this book is concise and it is practical.

Whether you have recently begun trading, or are someone who is interested in starting a career in trading, or perhaps just someone who is sheltering in place under a stay-at-home order with time on their hands and an inquiring mind, this book will equip you with an understanding of where to start, how to start, what to expect from day trading, and how you can develop your own strategy. Simply reading this book will not make you a profitable trader. Profits in trading do not come from reading one or two books, but, as I will explain later, profits can come with practice, the right tools and software, and proper ongoing education.

I have again included at the back of this latest edition of my book a handy and helpful glossary of the most common terms you will come across in day trading. If, as you are reading this book, you come across a term or phrase that you don't recall the meaning of, please go and have a look at its definition in the glossary. I've used easy to understand language to explain the "lingo" of day traders.

Intermediate traders, those who have prior trading and investing experience in the markets, may benefit from this book's overview of some of the classic strategies that the majority of retail traders use effectively. If you don't consider yourself a novice trader, then you may wish to jump ahead and start reading at Chapter 7 for an overview of these important day trading strategies. However, I encourage you to skim through the earlier chapters as well. Becoming a consistently profitable trader will not require you to master complicated new trading strategies every day. The strategies described in Chapter 7 are ones that traders have been successfully using for more than a decade now. They have worked so far and need to be mastered. Work on simple, well-known strategies, but adjust them over time to complement your own personality and whatever the current market conditions are. Success in trading is not a revolution, it is an evolution.

The market has changed, and it's changing even now as you read this book. In 2016, a day trader of over twenty years named Kem emailed me and asked for some guidance. She was a more experienced trader than I was, but she always traded a certain basket of stocks every day, and with the growing prevalence of algorithms and high frequency trading (abbreviated by many to "HFT"), she needed to adapt to the "new" market and learn a new style of day trading for a living, taking into account all of the social and technological changes that were unfolding. Figure 1.3 below is the review she wrote in 2016 for the first edition of *How to Day Trade for a Living*.

"*I'm a very experienced day trader of over 20 years. With the coming of HFT and other changes, it has been necessary to adjust my methodology. Scanning for stocks in play and trading unknown stocks is an approach I have resisted for my entire career but I think I have to go there now. I won't do it without a solid method/plan and a hard set of rules. I'm not too proud to look at a "beginner" book to figure out how to do this. This book is exceptional. It gave me what I wanted and I will build on the information using what I already know. The author is an engineer and being of a methodical/mechanical mindset myself, I was happy with the way he laid it all out. There is also good information on other topics for real beginners such as the importance of risk management, emotional control which are important.*

"I will recommend this book to people who ask me how to begin day trading."

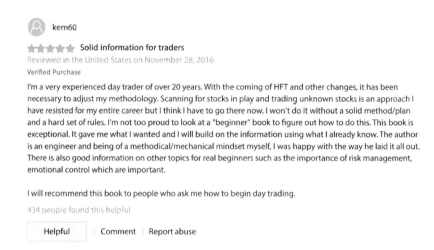

kem60

★★★★★ Solid information for traders
Reviewed in the United States on November 28, 2016
Verified Purchase

I'm a very experienced day trader of over 20 years. With the coming of HFT and other changes, it has been necessary to adjust my methodology. Scanning for stocks in play and trading unknown stocks is an approach I have resisted for my entire career but I think I have to go there now. I won't do it without a solid method/plan and a hard set of rules. I'm not too proud to look at a "beginner" book to figure out how to do this. This book is exceptional. It gave me what I wanted and I will build on the information using what I already know. The author is an engineer and being of a methodical/mechanical mindset myself, I was happy with the way he laid it all out. There is also good information on other topics for real beginners such as the importance of risk management, emotional control which are important.

I will recommend this book to people who ask me how to begin day trading.

434 people found this helpful

Helpful | Comment   Report abuse

Figure 1.3: Screenshot of a 2016 Amazon review stressing the need for even the most experienced of traders to be flexible and open to changing their trading methods in order to adapt to changes in the markets.

I salute Kem. She was an experienced day trader, but after a period of self-reflection, she realized she needed to adjust to the new markets.

Regardless of your level of experience, in my opinion, the most important lesson that you can learn from reading this book is that you will not get rich quickly by day trading. Day trading is not the same as gambling or playing the lottery. This is the most important misconception that people have about day trading and I hope you will come to the same conclusion after reading this book. Day trading looks deceptively easy. Brokers do not normally release customer statistics to the public but, in Massachusetts, a state court did order the release of the records of financial brokers. Those records indicated that after six months of trading, only 16% of day traders actually made money. It is very easy to be one of those 84% of traders who are losing money.

This brings you to my first rule of day trading:

RULE 1	Day trading is not a strategy to get rich quickly.

Stay away from anyone who thinks the stock market is a get–rich–quick scheme. In light of the 2020 COVID-19 pandemic and social distancing guidelines, Figure 1.4 below shows two particularly important social distancing directives. One protects your health; the other protects your wealth! Stay away from anyone who think stocks are designed to help you get rich overnight!

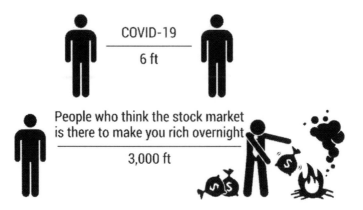

Figure 1.4: Images of a social distancing guideline related to COVID-19 (to protect your health), and a social distancing guideline related to those who want to make you rich overnight via the stock market (to protect your wealth). (For my non-American friends, 6 feet is about 1.8 meters, and 3,000 feet is about 900 meters.)

Stories abound of people who jump into the stock market without any plan. I'll review some of those stories in Chapter 10.

A very common misconception that people have about day trading is that it is easy: just *"Buy low and sell high!"* or *"Buy the dip, sell the rally!"*. Again, day trading looks deceptively easy, but it is not. If it were that simple, everyone would be a successful trader and each year we would not see such a high failure rate amongst active traders. You must always remember that day trading is difficult and will not make you rich quickly. If you have this misconception, and if you want to get rich quickly and easily in the stock market, you should stop reading this book right now and spend the savings that you put aside for day trading on a nice family vacation. It would be much more satisfying to spend your money that way, rather than losing it in the stock market.

Having mentioned all of these points, day trading can be a profitable profession. But keep in mind that it's a highly demanding professional career and most definitely not a casual activity for beginners. It takes time to become a consistently profitable trader. Many traders will fail in the long and at times fatal day trading learning curve.

Chapter 10 focuses on the real actionable steps you must take to successfully enter the world of day trading but, again, be aware that day trading demands a brutal learning curve. Although there are many things that you can do to speed it up, you unfortunately cannot make it disappear. Trading in a simulator account is expediting your learning curve exponentially. One day of trading in a simulator can be worth weeks of training in real accounts or offline.

Often I am asked how long it takes to start making money as a trader. You may have heard it can take a year. Some professional traders may say it is not possible to make money for two years. I have found that most of the better traders in our community consistently make money before the end of their sixth month. But for others it can take a year. On average, it usually takes from six to eight months. It always amuses me to see books and online educational courses that advertise teaching a simple strategy to make you money from "day one" or after a week or even after just one month.

I am always intrigued to meet people who actually believe that advertising and are willing to pay for those products. Placing buying and selling orders in front of a screen, where all of the images and variables are moving exceptionally quickly, demands the highest levels of concentration and discipline. But, unfortunately, day trading attracts some of the most impulsive and gambling prone people out there.

With that said, the times have changed to the benefit of retail traders. Commissions used to be very high and it's been only recently that brokerage firms have reduced their commissions significantly. Direct-access software and other important technology which permit the fast execution of trades used to be available only to the Wall Street elites. "Normal" traders such as you and I did not have access to either the proper technology nor the proper education and training necessary to be a profitable active trader. This has definitely changed in the last decade. More affordable technology, including platforms and scanners, as well as discount brokers (also known as direct-access brokers), are now available at a significantly lower cost for everyone.

No one really knows the exact statistics, but some (now dated) reports from brokerage houses noted that only 10% of traders made money after two years. I shared just a few pages ago a 16% success rate disclosed in court records in the state of Massachusetts. Although a 90% (or 84%) failure rate is scary and disappointing, it is not uncommon in business. According to several published studies, the failure rate of startups and new businesses is at or around 90% after four years of operation. Even in typical and standard careers such as engineering or law, a great number of graduates move to other fields for better career growth and opportunity. I found out at a 2019 reunion of my alma mater's Chemical Engineering class that only 15% of the students I graduated with were still practicing chemical engineering. 15%! 85% have moved to other areas not related directly to our undergraduate education. We may not call this a failure for graduates per se, but it obviously shows that training in classical chemical engineering does not mean a lifetime career for all graduates. I myself have not practiced engineering for over seven years now, primarily because this profession did not provide sufficient financial support for my family.

In day trading, you will be competing with the sharpest minds in the world. You have to consider the market as a massive group of traders, situated all around the world, some experienced and some novice, some working from their homes and some working for large firms, all wanting to keep their money, and all wanting to help themselves to your money.

This leads to my second rule of day trading:

| RULE 2 | Day trading is not easy. It is a serious business, and you should treat it as such. |

Day trading is not a hobby. It's not a weekend pursuit. You need to study and prepare to enter the world of day trading as seriously as a student would study while in university or trade school. And, once you begin trading with your real money, you need to treat it as your career. You need to get up early, get dressed, and be seated in front of your trading station, just as if you were getting ready to go to any other job. You can't be casual about it. You can be successful, but in order to succeed, you have to be better prepared than many of the other traders who you are competing against. A significant part of achieving that success is to learn how to control your emotions. You need to enter each trade with a well-thought-out plan and then stick to it. As I am fond of saying, you need to stick to your trading plans like glue! You cannot allow your emotions to get the better of you in the midst of a trade.

You cannot be an emotional person when trading. You have to be "calm, cool and collected" as the saying goes. You have to somehow find a way to control your emotions. I personally believe you must start developing the discipline of a winner, and I'll expand upon that thought more in Chapter 8 when I share with you a lunchtime walk I took along Wall Street in New York City back in 2014.

So, then, what is day trading? In reality, day trading is a profession, very much like medicine, law and engineering. Day trading requires the right tools and software, education, patience and practice. In order to learn how to trade with real money, you will have to dedicate countless hours to reading about trading styles, observing experienced traders, and practicing in simulator accounts. An average successful day trader can make between $500 and $1,000 every day. That's equal to $10,000 to $20,000 a month (based on about twenty trading days in a month), and that equals some $120,000 to $240,000 a year. Why would anyone expect a job that pays this well to be easy? Doctors, attorneys, engineers and many other professionals go through years of school, practice, hard work and examinations to earn a similar income. Why should day trading be any different?

And therefore, if it isn't easy, and it doesn't make you rich quickly, why would you ever want to day trade?

What makes day trading attractive is the lifestyle. You can work from home, work only for a few hours each day and take days off whenever you wish to. You can spend as much time as you want with your family and friends without requesting vacation time from a boss or manager. You are the boss. Since day trading is a form of self-employment, you are the CEO and you make the executive decisions for your business. I mentioned my love of traveling earlier in this chapter. I was able to travel to twenty-seven countries in 2019, and most of those times I was able to trade with my laptop and a few portable screens. I did not need to request time off, bank my vacations or ask permission from my manager.

The lifestyle is extremely attractive and, of course, if you master the profession of day trading, you can potentially make thousands of dollars every day, far more than in most other professions. I personally know some traders who average over $2,000 every day. Some days are lower and some days are higher, but over the long term they have a profit of over $2,000 every day. No matter where you live and how you live, $2,000 a day is a substantial amount of money and can contribute to a very satisfying lifestyle. If you learn how to day trade properly, your reward is the trading skills to trade profitably in any market, from anywhere, and for the rest of your trading career. Essentially, it is a license to print money. But it takes time and experience to develop skills for this new career. How much you can expect to make is also correlated directly to how much capital you have available for trading. If you have a small amount of capital for trading, such as $5,000, you cannot expect a $2,000 return per day. It may be possible in one or two lucky days, but it certainly is not realistic nor sustainable. It is hard to make a living with such a small account.

If you want to own your own business, day trading is a simple place to start. Take a moment and compare day trading with opening a pizza shop or a restaurant. If you want to open a restaurant, you'll have to spend large amounts of money on rent, equipment, staff hiring and training, insurance and licenses – and you still won't be guaranteed to earn money from your restaurant. Many businesses are like that. Day trading, on the other hand, is very easy to set up and start. You can open a trading account today, at no cost, and then start trading tomorrow. Of course you should not do that until you educate yourself, but the logistics of commencing day trading are extremely easy compared to many other businesses and professions.

Day trading is also an easy business to manage the cash flow of. You can buy a stock, and, if things go badly, you can immediately sell it for a loss. Compare that to people who have import-export businesses and are importing goods from other countries. There are plenty of things that can go wrong when purchasing shipments of goods to sell in your own country - problems with vendors, transport, customs, distribution, marketing, quality and customer satisfaction - plus, your money is locked in for the entire process. Unless everything goes well, you can't do anything about it. At times you cannot even accept a small loss and easily step away from your business. With day trading, if things go wrong, you can come out of the trade in a few seconds with an action as quick and simple as a click (and, of course, a small loss). It is easy to start over in day trading and that is a highly desirable aspect of any business.

Closing a day trading business is also easy. If you think day trading is not for you, or if you don't make money from it, you can immediately stop trading, close your accounts and withdraw your money. Aside from the time and money that you have already spent, there are no other costs or penalties. Closing other professional offices or businesses are not nearly as straightforward. You cannot as easily close your store, office or restaurant, lay off your staff and walk away from your lease and equipment.

Why then do most people fail in day trading?

I will explain specific reasons behind this important question in Chapters 8 and 10 but, overall, in my opinion, the most common reason that people fail in day trading is that they do not regard it as a serious business. They instead treat it as a form of gambling that will quickly and easily make them rich.

Others decide to become involved in trading because they think it will be fun or entertaining, or an interesting hobby of some kind. They might be drawn to trading because they consider it a "cool" thing to do, something that will bring them prestige or perhaps make them more attractive to others.

Losing amateurs trade for the thrill of short-term gambling in the markets. They play around a little bit in the market but never commit themselves to acquiring a proper education or an in-depth awareness of day trading. They may get lucky a few times and make some money, but eventually the market will punish them.

This is actually my own story. At the beginning of my trading career, a company then called Aquinox Pharmaceuticals Inc. (ticker: AQXP) announced some positive results for one of its drugs, and its stock jumped from $1 to over $55 in just two days. I was a beginner at the time. I purchased 1,000 shares at $4 and sold them at over $10. I was thrilled. What looked like a very good thing however, turned out to be very bad. I had made over $6,000 in a matter of minutes. And on my first day of trading with real money! I was left with the impression that making money in the market was easy. It took me time and several severe losses to get rid of that very mistaken notion.

It was pure luck. I honestly had no idea what I was doing. In just a few weeks I lost that entire $6,000 by making mistakes in other trades. I was fortunate because my first stupid trade was my lucky one. For many people, their first mistake is their last trade because they blow up their account and have to desperately say good-bye to day trading.

New day traders should never lose sight of the fact that they are competing with professional traders on Wall Street and other experienced traders around the world who are very serious, highly equipped with advanced education and tools, and most importantly, committed to making money.

Never forget Rule 2: day trading is a business, and it's an intensely serious one. You have to wake up early in the morning, do your preparations every day on the stocks that you plan to trade, and be thoroughly prepared before the market opens. Imagine for a moment that you have opened a restaurant. Can you afford not to be ready for your customers when you open your doors? You can't close the restaurant at lunchtime because you aren't feeling well or you're not in the mood or you didn't have time to order enough groceries for the kitchen staff to prepare meals with. You must always be ready. The day trading business is no different.

Day trading requires the proper tools, software and education. As with any business, you must have the right tools to succeed. So, what are the basic tools you need for your day trading business?

1. **Business Plan:** like any other business, you need to have a solid business plan for your day trading including what strategies you will use and how much you will invest in your education, a computer and screens, scanner software (if you are not making use of someone else's), platforms, and other tools. I always advise individuals to budget at least $1,500 for education for their first year. Yes, $1,500 might be a lot of money for one week or one month of training, but over the course of your lifetime it is a very manageable investment, even for people who are not financially blessed but are ready to begin trading. For this 2020 edition of my book, I have included a new section (found in Chapter 10), that discusses how to put together your day trading business plan.

2. **Education:** it always amazes me when I see people start a new business without proper education and training. Day trading is a business that requires a serious education and consistent practice. Would you start performing surgery just by reading one or two books? Would you be able to practice law or engineering just by combining the reading of a book with the watching of a handful of YouTube videos? No. A day trading

career is no different. Seek a solid education and practice for at least three months in simulators before trading with real money. Many people think that trading can be reduced to a few rules that they can follow every morning: always do this and always do that. In reality, trading isn't about "always" at all; it is about each situation that presents itself and it is about each individual trade.

3. **Startup capital (cash):** like any other business, you need some money to start your trading business, including money for buying a good computer and four monitors, plus sufficient capital to actually begin trading with. Many businesses, including day trading businesses, fail because the entrepreneur founders lack adequate startup capital and cannot keep tight control of their overhead costs. It will take time before you will make a living out of day trading. You need sufficient startup cash to sustain break–even operations at the beginning. Often, new traders will cut back on the essentials, such as paying for the right education, tools and platform, in order to preserve their capital. They are trying to do too much with too little. This creates a death spiral of distress and emotional trading. Adequate startup capital enables new traders to make beginner's mistakes and address their weaknesses early in their day trading career and before they are forced out of the

trading business. The amount of capital you have available for trading is also an important component of your daily goals, especially if you desire to make a living from trading. When traders are undercapitalized but still hope to trade for a living, they are more likely to take higher risks to achieve their desired returns. That, unfortunately, will most likely destroy their account.

4. **Right tools and services:**
   a. High-speed Internet service.
   b. The best available broker.
   c. A fast order execution platform that supports Hotkeys.
   d. A scanner for finding the right stocks to trade.
   e. Support from a community of traders.

Some of these tools must be paid for every month. Just as other businesses have monthly bills for electricity, software, licenses and leases, you have to be able to pay your Internet provider's monthly bills, your broker's commissions, scanner costs (if not sharing someone else's) and trading platform fees. If you are part of a paid chatroom or community, you can add the cost of that membership to this list too.

It is also important to mention that most of the strategies and other information in this book are geared toward day trading in the U.S. stock market.

The U.S. stock market is the most volatile and most liquid stock market in the world. Day trading is really hard, if not impossible, in markets that do not have much volatility or are not regulated. Several other international markets are also available to trade in though, including Canada's Toronto Stock Exchange, the Shanghai Stock Exchange, the London Stock Exchange, and Germany's Deutsche Börse AG. I personally do not trade them, and do not have much information available about them. I only actively trade in the U.S. market and most tools in this book are really only appropriate for that market. I in fact recommend that you only day trade in the U.S. market. However, you do not need to be a resident of the United States to be able to trade in that market. Almost all brokers open brokerage accounts for people of any nationality. As I wrote earlier, I am Canadian and live in Canada, but I am easily able to trade in the U.S. market. If, like me, you are not resident in the United States, do reach out to the brokerage firm of your choice and they will more than likely open up a suitable account for you.

CHAPTER 2

HOW DAY TRADING WORKS

In this chapter I will review many of the basics of day trading and hopefully answer your questions about what day trading is and how it works. This chapter will also introduce some of the main tools and strategies that you'll come across later in this book. Of course, tools are of no value unless you know how to properly use them. This book will be your guide in learning how to use these tools.

DAY TRADING VS. SWING TRADING

A compelling question to begin with is: What do you look for as a day trader?

The answer is simple. First, you're looking for stocks that are moving in a relatively predictable manner. Secondly, you are going to trade them in one day. You will not keep any position overnight. If you buy stock in Apple Inc. (ticker: AAPL) today, for instance, you will not hold your position overnight and sell it tomorrow. If you hold onto any stock overnight, it is no longer day trading, it's called *swing trading.*

Swing trading is a form of trading in which you hold stocks over a period of time, generally from one day to a few weeks. It is a completely different style of trading, and you shouldn't use the strategies and tools that you use for day trading to do swing trading. Do you remember Rule 2, where I mentioned that day trading is a business? Swing trading is also a business, but a completely different kind of business. The differences between swing trading and day trading are similar to the differences in owning a restaurant and owning a food delivery company. They both involve food, but they are very different: they operate with different time frames, regulations, market segments and revenue models. You should not confuse day trading with other styles of trading just because the trading involves stocks. Day traders always close their positions before the market closes.

Many traders, including myself, do both day trading and swing trading. We are aware that we are running two different businesses, and we have gone through separate educational programs for these two kinds of trading. One of the key differences between day trading and swing trading is the approach to stock picking. I do not swing trade and day trade the same stocks. Swing traders usually look for stocks in solid companies that they know won't lose their entire value overnight. For day trading, however, you can trade anything, including companies that will soon go bankrupt, because you don't care what happens after the market closes. In fact, many of the companies that you will day trade are too risky to hold overnight because they might lose much of their value in that short of a period of time.

You have now reached Rule 3 of day trading:

RULE 3	Day traders do not hold positions overnight. If necessary, you must sell with a loss to make sure you do not hold onto any stock overnight.

Several traders over the years have emailed me about this rule, and wondered why I advise them to close their position at the end of the day, even with a loss? Of course I do not want you to lose money, but I often see traders suddenly change their plan at the end of the day because they do not want to accept a small loss. They should get out of a losing trade, but they instead suddenly decide to stay in the trade and hold it overnight, in the "hope" that perhaps a stock will come back the next day. I myself have turned some of my day trades into swing trades, and I paid a heavy price for that. Often, many of the stocks we day trade will lose even more of their value overnight. As a day trader, you must stick to your daily plans. You should never change a day trade that was supposed to close at the end of the day into a swing trade. It's a common human inclination to accept profits quickly but to also want to wait until losing trades return to even.

It's also very important to remember that "trading" is different from "investing". My friends will often ask me:

"Andrew, you are a trader, can you teach me how to trade too?"

When I sit down with them and listen to their expectations, I realize that most of them want to invest their money, they are not looking for a new or additional career as a trader. They actually want to invest their money themselves rather than settle for the gains that typical mutual funds offer. They are not looking to become a trader. They don't realize the differences and are incorrectly using the words investing and trading interchangeably. Most of them have some money in their savings or retirement accounts and would like to grow that investment at a faster rate than what mutual funds or other managed investment services offer. I explain to them the differences between a trader and an investor, to ensure they are clear about a trading career. Of course, most of them are not ready to become a trader.

I am also often asked to give my opinion on the market or on a specific stock. For example, my friends and family will ask me:

"Andrew, do you see the market up or down from here until the end of the year?" or *"Apple is selling off, is it a good buy now? Do you think it will go higher?"*

My answer is: "*I have no idea.*"

I am a trader. I am not an investor. I do not study long-term trends nor am I trained as an investor. I have never developed a long-term investing strategy. I am not sure where the overall market is headed in six months or where for that matter Apple will trade even tomorrow. My business is called trading, not investing. I do not care where AAPL will trade in two years. I personally wish that it will trade higher, but, as a trader, my personal wishes are irrelevant. If AAPL is that day a Stock in Play (see Chapter 4) and weak, I am shorting it. If AAPL is strong, I am long. I'll explain "short" and "long" in the next section. As a day trader, I am trained for short-term intraday trading, nothing more. I am only interested in what stocks will move the most today. How I can make money today is my obsession and my expertise.

I have some understanding of the overall market situation, if it is bullish, bearish or neutral, but that is because I am also a swing trader. You as a stock market day trader will not necessarily need to know about the market direction in the near future. You are a day trader, your time span is measured in seconds and minutes, rarely in hours, and certainly not in days or weeks or months.

BUYING LONG, SELLING SHORT

Day traders buy stocks in the hope that their price will go higher. This is called *buying long*, or simply *long*. When you hear me or another trader say, "*I am long 100 shares AAPL*," it means that we have bought 100 shares of Apple Inc. and would like to sell them higher for a profit. Going long is good when the price is expected to go higher.

But what if prices are dropping? In that case, you can *sell short* and still make a profit. Day traders can borrow shares from their broker and sell them, hoping that the price will go lower and that they can then buy those shares back at a lower price and make a profit. This is called *selling short*, or simply *short*. When people say, "*I am short Apple*," it means they have sold short stocks of Apple and they hope that the price of Apple will drop. When the price is going lower, you owe 100 shares to your broker (it probably shows as -100 shares in your account), which means you must return 100 shares of Apple to your broker. Your broker doesn't want your money; they want their shares back. So, if the price has gone lower, you can buy them cheaper than when you sold them earlier and make a profit. Imagine that you borrow 100 shares of Apple from your broker and sell them at $100 per share. Apple's price then drops to $90, so you buy back those 100 shares at $90 and return them to your broker. You have made $10 per share or $1,000. What if the price of Apple goes up to $110? In that case, you still have to buy 100 shares to return to your broker because you owe your broker shares and not money. Therefore, you have to buy 100 shares at $110 in order to return 100 shares to your broker, and you will have lost $1,000.

Short sellers profit when the price of the stock they borrowed and sold drops. Short selling is important because stock prices usually drop much more quickly than they go up. Fear is a more powerful feeling than greed. Therefore, short sellers, if they trade right, can make astonishing profits while other traders panic and start to sell off.

However, like anything in the market that has great potential, short selling has its risks too. When buying stocks of a company for $5, the worst case scenario is that the company goes bankrupt and you lose your $5 per share. There is a limit to your loss. But if you short sell that company at $5 and then the price, instead of going down, starts going higher and higher, then there won't be any limit to your loss. The price may go to $10, $20, or $100, and still there will be no limit to your loss. Your broker wants those shares back. Not only can you lose all of the money in your account, but your broker can also sue you for more money if you do not have sufficient funds to cover your shorts.

Short selling is a legal activity for several good reasons. First, it provides the markets with more information. Short sellers often complete extensive and legitimate due diligence to discover facts and flaws that support their suspicion that the target company is overvalued. If there were no short sellers, the price of stocks could unreasonably increase higher and higher. Short sellers are balancing the market and adjusting prices to their reasonable value. Their actions are conducive to the health of the market.

If the price is going to go lower, you may correctly ask, why does your broker allow you to short sell instead of selling stock themselves before the price drops? The answer is that your broker prefers to hold their position for the long term. Short selling provides investors who own the stock (with long positions) with the ability to generate extra income by lending their shares to the short sellers. Long-term investors who make their shares available for short selling are not afraid of short-term ups and downs. They have invested in the company for a good reason and they have no interest in selling their shares in a short period of time. They therefore prefer to lend their shares to traders who wish to make a profit from short-term fluctuations of the market. In exchange for lending their shares, they will charge interest. Therefore, by short selling, you will need to pay some interest to your broker as the cost of borrowing those shares. If you short sell only during the same day, you usually will not need to pay any interest. Swing traders who sell short usually have to pay daily interest on their short stocks.

Short selling is generally a dangerous practice in trading. Some traders are long-biased. They only buy stocks in the hope of selling them higher. I don't have any bias. I will short sell when I think the setup is ready, and I will buy whenever it fits my strategy. Having said that, I am more careful when I short stocks. Some of the strategies that I explain in this book work only for long positions (Bull Flag and Bottom Reversal). Some strategies work only for short selling (Top Reversal) and others will work in both long and short positions depending on the setup. I explain these positions in detail in the coming pages.

RETAIL VS. INSTITUTIONAL TRADERS

Individual traders, like you and I, are called *retail traders*. We can be part-time traders, or full-time traders, but we're not working for a firm and we're not managing other people's money. We retail traders are a small percentage of the volume in the market. On the other hand, there are the so-called *institutional traders* such as Wall Street investment banks, proprietary trading firms (called prop traders), mutual funds and hedge funds. Most of their trading is based on sophisticated computer algorithms and high frequency trading. Rarely is any human involved in the day trading operations of these large accounts. Through whatever means, institutional traders have considerable money behind them and they can be very aggressive.

You may correctly ask, *"How can an individual trader, like you and me, coming later to the game, compete against institutional traders and win?"*

Individual traders have a tremendous advantage over institutional traders. Banks and other institutions are compelled to trade, often in large volumes, and some-times with little regard to price. They are expected to be constantly active in the market. Individual traders, on the other hand, can decide whether or not they want to trade, and they can bide their time until opportunities present themselves.

Ironically, large numbers of individual traders miss out on their advantage by overtrading. Instead of being patient and exercising the self-discipline of winners, they succumb to greed, trade unwisely and unneces-sarily, and become losers.

I always use the analogy of retail day trading and guerrilla warfare. Guerrilla warfare is an irregular approach to warfare in which a small group of combat-ants, such as paramilitary personnel or armed civilians, use hit-and-run tactics like ambushes, sabotage, raids and petty warfare to maneuver around a larger and less-mobile traditional military force. The United States military is considered to be one of the most formidable fighting forces in the world. However, they suffered significantly as a result of jungle warfare tactics used against them in North Vietnam. Earlier examples include the European resistance movements which fought against Nazi Germany during World War Two.

In guerrilla trading, as the term suggests, you are in hiding, waiting for an opportunity to move in and out of the financial jungle in a short period of time to generate quick profits while keeping your risk to a mini-mum. You don't want to defeat or outsmart investment banks. You are simply waiting for an opportunity to reach your daily profit target.

As a retail day trader, you have another distinct advantage over institutional traders in that you can exit your losing positions quickly. As I will discuss later, you must determine your exit plan if a stock trades against you. A new trader should start with trading one standard lot, 100 shares. One hundred shares is low risk, and although it's also a low reward for the trader, you need to start somewhere. New traders should start out with trading 100 shares. If their stop loss hits, they really have no excuse about why they couldn't get out. Even for an illiquid stock (a stock that is hard to sell) that is traded with very low volume, 100 shares is nothing.

Institutional traders, on the other hand, may have a 1,000,000 share position with which to work. It takes some time to unravel such a large position, not one click of a mouse (or in the case of most active day traders, a tap of a Hotkey, exceedingly faster than clicking a mouse), and losses can be significant. Day traders trade with much smaller size and can get out of their losing trade for a very small loss. In fact, a good day trader can take numerous losses of as little as one penny. So you must learn to exploit one of your huge advantages. And this means stopping out a stock when it trades against your exit price.

As a day trader, you profit from volatility in the stock market, which is more apt to occur in morning trading than later in the day. If the market or stock prices are not moving much, you most likely are not going to make any money; only high frequency traders make money under these circumstances as they have access to low commissions and can trade large volumes of shares with low fees. Therefore, you need to find stocks that move to the upside or to the downside. Not every move of a stock's price is tradeable or even recognizable by traders. The job of a good trader is to find recogniz-able and consistent patterns that you know from the past and then trade them. There are many "big" moves in the market, and most traders think they should be doing their best to catch and trade every single one of them. That is a mistake. Your job as a trader is to stick to consistent patterns that have earned your trust because of their past performance. Institutional traders, on the other hand, are trading with very high frequency and will profit from very small movements of price, or as it is sometimes called, from "choppy price action".

It is extremely important to stay away from stocks that are being heavily traded by institutional traders. As an individual retail day trader, you must stick to your retail trading territory. You will not trade stocks that other retail traders are not trading or not seeing. The strength of retail day trading strategies is that other retail traders are also using them. The more traders using these strategies, the better they will work. As more people recognize the line in the sand, more people will be buying at that point. This, of course, means the stock will move up faster. The more buyers, the quicker it will move. This is why many traders are happy to share their day trading strategies. It not only helps other traders to become more profitable, but it also increases the number of traders who are using these strategies. There is no benefit in hiding these methods or keeping them secret.

HIGH FREQUENCY TRADING (HFT)

As I mentioned just a few pages ago, most of the Wall Street investment banks, mutual funds, prop firms, and hedge funds base their trading on sophisticated computer algorithms and high frequency trading (HFT).

You may have heard about the mysterious "black box", the top secret hidden computer programs, formulas and systems that manipulate the stock market. Some will say that since you can't beat a computer or HFT, why even bother trying. To me, this is simply an excuse for not doing well and not working hard enough. I and many other successful day traders have beat the "black box", and have profited very nicely in the process.

In all honesty, yes, HFT has made trading more difficult and complicated for the individual day trader. It can frustrate you. Stress you out. Some of these programs are deliberately designed to go after and beat us day traders.

The best way to overcome them is to be very selective in when you make a trade and to monitor the price action very, very closely. Be that guerrilla trader. Find a Stock in Play (described in detail in Chapter 4). Find the moments when the computer formulas and algorithms cannot take your money. Find your entry point. Make your move. Make your exit. Take your profit.

I believe one of the most significant challenges with these "black boxes" is that the computer programmers who work so many hours each day on the formulas don't have a clue how to day trade themselves. Past market data is very valuable for both you and for their computers, but the stock market is not 100% predictable. It is always changing. There is an uncertainty about it that no computer programmer can fully prepare for in advance. It's impossible for them to upload every single variable. As you observe the market, in real time, you will see those unpredictable moments and you will profit in them. You must be very strategic with every trade you enter. Never forget that in the equally strategic world of chess, Garry Kasparov did win some of his rounds against IBM's Deep Blue. More recently, even IBM's Watson got answer after answer wrong when playing on *Jeopardy!*

You must also remember that any one organization's powerful "black box" is trading against all of the other organizations' powerful "black boxes" and thus they are destined to fail. Not all of them can win. As you practice and gain experience in day trading, you will learn to identify different algorithms and how to trade against them. You can succeed and they can fail. They have actually failed miserably.

Of the various HFT programs that are currently operating, one of the least effective is the so-called *"Buy the New Low"* program. When a stock reaches a new intraday low, many day traders will go short to ride the downside momentum. This program then begins to buy the shorts from those day traders to push the price higher. This causes day traders to panic and to cover their shorts. Because the organizations behind HFT programs have almost limitless buying power, the plan sounds flawless. The plan quickly breaks down, however, when another large institutional seller also gets behind the trade and decides to dump their large positions. This means that regardless of how many shares the program buys, the stock will simply not push higher because institutional sellers and day traders will continue to dump their shares on it.

A now-classic example of the failure of this sort of HFT is presented in the book, *One Good Trade*, by my friend and acknowledged great trader, Mike Bellafiore. In September 2008, the investment bank Lehman Brothers Holdings Inc. (ticker: LEH, now delisted after bankruptcy), Federal Home Loan Mortgage Corp (then ticker: FRE), and many other mortgage holdings and investment banks all suffered a massive drop in price. Programs tried to buy their already broken stock to squeeze and burn the short sellers, but the stock price never went higher. Day traders and huge institutional sellers dumped their shares on the program. The programs and their developers were obliterated and left holding huge quantities of worthless shares of LEH and FRE, as well as other bankrupted holdings.

You will read over and over again in this book how important it is to do your homework. To prepare. To practice. To be disciplined. To be smart. To make smart trading moves. You will not win every round against algorithms and HFT, but you can win some of the rounds, and you can profit. You must be able to identify the different algorithmic programs so that you can trade against them. This takes some experience, good mentoring, and practice.

HFT programs should be respected but not feared. Always remember that the market is a dynamic and ever-changing place. What works today for traders may not work tomorrow. And because of this, HFT and computerized trading can never completely rule trading. There will always be the need for an intelligent trader who understands the market and price action in real time. And since the market is always changing, it is impossible to program all of the different variables that eliminate the need for trader discretion. There isn't an algorithm that can be programmed to trade against the well-trained and disciplined trader. There are just too many variables in the markets.

I always remind my trading colleagues who are annoyed by computers that there is really a much larger lesson here. As a day trader, you can complain about anything that takes your money, including of course the annoying algorithmic programs. If you don't do your homework, and are unprepared and uneducated when you start your trading, they will indeed take your money. But you have a choice to either spend your energy complaining or to instead compete with them. I encourage traders to figure out how to use the programs to their advantage. For example, when a program forces short sellers to cover fast, ride *the short squeeze* on the upside with the program. Find the spots where the algorithms cannot take your money and discover the stocks where you can beat the programs. This is just another reason why you must be in the *Stocks in Play* (read Chapter 4).

You won't get anywhere in day trading by complaining about algorithms. What will that accomplish? How will that help you make money? Many retail day traders are consistently making profits by day trading from their home offices. As I have written, new traders have a choice. The market is simply a pattern–solving exercise. Every morning, you need to solve a new puzzle. The algorithms and HFT make it more difficult to decipher these patterns, but they do not make it impossible. Yes, there will always be obstacles and unfair situations in the stock market for retail traders like you and me. We should take small and consistent steps and work harder to profit in the market with its ever-changing situations. But what we should not do, what a trader must never do, is to make excuses.

TRADE THE BEST, LEAVE THE REST

As part of the algorithmic trading by computer systems, the majority of stocks will trend with the overall market unless they have a reason not to. So, if the market is moving up, the majority of stocks will be moving up. If the overall market is going down, the prices of the majority of stocks will also go down. But, remember, there will be a handful of stocks that will buck the trend of the market because they have a catalyst. These are the *Stocks in Play*. This is what retail traders are looking for – that small handful of stocks that are going to be running when the markets are tanking, or tanking when the markets are running.

If the market is running, and these stocks are running too, that's fine. You just want to ensure you are trading stocks that are moving because they have a *fundamental reason* to move and are not just moving with the overall market conditions: these are the Stocks in Play. You may ask, what is the fundamental catalyst for these Stocks in Play that make them suitable for day trading? Stocks in Play generally have unexpected fresh news, either positive or negative. Here are some examples:

- Earnings reports
- Earnings warnings or pre-announcements
- Earnings surprises
- FDA approvals or disapprovals
- Mergers or acquisitions
- Alliances, partnerships, or major product releases

- Major contract wins or losses
- Restructurings, layoffs, or management changes
- Stock splits, buybacks, or debt offerings

When I do reversal trades (explained in Chapter 7), my favorite reversal trades are on stocks that are selling off because there has been some bad news regarding that company. If there is a quick sell off because of bad news, many people will notice and start monitoring the stock for what is called a Bottom Reversal. If stocks are trending down with the overall market, such as oil was some time ago, you cannot do a good reversal trade. Their value pops up by 10 cents, and you think it's a reversal, but then they are sold off for another 50 cents. They're selling off because they're trending with both the overall market and their sector. Oil was a weak sector for a while in 2014 and 2015 and the majority of the oil and energy stocks were selling off. When a sector is weak, that is not a good time to make a reversal trade. That's where you have to differentiate.

So here's the fourth rule of day trading:

RULE 4 — **Always ask, "Is this stock moving because the overall market is moving, or is it moving because it has a unique fundamental catalyst?"**

That's when you have to do a little bit of research. As you become more experienced as a trader, you will be able to differentiate between catalyst-based price action and general market trending.

As discussed, you must be careful that you as a retail trader are not on the wrong side of the trade against the institutional traders. But how do you stay out of their way? Instead of trying to find institutional traders, you find out where the retail traders are hanging out on that day and then you trade with them. Think about a schoolyard for a moment. You don't want to be off in the sandbox doing your own thing, trading a stock that no one is paying attention to. You're in the wrong place. Focus where everyone else is focused: focus on the stock that is moving every single day and receiving literally a ton of action. That is what day traders will be looking at.

Can you day trade stocks like Apple or Microsoft or Coca-Cola or IBM? Of course you can, but these are slow moving stocks that are dominated by institutional traders and algorithmic traders, and in general terms they are going to be very hard to day trade. Think of it as the equivalent of hanging out in that isolated sandbox instead of hanging out with your peers in the playground where the cool cats are.

How do you determine what retail traders are focused on and your place in that playground?

There are a couple of ways to find your best place. One is by watching day trading stock scanners. I explain later in Chapters 4 and 7 about how I set up my scanner.

The stocks that are gapping significantly up or down are going to be the stocks that retail traders are watching. Secondly, it's good to be in touch with social media and a community of traders. *StockTwits* and *Twitter* are usually good places to learn what is trending. If you follow a handful of traders, then you'll be able to see for yourself what everyone is talking about. There is a huge advantage to being in a community of traders, such as a chatroom, and there are many chatrooms on the Internet.

If you're trading completely on your own, you're off in the corner of that proverbial playground. You're not in touch with what other traders are doing, and inevitably you will make it really hard on yourself because you will not know where the activity is. I have tried blocking out social media and trading in a bubble, basically doing my own thing, and it did not work. Draw on the laws of high school survival to guide you!

A little more about what I do. As a day trader, I don't trade based on a company's fundamentals such as product, earnings, earnings-per-share growth and financial statements. As I mentioned earlier, I'm not a value investor and I'm not a long-term investor. I don't trade Options or Futures either, but I do use Futures to gain an understanding of the overall market direction in the near-term future. I am an intraday equity (stock) trader. I am also a swing trader. In swing trading, I personally do care very much about the fundamentals of the companies I choose to trade: their earnings, dividends, earnings-per-share, and many other criteria.

But swing trading is not the focus of this book, so I won't pursue that topic for now.

I'm also a Forex (Foreign Exchange Market) trader and sometimes I trade commodities and currencies. But, in the mornings, I am mostly an equities day trader and I focus on the real stocks. The majority of day traders don't trade penny stocks or on the over-the-counter (OTC) market. Penny stocks are extremely manipulated and they do not follow any of the rules of the standard strategies. We trade real stocks. Sometimes we may be trading Facebook, Inc. (ticker: FB), and sometimes we may be trading Apple Inc. (ticker: AAPL), but we will always be trading the stocks that are having a big day. You may be surprised, but on almost every single day in the market, there's a stock having a big day because the company has released earnings, had a newsbreak, or had something bad or good happen to it. These are the fundamental catalysts that you must look for.

What does my day look like as a day trader? You will read about it in detail in Chapter 8, but my trading day typically starts at around 6 a.m. (which is 9 a.m. New York time) with pre-market scanning. I'm scanning to see where there is volume in the market. As early as 8:30 a.m. New York time, you'll know what stocks are gapping up or gapping down. I then start scouring through the news for catalysts that explain the gaps. I start to put together a watchlist (the list of stocks I will monitor during the trading day). I rule some out and then I pick and choose which ones I do and don't like. By 9:15 a.m. New York time I am in our chatroom, going over my watchlist with all of our traders. By 9:30 a.m., when the bell rings, my plans are ready.

From when the market opens at 9:30 a.m. until around 11:30 a.m. New York time is when the market will have the most trading volume and also the most volatility. This is the best time to trade and to especially focus on momentum trading (which will be explained later). The advantage of having high trading volume is that it provides liquidity. Liquidity is one of the most important elements of trading. This means that there are plenty of buyers and plenty of sellers, which in turn means that you can easily get in and out of trades without being worried about whether your orders will get filled or not.

Around Mid-day (12 p.m. to 3 p.m. New York time), you can have good trading patterns but you may not have the volume to trade them. Low trading volume, as explained before, means a lack of liquidity, which makes it harder to get in and out of stocks. This is especially important to consider if you want to take large shares. In addition, trading low volume stocks will make you vulnerable to high frequency trading and algorithms. My focus has always been on trading at the market's opening, which is 9:30 a.m. in New York (Eastern time). I personally trade only within the first one or two hours of the market's opening. I rarely make any trades after 11:30 a.m. New York time.

On a good day, I have reached my goal by 7:30 a.m. Pacific time (10:30 a.m. New York time). If it's just an average day, by lunchtime I have almost always hit my goal for the day and I'm generally sitting on my hands unless there is that perfect setup. From 4 p.m. until 6 p.m., I am either in trading courses with our traders or reviewing my trades from the day.

I avoid pre-market trading because there is very low liquidity as there are very few traders trading. That means stocks can pop up a dollar, then drop a dollar, and you can't get in and out with large shares. You have to go really small, and you have to use such small positions that, for me at least, it's just not worth it. If you don't mind trading in small shares, then you can certainly trade pre-market, but you need to first ensure your broker will allow you to do pre-market trading.

I live in Vancouver, Canada, so in my time zone the market opens at 6:30 a.m. Pacific time. This means that my days start really early. The great advantage for me is that I can be finished trading before many of the people in my city are even out of bed. I can then spend the rest of my day skiing, climbing, with family and friends, or focusing on other work and the other businesses that I have. In day trading, losing money is very easy. Once you have reached your daily profit goal, it is best to stop trading or switch to trading in your simulator.

CHAPTER 3

RISK AND ACCOUNT MANAGEMENT

I've learned, and at times the hard way, that success in day trading comes from three important skills: 1) learning and mastering one or a few proven trading strategies; 2) proper risk management (knowing how much of a size to enter a trade with and knowing when to properly exit a trade); and, as has been emphasized several times already in this book, controlling your emotions and having a sound psychology. It's just like a three–legged stool, you remove one leg and it will collapse. For success in trading, you need to master it all. Successfully mastering a few things at the same time is in fact common to all performance–based disciplines.

To be a successful and competitive athlete, for example, you need to master what *Nike* calls the five facets of training: Movement, Mindfulness, Recovery, Nutrition and Sleep. I really believe that to be successful in any career or endeavor, you need these same five facets, albeit with a little bit of tweaking specific to the situation. There is nothing in the world more comparable to trading than highly competitive professional athleticism. Borrowing on the concept introduced by Nike, I believe success in trading comes from mastering these five facets: Technical Knowledge, Risk Management, Nutrition, Sound Psychology and Sleep.

That is why at Bear Bull Traders, we try to touch upon and guide the community in all of these areas, as they all contribute to your success. If you do not believe, for example, in the role of nutrition or proper sleep when it comes to your trading, try to trade when highly caffeinated, when under the influence of a substance, or when lacking sleep, and you'll see the results for yourself. (I strongly recommend trading in a simulator for this test!) There is considerable evidence and scientific research studies documenting the effects of food, sleep and stimulants on a person's cognitive ability and fast decision-making.

Often, beginner traders who fail to make money in the markets get frustrated and go out and try to learn more about how the markets work, study new strategies, adopt additional technical indicators, follow some different traders, and join other chatrooms. They don't realize that the main cause of their failure is often a lack of self-discipline, the making of impulsive decisions and sloppy risk and money management, not their technical knowledge. You are the only problem you will ever have for your trading career and, of course, you are the only solution to this problem.

Each of the strategies outlined in this book has been demonstrated, if executed properly, to show positive expectancy. But, before you begin your first trading day, you have to realize and accept in your mind that there will be days when you will lose money. Maybe even very badly. It happens to the most experienced of traders and it will happen to you. Something completely unexpected can happen in the middle of your trade. Please believe me, there is no magic formula for success in trading. It will take hard work, determination and resilience in order to escape failure.

One of my favorite trading expressions is *"live to play another day"*. This simple saying says so much about the mindset of a professional trader. If you survive the learning curve, then the good times will come and you can become a consistently profitable trader. But you have to survive. And many just can't.

A common reason for the failure of new day traders is that they cannot manage their early losses. Accepting profits is easy to do, but it is much more difficult, especially for beginners, to overcome the temptation to wait for losing trades to return to the break-even point. They'll often say, *"I'll just give this trade a bit more room."* Waiting for something that is not likely to happen can result in serious damage to their accounts.

As Dr. Alexander Elder writes in his book, *Trading for a Living*, to be a successful trader, not only must you learn excellent risk management rules, but you also need to firmly implement them. Experienced traders keep an eye on the trade they're in and the cash they have in their account as carefully as scuba divers watch their supply of oxygen. You must have a line in the sand that tells you when to get out of a trade. That is what we call having a "stop loss". It's going to be necessary from time to time to admit the trade did not work and say, *"The setup isn't ready yet."* Or perhaps, *"I'm getting out of the way."* And that acknowledgement must come in a timely fashion, and not too late in the trade! Waiting too long to exit a trade can literally wipe out your entire account.

It can happen to almost any of us, at any stage of our career. In June 2020, I entered a mindless trade on American Airlines Group Inc. (ticker: AAL) without any stop loss in mind. Traders in our community warned me not to do it, as I show all of my positions in the chatroom. Nevertheless, for some reason, I was much too confident. I did not even have a stop loss in mind. I eventually had to accept a $25,000 loss on a trade that I should have only accepted a $1,000 loss on.

That trade notwithstanding, I'm a consistently profitable trader, but I still lose almost every day. That means I must have found a way to be a really good loser. Lose gracefully. Take the losses and walk away, and then come back and look for another trade.

If a trade goes against you, exit the trade. In day trading, the unexpected will occur, this is the name of the game. There is always another trade and another day. Holding a position that is trading against you because you are primarily interested in proving your prediction to be correct is bad trading. Your job is not to be correct. Your job is to make money. This career is called trading, not predicting.

I can't emphasize enough how important it is to be a good loser. You have to be able to accept a loss. It's an integral part of day trading. In all of the strategies that I explain in this book, I will let you know what is my entry point, my exit target, as well as my stop loss.

You must follow the rules and plans of your strategy, and this is one of the challenges you will face when you are in a bad trade. You may very likely find yourself justifying staying in a bad trade by saying, *"Well, you know, it's Apple, and they make really great smartphones. They're definitely not going out of business. I'll just hold this a little longer."*

You do not want to experience that sort of wishful thinking. In the American Airlines trade I just mentioned, it crossed my mind that the U.S. government would eventually do something to save airlines, wouldn't they? And do that "something" right that very moment when I was in the midst of my trade? I forgot about trading rules, I forgot about trading patterns, and instead I "hoped" that something unexpected would save me. You must follow the rules of your strategy. You can always get back in, but it's hard to recover from a big loss. You may think, *"I don't want to take a $50 loss."* Well, you definitely don't want to take a subsequent $500 loss, and certainly not a $25,000 loss in front of your peers, like I did. And if you ended up taking such a big loss, it would be really hard to recover from that. Many beginner traders can never recover from a big loss. Take the small losses, get out, and come back when the timing is better.

Every time you enter a trade, you exposed to a risk. How do you minimize that risk? You need to find a good setup and manage the risk with proper share size and stop loss.

Here is my next rule:

RULE 5

> **Success in day trading comes from risk management - finding low-risk entries with a high potential reward. The minimum win:lose ratio for me is 2:1.**

A good setup is an opportunity for you to get into a trade with as little risk as possible. That means you might be risking $100, but you have the potential to make $500. You would call that a 5 to 1 profit-to-loss ratio. On the other hand, if you get into a setup where you're risking $100 to make $50, you have a less than 1 risk/reward ratio (in this case 1 to 2), and that's going to be a trade that you should not take. The minimum risk/reward ratio a day trader should take is 2 to 1.

Good traders will not take trades with profit-to-loss ratios of less than 2 to 1. That means if you buy $1,000 worth of stock, and are risking $100 on it, you must sell it for at least $1,200 so you will make at least $200.

Of course, if the price comes down to $900, you must accept the loss and exit the trade with only $900 (a $100 loss).

Let me explain the risk/reward ratio in a real trade that I took. Molina Healthcare, Inc. (ticker: MOH) was on my watchlist on February 16, 2017. At the Open (at 9:30 a.m.) it was strong and it then went higher. I was watching it. Suddenly, around 9:45 a.m., MOH started to sell off heavily below Volume Weighted Average Price (VWAP, see Chapter 5 for some detailed commentary on my indicators). I decided to sell short MOH below VWAP at around $50. My profit target was the next daily support of $48.82. That was a $1.20 reward per share. My stop loss naturally should have been when the price of MOH went above VWAP, which in this case was $50.40, as marked in Figure 3.1 below. I could risk $0.40 per share in the hope of rewarding myself $1.20 per share. That is a 1:3 risk/reward. I indeed took this trade.

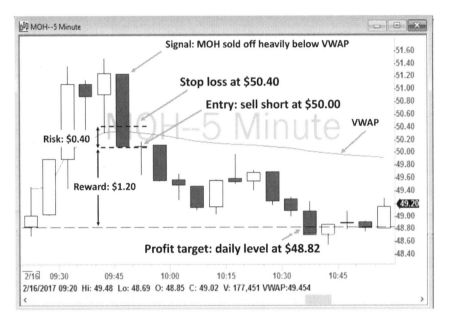

Figure 3.1: Screenshot of my trade on MOH on February 16, 2017 showing my entry, exit and stop loss. As you can see, the profit-to-loss ratio is 3 to 1.

Now imagine if, in the above example, you missed the opportunity at 9:45 a.m. when the stock was being traded at around $50.20, and instead you went to go short a few minutes later at around $49.60 with the profit target of $48.82. In this case, your reward would be around $0.80 per share, but your stop loss should be above VWAP at around $50.20. In this case, you are then risking $0.60 per share to reward yourself $0.80 per share. This 1.3 ratio ($0.80/$0.60) is not a favorable profit-to-loss opportunity that I want to base a trade on. In this case, I would accept that perhaps I missed the opportunity. You may say, OK, if my entry is at $49.60, I will define a closer stop loss to have a more favorable profit-to-stop loss ratio? The answer is NO. Your stop loss should be at a reasonable technical level. Any stop loss below VWAP is meaningless in this case, because the stock can make a normal pull back toward VWAP at any time and then continue to sell off toward your target. This is actually what happened when, at around 10:20 a.m., MOH's price pulled back toward VWAP, but did not reach to VWAP, and then sold off toward $48.80. I've marked this in Figure 3.2 below. If you had defined a stop loss anywhere below VWAP, most likely you would have been stopped out at a loss.

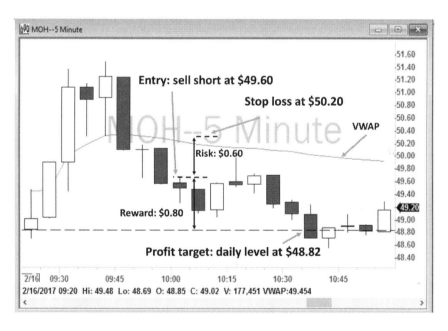

Figure 3.2: Screenshot of MOH on February 16, 2017. This is the example of a bad risk/reward. As you can see, the profit-to-loss ratio is less than 2 to 1 and is not tradeable. You have missed the opportunity.

If you cannot find a setup with a good profit-to-loss ratio, then you should move on and keep looking for another trade. As a day trader, you are always looking for opportunities to get a low-risk entry with a big reward, or as we call it, a favorable risk/reward. Being able to identify setups that have a proper and favorable risk/reward is one of the important parts of the learning process. As a beginner trader, you of course may not be able to differentiate and recognize these setups. It may be difficult for you to recognize what a home run ABCD Pattern is and what will end up being a "false breakout". That's something that comes with both experience and training. We will cover this in more depth in the coming chapters. You can learn from videos on YouTube and Google. You can also join our Bear Bull Traders chatroom where I and other experienced traders in our community explain our thought process in real time while we are trading. You will be able to observe us, our shared screen including scanner, and our trading platform. As a member of our community, you can also access our scanner for your own searches.

Using a 2 to 1 win:lose ratio, I can be wrong 40% of the time and still make money. Again, your job as a day trader is managing risk, it is not buying and selling stocks. Your broker is buying and selling stocks for you in the market. Your job is to manage your risk and your account. Whenever you click "buy" in your trading platform, you expose your money to risk.

How then do you manage that risk? There are essentially three steps to follow. You need to ask yourself:

1. Am I trading the right stock?

Do remember that risk management starts from choosing the right stock to trade. You can have the best platform and tools and be a master of many strategies, but if you are trading the wrong stock, you will definitely lose money. Chapter 4 focuses on finding the right Stocks in Play for day trading. I will explain in detail how to find stocks that are suitable for day trading and what criteria you should look for in them. You must avoid stocks that (1) are heavily traded by computers and institutional traders, (2) have small relative trading volume, (3) are penny stocks and are therefore highly manipulated, and (4) don't have any reason to move (no fundamental catalysts). I will explain these points in more detail in Chapter 4.

2. What share size should I take?

One share, 10 shares or 100 shares? What about 1,000 shares? This depends on your account size and your daily target. If you are targeting $1,000 a day, then ten or twenty shares might not be enough. You either have to take more shares or increase your account size. If you don't have enough money to trade for a $1,000 daily target, you should lower your daily goal.

I am holding around $50,000 in my trading account and I usually choose 2,000 shares to trade. My daily goal is $500 or around $120,000/year. That is sufficient for my lifestyle. What is your trading goal?

3. What is my stop loss?

An easy way to remember what your stop loss should be is to think about a carton or jug of milk. That's right. Milk. 2%. You should never risk more than 2% of your account on any given trade. If you have saved up sufficient funds and have $50,000 in your account, you should never put more than 2% at risk – in this case, $1,000. If you have only been able to save up a modest amount of funds for day trading, then you have no choice but to trade in smaller numbers of shares. Make it one of your unbreakable rules. It will be difficult to move on, but if as you stare at your monitors you see a possible setup that could cost you more than 2% of your trading account, just move on and look for another trade. With every single trade you make, you should always ensure that at least 98% of your account is protected.

THREE-STEP RISK MANAGEMENT

Step 1: Determine your maximum dollar risk for the trade you're planning (never more than 2% of your account). Calculate this before your trading day starts.

Step 2: Estimate your maximum risk per share, the stop loss, in dollars, from your entry. I will explain later in this book what the stop loss should be depending upon which specific strategy you are planning to trade.

Step 3: Divide "1" by "2" to find the absolute maximum number of shares you are allowed to trade each time.

To better illustrate this, let's return to the example of MOH from a few pages back. If you have a $40,000 account, the 2% rule will limit your risk on any trade to $800. Let's assume you want to be conservative and risk only 1% of that account, or $400. That will be Step 1.

As you monitor MOH, you see a situation develop where the VWAP Strategy (see Chapter 7) may very well work in your favor. You decide to sell short the stock at $50, and you want to cover them at $48.82, with a stop loss at $50.40. You will be risking $0.40 per share. That will be Step 2 of risk control.

For Step 3, calculate your share size by dividing "Step 1" by "Step 2" to find the maximum size you may trade. In this example, you will be allowed to buy a maximum of 1,000 shares.

In this case, you may not have enough cash or buying power to buy 1,000 shares of MOH at $50 (because you have only $40,000 in your account). So instead you will buy 800 shares or, perhaps, even 500 shares. Remember, you can always risk less, but you are not allowed to risk more than 2% of your account under any circumstance.

With the strategies introduced in the pages to come, I explain where my stop loss would be based on technical analysis and my trade plan. I cannot consider maximum loss for your account because I of course don't know your account size. You need to make that judgment for yourself. For example, when your stop would be above a moving average (see Chapter 5 for information on the indicators on my chart), you need to calculate and see if that stop would be bigger than your maximum account size or not. If break of moving average will yield a $600 loss, and you have set a $400 maximum loss per trade, then you should either take fewer shares in that trade or not take that trade at all and wait for another opportunity.

You may correctly argue that it will be difficult to calculate share size or stop loss based on a maximum loss on your account while you are waiting to jump into a trade. You will need to make a decision fast or else you will lose the opportunity. I understand that calculating your stop loss and maximum loss in your account size in a live trade is difficult. Remember Rule 2? Day trading is not supposed to be easy. Trading needs practice and I strongly recommend that new traders paper trade under supervision for at least three months in a live simulated account. It sounds crazy at the beginning, but you will quickly learn how to manage your account and your risk per trade. You will be amazed at how rapidly the human brain can do calculations on what share size to take and where to set the stop loss.

TRADING PSYCHOLOGY

A burning question for many when they begin their trading career is: *"Why do most traders fail?"*

To answer that, let's imagine three different traders place the exact same trade and all of them lose money. However, the way they react to their losses can be the catalyst that determines their eventual trading results. One trader might become discouraged, curse the market, and give up for the day. Another trader might become frustrated, trade more aggressively to recoup his earlier loss, and end up losing even more that day. A third trader will take a break from trading, walk out for a few minutes to reassess her emotions, come back to re-evaluate her strategy, wait for a clear signal of opportunity, and then place a good trade that brings her even by the end of the day.

What is fundamentally different about these traders?

The answer to these two questions is that success and failure are based on how traders behave and how they control their emotions. That is what distinguishes the winners from the losers.

A key reason why many traders fail is that they take negative events and losses in trading personally. Their confidence and peace of mind are connected to their trading results. When traders do well, they feel good. When they encounter losses, they become discouraged, doubtful, and frustrated, questioning themselves, their strategy and their career. Instead of dealing directly and constructively with their losses, they react to the emotions triggered by personalizing the events.

Successful traders are those who trade for skill and not for the money. Almost all professional traders hide their unrealized profit and loss (P&L) column while in a trade. They have no interest in seeing how much they are up or down. They focus on the perfect execution of a profit target or a stop loss level. Consistently profitable traders take every negative or positive trade they make as an opportunity to improve themselves.

Day trading requires you to make quick decisions while at the same time being very disciplined. That is why it is such a demanding career. Every morning, you should scan the market, find the opportunities, and sometimes in a matter of seconds make decisions on whether you should buy or sell or sell short the Stock in Play, and you need to make that call with a high degree of discipline.

One of the key contributors to traders' self-discipline is their physical and mental health. People who eat well-balanced nutritional meals, exercise regularly, maintain proper body weight and fitness levels, and get adequate rest are likely to have the levels of energy and alertness that are required to make them effective traders. You may be surprised to read this, but your state of alertness, your energy level, and your overall health have a significant impact on your daily trading results. Those who neglect these aspects of their well-being or, even worse, abuse alcohol or drugs, will find it difficult to concentrate and make good decisions.

Fatigue, physical tension, and ill health will often affect your concentration and adversely affect your sound decision-making process. It is difficult to make and sustain the required mental efforts for day trading when you lack proper sleep or feel down from a lack of exercise. Very often, your moods are influenced by your physical state, even by factors as delicate as what and how much you eat. Keep a daily record of both your trading results and your physical condition and you will see these relationships for yourself. Begin preventive maintenance by keeping your body, and thus your mind, in their peak operating condition.

Aspects of personal lives outside of trading can also impact the effectiveness of a trader. Changes in personal relationships such as a breakup or divorce, family issues like illness, and financial problems can reduce a person's ability to focus and make appropriate decisions. For example, it is common for young traders to experience more stress after they have married, had children, or purchased a new home, because these added financial responsibilities create additional worry and stress (but also hopefully much pleasure!).

It certainly took time, but I found that the more and more I practiced, the more effectively I was able to execute my trading strategies (which I will explain later). Real success though did not come until I was able to control myself and practice self-discipline. It's very challenging to predict what the stock markets will do on any given day. Your success will be very limited, and any success will almost exclusively be based on pure luck, if you yourself do not know in advance what you will do before you enter a trade. You need to have a well-thought-out plan and you need to follow that plan. New trading strategies, tips from chatrooms or from this book, or even the most sophisticated software imaginable, will not help traders who cannot handle themselves and control their emotions.

For every trade, you must ask yourself some questions:

- Does this trade complement my trading personality and my risk tolerance?
- What strategy will this trade fit into?
- If this trade goes the wrong way, where is my stop?
- How much money am I risking in the trade, and what is the reward potential?

This is what many traders find difficult. All of these decisions, the very process of ensuring these decisions fit into your risk tolerance and your strategy parameters, are a tough multitasking call. Not only is it multitasking, but it is multitasking while under stress.

I understand that stress. There have been times when I've been in the trade, had an $80,000 position, and all I needed to do was to sell. But as I was looking at my keyboard, I found myself frozen like the proverbial deer in the headlights. I couldn't even figure out which keys to punch. This sort of paralysis is not unusual when you're overwhelmed. It happens to every single one of us. But remember, confidence in trading doesn't arise from being right and profitable in all of your trades, it comes from surviving the occasions of being wrong and losing money.

Trading is stressful. Day trading is perhaps the most stressful of all types of trading. One mistake can ruin your month. One missed proper profit taking can ruin your week. There is a fine line between being a good trader and being a losing trader. If you are under pressure, don't make any trades. Take a walk to release your stress and do not restart trading until you are once again focused and calm. Trading professionals will often refresh their minds by going for a run after a bad loss, and then come back to restart trading, but in a simulator and not live, until they are back on track emotionally.

Review the results of your decisions and constantly be analyzing your performance.

- Are you trading profitably over time? How is your cumulative profit and loss? Your net equity curve (your profit and loss after deducting your broker's commissions and fees)?

- Have you had several winning days in a row or have you had several losing days in a row?

- If you are on a losing streak, will you be in touch with your own emotions and maintain your composure, or will you let your judgment be impaired? You need to connect with your community or accountability group and ensure you have a trading "buddy" or mentor who will also monitor your performance and provide feedback.

I cannot emphasize enough just how important the following steps are: you must take the time to prepare, you must work hard, you must plan your trades, you must take the time afterward to review your trades, and you cannot do it alone. You cannot succeed on your own. There is so much value in sharing ideas and learning from a community of traders and, should you have one, your mentor.

Consider skill and discipline to be your trading muscles. Muscles require exercise to grow and, once you've grown them, they need to be exercised or you will lose them. That's what I experience every day: continually exercising my ability to practice self-control and discipline. The good news is that many of the skills you learn from trading are comparable to learning how to drive. Once you've learned it, driving is a skill that can't be taken away. Do you remember the very first time you went driving? I sense it was a very intimidating and multitasking endeavor. Now though, you can drive without really thinking about it. It's the same for trading. Once you've learned it, skills such as identifying a good stock to trade or how to enter and exit a trade will not go away. But remember, discipline is something you will need to constantly work at in order to be a successful trader. Discipline has always been a continuous endeavor. For example, when can you say you are finally fit and are in great physical shape? Never. You must always be disciplined with your diet, with your exercise, and with your sleep.

You've entered a profession in which you will always be learning and practicing discipline and mindfulness. That's great and it's very stimulating. But it's important to remember that if you start to get over-confident and think you've outsmarted the market on trading wisdom, or that you don't need to learn anymore, you'll often get a quick reminder from that market: a slap in the face! You'll lose money and you will see that the market is correcting you.

I cannot emphasize enough that being able to make quick decisions and being able to make and then follow your trading rules are critical for success in the market. As you continue through this book, you are going to read much about risk management. Everything that traders do comes back to risk management because ultimately it is the most important concept for a trader to understand. All day long, you are managing risk. Related to this is the ability to manage risk so that you will make good decisions - even in the heat of the moment.

That's the next rule of day trading:

RULE 6

Your broker will buy and sell stocks for you at the Exchange. Your only job as a day trader is to manage risk. You cannot be a successful day trader without excellent risk management skills, even if you are the master of many effective strategies.

As mentioned before, day trading is a very serious pursuit. You must treat it as such. Only you can decide how much of your account you can afford to potentially lose at any one time. You have to take into consideration your finances, your skill and your personality. But never forget the previously explained 2% rule. Do not take a trade if more than 2% of your account will be put in jeopardy. It very simply is not worth the risk.

There's a very basic truth that you must accept: you should not expect to be right all of the time. It's impossible to be. Trading is based on probabilities, and it requires a great deal of patience to identify setups with attractive risk/reward potential. I'm a consistently profitable trader, but 30% of my trades result in a loss. I don't expect to be right every single trade. If you owned a small business, you wouldn't expect it to be profitable every single day. There would be days when you wouldn't have enough customers or sales even to support your staff or your lease, but these would be more than offset by days when your business prospered.

If you examine the work of most successful traders, you will notice that they all take many small losses. Their results are littered with numerous small losses of 7c (cents), 5c, 3c, and even 1c per share. Most good day traders have few losses that are more than 30c per share. Most winning trades should work for you right away.

One of the fundamentals you must learn from this book is that every day trading strategy comes with a stop loss level and you must stop out from stocks that trade against your strategy. Imagine for a moment that you are shorting a stock below an important resistance level and you are waiting for the price to go lower. That is fine. But suddenly the price turns against you and breaks the resistance level and trades higher. Now your original trade plan is obsolete. You have no reason to stay in the trade. You cannot wait in the trade in the hope that the stock may trade lower again. That is wishful thinking. You can wipe out your trading account with ONE crazy move. The stock may or may not trade lower again, but above the resistance level you have no reason to be short in the stock. If the stock was weak and comes back below the level, you may enter the trade again. Commissions are cheap, so accept a small loss and get out. You can always get back into the trade when the setup is ready.

Those who never master this fundamental rule will fail. This is a common problem amongst new traders: they don't accept the small loss. You must work at this while trading in a simulator. You should move to live

trading only if you have mastered accepting and respect-
ing your stop loss. If you don't know where your stop
loss is or where it should be, it means that you probably
should not be in the trade in the first place. It means
you have not planned it correctly. It also means you
should step back, review your strategies, and return to
trading in the simulator.

Consistently profitable traders make sound and
reasonable trades. They accept that they cannot control
the market or results on every single trade, but they
stick to their plan and control their capital. Often you
can review your profit and loss at the end of the month.
Professional traders often review their P&L quarterly,
and then make a decision on their performance and
adjust their trading strategies accordingly.

Many traders think a good trading day is a positive
day. Wrong. A good trading day is a day that you were
disciplined, traded sound strategies and did not violate
any trading rules. The normal uncertainty of the stock
market will result in some of your days being negative,
but that does not mean that a negative day was a bad
trading day.

CHAPTER 4

━━━━━━

HOW TO FIND STOCKS FOR TRADES

"*You are only as good as the stocks that you trade.*" This is a famous expression in the trading community. There are too many new traders who do not know what a good stock to day trade is nor how to find one, and they waste too many trading days mistakenly believing that the market is impossible to day trade in.

You can be the best trader in the world, but if your stocks do not move, nor have enough volume, then you cannot make money consistently. My previously mentioned friend, Mike Bellafiore, who is the co-founder of SMB Capital (a proprietary trading firm in New York City), writes in his amazing book, *One Good Trade*, that trading a stock that doesn't move is a trading day wasted. As a day trader, you must be efficient with your time and buying power (which will be explained in Chapter 5).

Now, we don't want stocks to just move, but we seek stocks where we can identify that they are about to move in a certain direction. It is possible that a stock that moves $5 intraday may never offer us excellent risk/reward opportunities. Some stocks move too much intraday without foreshadowing their direction.

Your next challenge as a new trader is to learn how to find proper stocks to play.

Many new traders understand how trading works and have a proper education and the right tools for day trading, but when it comes to actually finding stocks to trade in real time, they are (and I don't want to sound mean) clueless. I certainly experienced this as a new trader myself. If you learn the strategies explained in this book, but you cannot make money consistently, it is possible that you are in the wrong stock. Again, you are only as good as the stocks you trade. You need to find the stocks that are in play by day traders or, as I call them, *Stocks in Play.*

There is more than one way to select Stocks in Play and make money trading them, and there is definitely more than one correct way. Some traders trade baskets of stocks and indexes. Some day traders, like another one of my friends, Brian Pezim, author of the best-selling book, *How to Swing Trade*, primarily trade Exchange-traded funds (ETFs). Many have developed proprietary filters to find stocks. Others concentrate on trading the markets as a whole with index Futures. Professional traders at the trading desks of the big banks often simply trade in a sector like Gold or Oil or Tech. But remember, we are retail traders with limited amounts of capital, so we must be efficient with selecting our Stocks in Play.

A Stock in Play is a stock that offers excellent risk/ reward setup opportunities - opportunities where your downside is 5c and your upside is 25c, or your downside is 20c and your upside is $1 - that's 1:5. You can regularly read a Stock in Play that is about to trade higher or lower from its present price. A Stock in Play moves, and these moves are predictable, frequent, and catchable. A good intraday stock offers numerous and excellent risk/reward opportunities.

Every day, there are a new series of stocks that are in play. Trading Stocks in Play allows you to be the most efficient with your buying power. They often offer much better risk/reward opportunities intraday and allow you to execute your ideas and trading rules with more consistency. Trading the right Stocks in Play helps you to combat algorithmic programs.

STOCKS IN PLAY

What are Stocks in Play? I explain in detail later in this book how to find them, but they could be, in no particular order:

- A stock with fresh news
- A stock that is up or down more than 2% before the market Open
- A stock that has unusual pre-market trading activity
- A stock that develops important intraday levels which we can trade off from

You must remember that retail trading does not work on all stocks. It only works on the stocks that have *high relative volume.* Some stocks like Facebook, Inc. (ticker: FB) will on average trade millions and millions of shares each day, while other stocks on average might trade only 500,000 shares each day. Does this mean you should trade FB only? No. High volume will be relative from one stock to another. You don't just look for high total volume. There are some stocks that on average will trade with much volume. You need to look for what's above average for that specific stock. Twenty million shares of FB traded in one day might very well not be higher than usual. Do not trade FB unless it has a very unusual trading volume. If trading volume is not higher than normal, it means that the trading is being domi-nated by institutional traders and high frequency trading computers. Stay away from it.

Figure 4.1: FB daily chart for winter 2019. Days that FB had a significant relative volume are marked. Those days were suitable for day trading FB.

Take a look at Figure 4.1 above, the FB daily chart for the winter of 2019. As you can see, there were only a handful of days that had high relative activity. They're marked with arrows on the chart. Interestingly enough, when you take a close look at the chart, you realize that on those days the stock gapped up or down. I marked those price gaps on the chart. If you wanted to trade FB, you should have traded it only on those days. The other days were comprised of just normal, high frequency, algorithmic trading. Retail traders should stay away from stocks that are trading normally.

The most important characteristic of high relative volume stocks is that these stocks trade independent of what their sector and the overall market are doing. When the market is weak, it means that the majority of stocks are selling off. It does not matter if it is Apple, Facebook, Amazon or ExxonMobil. When the market is strong, the prices of the majority of stocks will be going higher. Similarly, when you hear someone say the market is "bear" or "collapsing", they don't mean a specific stock. They mean that the whole stock market is losing its value – all stocks together. The same is true for specific sectors. For example, when the pharmaceutical sector is weak, it means all of the pharmaceutical companies are losing their values together.

How do you recognize the behavior of the market? Index funds such as the Dow Jones Industrial Average (ticker: DIA) or the SPDR S&P 500 ETF Trust (ticker: SPY) are usually good indicators of what the overall market is doing. If the DIA or SPY are red, it means that the overall market is weak. If the DIA or SPY are strong, then the overall market will be going higher.

The behavior of stocks that have high relative volume is independent of the overall market; they are Stocks in Play. Every day, only a handful of stocks are being traded independently of their sector and the overall market. Day traders trade only those stocks. I sometimes call those stocks "*Alpha*". In the animal kingdom, alpha is a predator at the top of a food chain upon which no other creatures prey. In day trading, Alpha stocks are the ones that are independent of both the overall market and their sector. The market and high frequency trading cannot control them. We call these Stocks in Play.

Therefore, the next rule is about Stocks in Play:

RULE 7

Retail traders trade only Stocks in Play, high relative volume stocks that have fundamental catalysts and are being traded regardless of the overall market.

We know we need high relative volume, but how much volume is enough. I don't trade stocks with an average daily volume of less than 500,000 shares. You need certain liquidity in the stock to be able to get in and out of the stock without difficulty. For example, if you buy JPMorgan Chase & Co. (ticker: JPM) at $105 and you set an exit price for $104.85, can you actually get out near $104.85? Or, because volume is so low, do you have to sell at $104.50 to exit? If you are trading JPM and you conclude you should exit at $104.85, but really you cannot exit until $104.50, then this is not a good trading stock intraday. Stocks in Play have sufficient liquidity so that you can exit without unexpected slippage.

What makes a stock a Stock in Play? Usually it is the release of fundamental news about the stock either the day before or during the same trading day. Important news or events for companies can have significant impacts on their value in the market and therefore act as fundamental catalysts for their price action.

As mentioned in Chapter 2, some examples of the fundamental catalysts for stocks that make them suitable for day trading include:

- Earnings reports
- Earnings warnings or pre-announcements
- Earnings surprises
- FDA approvals or disapprovals
- Mergers or acquisitions
- Alliances, partnerships, or major product releases
- Major contract wins or losses
- Restructurings, layoffs, or management changes
- Stock splits, buybacks, or debt offerings

I check the news on all stocks up or down more than 2% pre-market and shortlist my Gappers watchlist (which I will explain further along in this book). Stocks in Play the day before are often still in play for a few days after.

In Chapter 7, I explain specific day trading strategies such as Momentum, Reversal, VWAP, and Moving Average. For the moment, your main question needs to be, how do I find the stock for each strategy? I categorize stocks for retail trading into three classes. Based on my experiences, this categorization provides some clarity on how to find stocks and on how to adopt a strategy for them.

FLOAT AND MARKET CAP

Before explaining the three categories, let me explain the definition of "*float*" and "*market capitalization*" or "*market cap*". Float means the number of shares available for trading. Apple Inc., for example, as of June 2020, had 4.33 billion shares in the market that are available for buying and selling. Apple is considered a "*mega cap*" stock. These stocks usually don't move much during the day because they require significant volume and money to be traded, so Apple shares might on average change by only $1 or $2 each day. They are not very volatile and therefore day traders don't like trading them. Day traders look for volatility.

On the other hand, there are some stocks that have very low float. For example, ThermoGenesis Holdings Inc. (ticker: THMO) has only about a 3.4 million-share float as of June 2020. This means that the supply of shares of THMO is low and therefore a large demand can very quickly move the price of the stock. Low float stocks can be volatile and move very fast. Most of the low float stocks are under $10 because they are early stage companies which for the most part are not profitable. They hope to grow, and by growing further, they issue more shares and raise more money from the public market and slowly become mega cap stocks. These low float stocks are also called "*small cap*" or "*micro-cap*" stocks. Day traders love low float stocks. Now let's return to those three categories.

The first category consists of low float stocks that are priced under $10. These stocks are extremely volatile, moving 10%, 20%, 100% or even 1,000% each day. Yes, there have been those kinds of moves! You must be careful with this category. Just as you can turn your $1,000 into $10,000 in a single trade, your $1,000 can just as easily turn into $10. Low float stocks under $10 are often highly manipulated and difficult to trade, and therefore only very experienced and highly equipped retail traders should trade these stocks. I personally rarely trade in them. If someone claims to have turned $1,000 into $10,000 in a month, and if it's true, they must have traded this type of low float stock. No beginner or even intermediate trader can trade with such accuracy and efficiency. If novice traders tried trading low float stocks that are under $10, they would more likely turn their $1,000 into nothing in a matter of days.

When it comes to low float stocks, the Bull Flag Momentum Strategy - which I detail later - works best. The other strategies in this book are not suitable for low float sub-$10 stocks.

You generally cannot sell short low float stocks that cost less than $10. For short selling, you need to borrow shares from your broker, and it's rare that a broker will lend you such volatile stocks. Even if your broker is willing to lend them to you, I strongly advise that you do not attempt to short sell them. They can easily surge and you will end up wiping out your account. You definitely can become a full-time profitable day trader without short selling risky stocks, so leave that to the Wall Street professionals.

Trading low float stocks is very difficult for the new trader. It is difficult to read the direction of their next move and therefore it is very difficult to manage your risk while trading them. I discourage new traders from trading low float stocks. When the new trader is wrong, the loss is such that it wipes out many gains.

The second category is *medium float* stocks in the range of $10-$100. These stocks have medium floats of around 20 million to 500 million shares. Many of my strategies explained in this book work well on these stocks, especially the VWAP and Support or Resistance Strategies. Medium float stocks that are more expensive than $100 are not popular among retail day traders and I myself avoid them. You usually cannot buy many shares of them because of their high price. Therefore, it is basically useless to day trade them. Leave them for the institutional traders.

The third category of stocks for trading is *mega cap* stocks like Apple, Alibaba, Yahoo, Microsoft and Home Depot. These are well-established companies that usually have over $500 million in public shares available for trading. These stocks are traded in millions of shares every day. As you may guess, these stocks move only when large institutional traders, investment banks, and hedge funds are buying or selling large positions. Retail traders like us, who typically trade 100 to 2,000 shares, usually cannot move the price of these stocks. Retail traders should avoid these stocks unless there is a good fundamental catalyst for them. From the strategies set forth in this book, Reversals and Moving Average Strategies usually work well on these stocks. Do not forget though, unless there is a fundamental catalyst, these stocks are being heavily traded by computers and high frequency traders and are not suitable for retail day trading.

The table below summarizes these categories:

FLOAT	PRICE RANGE	MY FAVORITE STRATEGY (CHAPTER 7)
Low float (less than 20 million)	Under $10	Only Momentum (Long)
Medium float (20-500 million)	$10-$100	All, mostly VWAP and Support or Resistance
Large float (+500 million)	Any (usually +$20)	All, mostly Moving Average and Reversal

Stocks in Play can be found in two ways:

- Pre-market morning watchlist
- Real time intraday scans

Let me explain how each day I find my Stocks in Play for trading.

PRE-MARKET GAPPERS

Experienced traders are sensitive to being in the right stocks at the right time. As I mentioned, traders are only as good as the stocks they trade. I and the traders in our community use a scanner every morning that is programmed to find Stocks in Play based on the following criteria:

- Stocks that in the pre-market gapped up or down at least 2%

- Stocks that have traded at least 50,000 shares in the pre-market

- Stocks that have an average daily volume of over 500,000 shares

- Stocks that have Average True Range of at least 50 cents (how large of a range in price a stock has on average every day)

- There is a fundamental catalyst for the stock

- As a rule, I do not trade stocks with an enormous short interest higher than 30% (the short interest is the quantity of stock shares that investors or traders have sold short but not yet covered or closed out)

Why these criteria?

When there are some fundamental catalysts, there will be unusual pre-market activity and a Stock in Play will have gapped up or down before the market opens with a significant number of shares being traded (such as 50,000 shares).

I look for highly traded stocks, so that buying and selling 1,000 shares won't be a problem. That is why I am looking at stocks with an average daily volume of over 500,000 shares. I also am looking for stocks that usually move in a good range for trading. That is why I look at Average True Range (ATR). ATR means how large of a price range a stock has on average every day. If ATR is $1, then you can expect the stock to move around $1 daily. That is a good number. If you have 1,000 shares, you may profit $1,000 from the trade. But if ATR is only 10 cents, then that trading range is not attractive for me.

Let's look at Figure 4.2, which is an example of how my watchlist will form. On June 1, 2020 at 9 a.m. New York time, my scanner showed these stocks:

Symbol	Price ($)	Vol Today	Chg Close	Chg Close	Flt (Shr)	Avg True	Shrt Flt (%)	Sector
SPCE	18.27	1.15M	1.23	7.2	175M	1.30	55.79	Other Services (except Public Administration)
GAN	23.00	171,397	1.11	5.1	57.5M	1.77	0.72	Professional, Scientific, and Technical Services
CRWD	90.65	118,055	2.84	3.2	113M	4.45	3.19	Manufacturing
MT	9.93	121,941	0.31	3.2	1.01B	0.65		Manufacturing
GPS	9.16	140,952	0.26	2.9	205M	0.86	21.18	Retail Trade
ZM	183.77	172,576	4.29	2.4	155M	10.07	6.22	Professional, Scientific, and Technical Services
LUV	32.78	437,858	0.68	2.1	507M	2.07	4.25	Transportation and Warehousing
BYND	131.00	166,490	2.71	2.1	57.3M	10.31	11.64	Manufacturing
AAL	10.72	1.23M	0.22	2.1	423M	0.80	55.83	Transportation and Warehousing
UBER	35.52	112,120	-0.80	-2.2	1.25B	1.92	3.32	Professional, Scientific, and Technical Services
M	6.19	745,931	-0.17	-2.7	309M	0.56	48.06	Retail Trade
GILD	75.50	573,123	-2.33	-3.0	1.25B	2.18	2.08	Manufacturing
CGC	16.60	386,862	-0.77	-4.4	201M	1.77		Manufacturing
PFE	35.67	778,526	-2.52	-6.6	5.55B	0.79	0.95	Manufacturing
ADAP	9.90	394,554	-1.17	-10.6	665M	1.18		Manufacturing
ABIO	9.95	162,733	-2.65	-21.0	1.59M	1.97	1.44	Manufacturing
EVH	6.95	106,156	-1.93	-21.7	81.1M	0.65	12.79	Administrative and Support and Waste Management and Remediation Services

Gappers Watch List (Pre-Market Movers): 9:00:00 - 9:04:59 6/01/2020

Figure 4.2: My Gappers watchlist on June 1, 2020 at 9 a.m. ET.

As you can see, I have highlighted the second "Chg Close" and the Float columns on my watchlist. The second "Chg Close" column represents how much the price of the stock has changed since the markets closed the previous trading day. In this instance, for example, the price of CrowdStrike Holdings Inc. (ticker: CRWD) has gapped up 3.2% in pre-market trading. From over 4,000 stocks, I now have only seventeen candidates (the stocks that have gapped up or down by at least 2%). I will go over each of them before the market opens at 9:30 a.m. I will check the news on each of them to learn why they gapped up or down. Is there a fundamental catalyst for that stock? Has there been any news coverage or extreme events for that company?

From those seventeen candidates (for that day, the number varies each day), I usually select two or three stocks to watch closely. You cannot watch seventeen stocks, and regardless, there are usually no more than two or three good candidates. I watch the best two or three candidates closely on my screens, looking for potential setups. I plan my trades before the market opens (I provide some thoughts on how to create if-then statements in Chapter 10) and then I wait for the market bell. I then trade my plan.

I mentioned above that, as a rule, I do not trade stocks with an enormous short interest, nor with a daily volume likely to be less than 500,000 shares intraday. A high short interest indicates traders or investors think a stock's price is likely to fall. But the challenge with high short interest is that these stocks are more prone to a short squeeze by bullish investors and traders. A short squeeze occurs when short sellers panic and are scrambling to return their borrowed shares, forcing prices to increase quickly and dangerously. You do not want to be stuck short in a short squeeze.

I am sometimes unable to identify a stock that fits these criteria for being in play on the Gappers scanner. In those cases, I watch my intraday real time scanner to find Stocks in Play for momentum or reversal or other types of trades. My first choice though will always be a Stock in Play that I find on my pre-market Gappers watchlist.

REAL TIME INTRADAY SCANS

For some strategies, you cannot find stocks in the pre-market. The Momentum, Top Reversal and Bottom Reversal Strategies explained later in this book are the types of strategies applicable for when a setup suitable for trading happens during trading hours. It is hard to find these stocks during a pre-market scan watchlist. For these strategies, I have specific scanners that look for these stocks and I will explain these scanners in detail in the next section.

Real Time Volume Radar

During the day, there may be some new Stocks in Play in the market that did not present as such when I was building my morning watchlist. Figure 4.3 below is a screenshot of a scanner on my Trade Ideas software that is set to find real time stocks for me that:

VolumeRadar: 10:55:00 - 10:59:59

Symbol	Price ($)	Chg Close	Vol Today (Shr)	Avg Vol	Pos Rng (%)	Rel Vol	Avg True	Sector
USG	30.54	8.8	3,059,686	918K		10.6	0.56	Manufacturing
RMD	67.89	-1.7	622,086	1.41M		3.23	0.99	Manufacturing
KLAC	68.74	1.8	706,826	1.51M		2.31	1.80	Manufacturing
HLF	62.30	3.0	1,853,963	3.26M		1.86	1.52	Wholesale Trade
HOG	51.83	-1.4	936,729	1.20M		1.34	1.28	Manufacturing
GOLD	98.37	-0.7	172,337	960K		0.56	2.77	Mining, Quarrying, and Oil and Gas Extraction

Figure 4.3: My intraday Volume Radar scanner looking for real time Stocks in Play.

1. Have gapped up or down at least $1
2. Have ATR of more than 50 cents
3. Have average relative volume of at least 1.5 (the stock is trading at 1.5 times its normal volume)
4. Have average daily trading volume of at least 500,000 shares

Those are my requirements for a stock to be in play. Having ATR of more than 50 cents is important because you want the stock to move enough during the day so you can make a profit out of its volatility. There is no point in trading a stock that is moving only 5 cents on average in a day.

I will also take a look at the sector of stocks. If I have a few stocks in one sector, there is a good chance that these stocks are not in play. They have high relative volume because their sector is under heavy trading by institutional traders. It is important to know that stocks usually trade with their sector. For example, when oil stocks are selling off, almost all of the oil companies sell off. Therefore, it is important to recognize Stocks in Play from the herd. Remember, you are only as good as the stock you trade, so if you are the best trader in the world, but in a wrong stock, you will lose money.

Real Time Bull Flag Momentum Scanner

For the Momentum Strategy, as I earlier explained, you need to find low float stocks that are moving. You cannot find these stocks unless you are using a good scanner. For a scanner, I use Trade Ideas software *www.Trade-Ideas.com*. Please check our website for the Trade Ideas link and information on a discount exclusive for members of our trading community.

M History: Intraday Bull Flag Momentum Scalping Strategy							— ☐ ✕
Time	Symbol	Price ($)	Vol Today	Rel Vol	Flt (Shr)	Vol 5 Min	Strategy Name
3:49:26 PM 8/29	NIHD	2.73	1.30M	3.18	92.4M	1,321	Medium-Float Bull Flag Momentum
3:49:01 PM 8/29	LNTH	9.70	1.44M	6.25	11.3M	917.2	Medium-Float Bull Flag Momentum
3:48:53 PM 8/29	LNTH	9.67	1.44M	6.24	11.3M	1,005	Medium-Float Bull Flag Momentum
3:48:18 PM 8/29	NIHD	2.69	1.27M	3.15	92.4M	1,078	Medium-Float Bull Flag Momentum
3:46:51 PM 8/29	NIHD	2.67	1.24M	3.11	92.4M	864.5	Medium-Float Bull Flag Momentum
3:46:32 PM 8/29	LNTH	9.66	1.40M	6.10	11.3M	764.6	Medium-Float Bull Flag Momentum
3:45:54 PM 8/29	CSTM	6.10	2.28M	3.33	70.0M	1,720	Medium-Float Bull Flag Momentum
3:45:27 PM 8/29	LNTH	9.58	1.38M	6.07	11.3M	925.0	Medium-Float Bull Flag Momentum
3:45:02 PM 8/29	SGU	8.90	131,484	3.00	51.7M	8,429	Medium-Float Bull Flag Momentum
3:43:59 PM 8/29	CSTM	6.09	2.25M	3.31	70.0M	1,441	Medium-Float Bull Flag Momentum
3:43:58 PM 8/29	TPIC	20.96	1.16M	4.99	11.2M	2,169	Daily Breakout Bull Flag Momentum
3:43:41 PM 8/29	LNTH	9.56	1.36M	6.02	11.3M	654.7	Medium-Float Bull Flag Momentum

Figure 4.4: My intraday real time Bull Flag Momentum scanner.

In Figure 4.4 above, you can see how I am scanning real time for my Momentum Strategy. During the day, the scanner is finding stocks that have high relative volume, low float, and high activity. I then check them in my trading platform and decide, based on my Momentum Strategy set out in Chapter 7, if I want to trade them.

Real Time Reversal Scanners

Top and Bottom Reversal Strategies are two other strategies that you cannot find stocks for in the pre-market. You must have an intraday real time scanner. Figure 4.5 below is an image of a Top and Bottom Reversal scan:

Time	Symbol	Price ($)	Vol Today	Consec Cndls	Rel Vol	Avg True	5 Min RSI (0
3:51:29 PM	ZG	34.80	648K	-4	1.12	1.13	23.8
3:49:21 PM	TRI	41.54	733K	-4	1.25	0.48	20.7
3:48:13 PM	TRI	41.55	718K	-4	1.23	0.48	21.9
3:45:45 PM	TRI	41.56	700K	-4	1.22	0.48	22.8
3:38:37 PM	MCHI	46.86	909K	-4	1.07	0.51	18.1
3:37:28 PM	MCHI	46.87	885K	-4	1.05	0.51	18.6
3:36:12 PM	MCHI	46.89	862K	-4	1.02	0.51	19.9
3:35:09 PM	MCHI	46.90	844K	-4	1.01	0.51	20.6
2:31:55 PM	SBAC	112.96	618K	-6	1.37	1.79	23.4
2:26:13 PM	SBAC	112.98	608K	-5	1.37	1.79	24.1
2:23:22 PM	PGR	32.33	2.00M	-4	1.55	0.39	23.4
2:21:22 PM	PGR	32.34	1.99M	-4	1.56	0.39	24.3
2:18:40 PM	RMD	67.51	2.48M	-7	5.79	0.89	19.2
2:12:47 PM	RMD	67.54	2.46M	-6	5.91	0.89	18.7
1:18:44 PM	AMT	115.03	923K	-5	1.29	1.31	26.1
1:16:34 PM	AMT	115.05	912K	-5	1.29	1.31	26.6
1:15:29 PM	AMT	115.07	910K	-5	1.29	1.31	27.3
1:14:14 PM	AMT	115.08	907K	-4	1.29	1.31	27.4

History: Top Reversal

Time	Symbol	Price ($)	Vol Today	Consec Cndls	Rel Vol	Avg True	5 Min RSI (0
2:36:54 PM	DATA	62.00	6.17M	4	7.76	1.49	53.2
2:27:42 PM	SGEN	47.83	535K	4	1.50	1.20	57.1
2:27:35 PM	FISV	104.19	711K	4	1.42	1.63	67.9
2:27:35 PM	FISV	104.19	711K	4	1.42	1.63	67.9
2:10:03 PM	DD	70.42	2.74M	4	2.23	0.90	73.1
1:46:26 PM	PVH	109.37	829K	5	2.10	2.41	64.6
1:40:54 PM	SHOP	42.20	1.20M	5	1.43	1.72	56.3
1:40:49 PM	MENT	23.68	2.26M	5	6.47	0.47	59.4
1:40:10 PM	PVH	109.36	807K	4	2.09	2.41	65.4
1:35:26 PM	SHOP	42.19	1.19M	4	1.45	1.72	55.7
1:35:14 PM	MENT	23.67	2.25M	4	6.56	0.47	58.3
1:32:41 PM	SWFT	19.48	1.32M	5	1.03	0.53	68.4
1:32:12 PM	DSW	26.01	1.07M	4	1.40	0.67	61.7
1:31:37 PM	ZAYO	29.37	1.14M	4	1.01	0.40	53.0
1:23:30 PM	AME	49.71	852K	4	1.08	0.83	68.0
1:20:12 PM	AME	49.70	848K	4	1.08	0.83	66.9
1:20:12 PM	AME	49.70	848K	4	1.08	0.83	66.9
1:20:12 PM	BA	134.14	1.96M	4	1.20	1.37	55.6

Figure 4.5: My intraday real time Reversal scanner.

As you can see, I am scanning the market real time to find stocks that are selling off or surging up so I can trade my Reversal Strategies.

I won't go into the details here about how to make these scans, but I will explain in Chapter 7 under each strategy the specifics of what to look for in stocks in each category. If you develop new strategies for yourself, you can also define new scanners for yourself. These scanners are highly adjustable and you can change the parameters as you like. These are the parameters that work for me, but as you gain experience and learn more about other strategies and your own preferred trading style, you may very well decide to define new scanners for yourself.

Many new traders don't initially need a scanner. Some day trading communities will let you observe their scanner in real time. These scanners are costly, so at the beginning of your career transition to day trading, you will probably want to keep your expenses down as much as possible.

PLANNING THE TRADE BASED ON SCANNERS

Once I find my Stocks in Play, I start to look for the individual trading patterns in them. I usually select three Stocks in Play and monitor their charts separately on three of my screens. When I see a potential strategy, I plan my trade. This is a fast decision-making process. Sometimes you have to plan a trade in a few minutes and at other times in just a few seconds. This is why you need months of training in simulator accounts to well understand the decision-making process.

I focus considerably on quality versus quantity. There are many, many traders out there and there are hundreds of strategies out there as well. I had to find the strategy that worked best for me, my personality and my account size. I've found a strategy that works really well for traders in our community as well as for my own personal trading. This strategy involves taking only the best setups and waiting, and not trading, until we see something that is actually worth trading.

Day trading can be a boring profession – most of the time you are just sitting and watching your list. In fact, if day trading is not boring for you, then you are probably overtrading.

If you require a reminder of the importance of patience in trading, here it is. There are plenty of traders out there who are making the error of overtrading. Overtrading can mean trading twenty, thirty, forty, or even sixty times a day. You'll be commissioning your broker to do each and every one of those trades, so you are going to lose both money and commissions. Many brokers charge $4.95 for each trade, so for forty trades, you will end up paying $200 per day to your broker. That is a lot. If you overtrade, your broker will become richer, and you will become, well, broker! As Dr. Alexander Elder writes in his book, *Trading for a Living*, "*Remember, your goal is to trade well, not to trade often.*

Another problem with overtrading is risk. While you're in a trade you are exposed to risk, and that's a place you don't want to be in unless you have proven that there is a setup in the strategy worth trading.

Here is my next golden rule:

RULE 8   **Experienced traders are like guerrilla soldiers. They jump out at just the right time, take their profit, and get out.**

The stock market is controlled by machines and highly sophisticated algorithms and, as a result, there is considerable high frequency trading. High frequency trading creates significant noise in the price action and is specifically designed to shake out retail traders like you and me. You must be smart. Don't expose yourself to them. Profitable traders usually make only two or three trades each day. They then cash out and enjoy the rest of their day.

As I mentioned earlier, scanners, especially real time scanners, are generally expensive. New traders, or even experienced traders who want to keep their costs down, can use scanners that are usually shared by communities. In our community, we show our scanners and share our Stocks in Play watchlist publicly every day with traders on our YouTube channel at *https://www.youtube.com/BearBullTraders/* In order to save some money, there's really no need to invest in a scanner when you are just beginning. You should wait until you are absolutely certain about pursuing this career.

CHAPTER 5

TOOLS AND PLATFORMS

Like beginning any other business or profession, to start day trading you require a few important tools. You will definitely need a broker and an order execution platform.

WHAT BROKER TO USE?

As you've been reading along, an obvious question that may have arisen in your mind is: How do I actually buy and sell stocks?

As an individual trader or investor, you cannot trade directly on a Stock Exchange. For that, you will need a "broker" or "brokerage account". A broker is simply an intermediary who gives people access to a Stock Exchange. They're very similar to real estate agents who facilitate real estate deals and receive a fee for their service. They are necessary evils; nobody wants to pay them the commission, but they offer essential services. In the past you had to telephone a brokerage firm to execute a trade, but now everything is processed electronically and all you do is login to their website (or online platform or mobile app). You can electronically transfer money from your bank account to your brokerage account and, in reverse, electronically withdraw your money back to your bank account.

For day trading, you need a good direct-access broker. In fact, you don't just need a good broker; you need an awesome broker. Your broker is your vehicle to trade. If you have a bad broker, you lose money, even if you are trading properly and accurately, because your broker eventually has to fill your order on time and at a good price. There are many brokers out there with various software and price structures. Many of them are great but expensive, others are terrible but cheap, and some of them are both terrible and expensive. For the sake of keeping this book short, I will not attempt even a brief review of the major ones. An online search of the topic can provide much more in-depth information about available brokers. However, I will share here what broker I and many of our community members are using and why. But before that, let me explain the pattern day trade (PDT) rule.

Pattern Day Trade Rule

The U.S. Securities and Exchange Commission (SEC) and the Financial Industry Regulatory Authority (FINRA) enforce laws that limit the number of trades a trader can make if they are undercapitalized. The rules adopt the term "pattern day trader", which includes any person that day trades (buys and then sells or sells short and then buys the same security on the same day) four or more times in five business days. Under the rules, a pattern day trader must maintain a minimum equity of $25,000 on any day that they day trade. The required minimum equity must be in their account prior to any day trading activities. If the account falls below the $25,000 requirement, the pattern day trader will not be permitted to day trade again until their account is restored to the $25,000 minimum equity level.

Although many new traders who do not have more than $25,000 in their account do not appreciate this rule, and see it as a barrier, it actually is in place to protect amateur traders from losing their limited capital to the high fees and commissions of brokers. It has been established to protect traders, and not to work against them.

This rule represents a minimum requirement, and some broker-dealers use a slightly broader definition in determining whether a customer qualifies as a "pattern day trader". Traders should contact their brokerage firms to determine whether their trading activities will cause them to be designated as pattern day traders.

This rule is strictly enforced by brokerages inside the United States due to their regulation by FINRA. However, offshore brokers, who have their main office and activities outside of the United States, are not subject to this rule and they do not enforce the PDT rule on their customers. This creates an opportunity for new traders who fall below $25,000 in their account to be able to day trade if they open an account with offshore brokers. Capital Markets Elite Group Limited (based in Trinidad and Tobago) and Alliance Trader (based in Jamaica) are examples of offshore brokers. These brokers offer no PDT restrictions to undercapitalized traders, and in return they offer a slightly higher commission fee structure.

Using these brokers does require some consideration. The U.S. SEC and FINRA strictly monitor and enforce regulations on U.S. brokers to ensure that customers and traders are protected from brokerage firms. Offshore brokers, on the other hand, are not regulated by U.S. authorities. Offshore brokers are regulated by authorities of the country they are operating in, but often these regulations and regulators might not be as strict and diligent as they are in the United States, and there is an inherently higher risk when working with them. I personally use offshore brokers, but I do not feel comfortable to keep large amounts of money in offshore brokerage accounts for the above-mentioned reasons. For example, I feel comfortable to have $5 to $10,000 in offshore brokerage accounts, but I do not keep $50,000 cash in such accounts. If you have over $25,000 available, there is really no need to use offshore brokers, and you can therefore day trade with U.S.-based brokers.

I recommend that traders who use offshore brokers withdraw their funds regularly, and if they can ever increase their account size to meet PDT rules, they should open an account with one of the U.S.-based brokers.

Other countries and jurisdictions might enforce similar PDT rules for their residents. I recommend that new traders contact their local brokers and ask about the minimum requirements for day trading in their jurisdiction.

Conventional Brokers vs. Direct-Access Brokers

Conventional online brokers usually direct customer trade orders to market makers and other liquidity providers through pre-negotiated order flow arrangements. This multi-step process often takes time - from a few seconds to several minutes. These brokers often do not offer a super-fast execution as their services tend to place a greater emphasis on research and fundamental analysis functions over speed execution. These brokers, at times called "full-service brokers", provide research and advice, retirement planning, tax tips, and much more. Of course, this all comes at a price, as commissions at full-service brokerage firms are much higher than those at direct-access brokers (which I will explain further below). Full-service brokers are usually well-suited for investors and retail swing traders, but due to the lack of speed execution, they are not a good choice for day traders.

As mentioned several times now, day traders need a fast and flawless order execution as their entry and exits are often only literally one or two seconds apart. I often get in and out of trades in a matter of a few seconds and people wonder how I can do it so fast. Direct-access brokers are the answer to this question. These firms concentrate on speed and order execution – unlike a full-service broker that focuses on research and advice to investors. Direct-access brokers often use complicated computer software that allows traders to trade directly with Stock Exchanges such as the Nasdaq and NYSE, or with other individuals, via electronic communication networks (ECNs). Direct-access trading system transactions are executed in a fraction of a second and their confirmations are instantly displayed on the trader's computer screen. This has opened up a new avenue for retail traders like us. Decades ago, it was almost impossible for a retail trader sitting in their home office to trade at the Exchanges. You needed to pick up the phone and talk to a broker and ask for trades, a process that might have taken minutes, if not hours. Today, active traders can receive fast transactions along with other services such as streaming quotes and market data, interactive charts, Level 2 Nasdaq quotes (which I will explain later in this chapter) and other real time features that previously were accessible only to Wall Street professionals. In the last few years, these brokers have cut down their costs significantly and increased efficiency, which provides traders like us a significantly lower commission than traditional full-service brokers.

Although direct-access brokers are a must for day trading, there are some disadvantages in using them, including volume requirements and technical knowledge. For example, some firms charge inactivity fees if a minimum monthly trading volume has not been met.

However, not all direct-access brokerages have minimum monthly trading volume requirements and with the new commission-free movement in the financial industry, it seems more and more brokers are now offering better packages and incentives to attract traders to their services. It's a good time to be a trader!

Another challenge is that new and inexperienced traders may find it difficult to become familiar with direct-access trading. Knowledge is required when dealing with processes and procedures such as making trade decisions and order routing. That is why I always recommend traders practice in their broker's simulator platform and ensure they are very familiar with the platform before they open a real account with that broker. In direct-access trading, you are only one click away from making a dangerous mistake and blowing up your account, while if you are on the phone with an agent in a full-service brokerage, the agent may catch your mistake or advise you before executing your order.

Please note that many brokerage firms have begun to offer both direct-access and full-service services (such as advice and research), so it is best to check their websites and inquire about their services.

For example, in Canada, BMO Bank of Montreal InvestorLine, RBC Direct Investing, and CIBC Investor's Edge are examples of full-service brokers that are generally not suited for day trading. On the other hand, Interactive Brokers Canada Inc. and Questrade offer both direct-access trading and full-service brokerage services.

In the U.S., some of the most well-known direct-access brokers are CenterPoint Securities, Lightspeed Trading, E*TRADE, and Interactive Brokers.

Interactive Brokers

I am currently using Interactive Brokers (also known as IB, *www.interactivebrokers.com*). Why? They are an inexpensive and established broker which offers discounted fees. In 2020, Barron's in fact rated IB as the best online broker. Based on quite a few different criteria, IB maintains the largest electronic trading platform in the United States and is also the largest broker on the Foreign Exchange Market (Forex). In addition, I appreciate their global presence as more than half of their customers are from outside of the United States. I was interested to learn that it was because of IB's lobbying that back in 1983 computers were first allowed on the trading floor. These days, it's hard to imagine trading, or doing anything in life, without access to computers!

Since 2019, IB has offered two types of accounts: IBKR Lite (commission free with access to an app and web-based platforms) and IBKR Pro (discounted commissions but not free) with access to an app and both web-based and direct-access platforms. Day traders should choose IBKR Pro or a similar service that offers fast execution of trades.

IB charges active traders a fee as low as $0.005 per share, which is incredibly low for brokers. They also offer most traders a 3.3:1 margin, which I will discuss the meaning of in just a few paragraphs.

As you investigate which broker might be best for you, please take a moment to read some commentary about various brokers on our website: *www.BearBullTraders.com*

Capital Markets Elite Group Limited

Capital Markets Elite Group Limited (*https://www.cmel itegroup.com*), not to be confused with the famous CME Group Inc., an American financial market company operating an Options and Futures Exchange, is an offshore broker that offers an excellent 6:1 margin for traders, higher than most brokers do. Since they are based outside of the U.S., the PDT rule does not apply to their clients. This results in CMEG being an alternative for those with less than $25,000 available for day trading. If you live in the U.S. and have under $25,000 available for day trading, you may be eligible to use CMEG as your broker.

Do remember that brokers will give you 3 to 6 times leverage. If you put in $30,000, you're going to have $180,000 in buying power (a leverage of 6:1 in this case). That leverage is called the "margin", and you're allowed to trade on margin, but you need to be responsible about it. It is easy to buy on margin, but it is also very easy to lose on margin. If you lose on margin, your broker takes the loss from your main money account. Therefore, margin is a double-edged sword. It provides you with an opportunity to buy more, but it also exposes you to more risk. There is nothing wrong with buying on margin, but you do have to be responsible.

Margin is like a mortgage for your house. You borrow a significant amount of money and buy a residence. Banks will give you a mortgage, but they won't take any responsibility or risk on it. For example, imagine that you put $100,000 down and borrowed $900,000 on a mortgage (10:1 leverage) from your bank to buy a $1,000,000 house. If the price of your house goes up to $1,200,000, you still owe the bank the original $900,000 plus their interest. So the extra $200,000 is your own profit that actually came from margin leverage. You couldn't have bought that house without mortgage leveraging. Now imagine that the price of the house drops to $900,000. You still owe the bank $900,000 plus their interest, so the drop has hit your main $100,000 and you have lost all of your original down payment of $100,000. That is the other side of leveraging. Therefore, you need to be responsible about when and how much you make use of your account margin.

When a broker notices that you are using leverage and losing money, they might issue a "*margin call*" to you. A margin call is a serious warning and day traders must avoid getting them. It means that your loss is now equal to the original money you had in your account. You must add more money or else your broker will freeze your account. If you are interested in learning more about margin, leverage or margin calls, check the broker's website, do some research on the Internet, or ask other traders in your chatroom.

Most day traders, including me, use a buying power of around $20,000 to $200,000. You'll remember that your "buying power" consists of your capital plus the leverage offered from your broker. My broker, Interactive Brokers, offers me a 1:3.3 margin. While leverage enhances returns, it also enhances losses. But since I don't hold positions for very long, almost always intraday, I do my best to minimize losses. CMEG is one of the few brokers that will give you a 1:6 margin. Your $5,000 in their account is equal to $30,000 in buying power for active trading.

Robinhood and Commission-Free Brokers

In April 2013, Robinhood Markets, Inc. was founded by Vladimir Tenev and Baiju Bhatt, who had previously built high frequency trading platforms for financial institutions in New York City (as I wrote about in Chapter 2, this is the type of trading the computer programmers on Wall Street work away at, creating algorithms and secret formulas to try to manipulate the market). The company's name comes from its mission to *"provide everyone with access to the financial markets, not just the wealthy"*. Tenev noted in an interview that, *"We realized institutions were paying fractions of a penny for trading and transactions,"* but that individual investors were typically being charged fees of $5 to $10 per trade, as well as being required to have account minimums of $500 to $5,000. They were right. Brokerage fees were very expensive up to that point and there was a demand from the Main Street people (such as you and I) to have access to better and more affordable tools in comparison with Wall Street. Robinhood is headquartered in Silicon Valley and similar to the philosophy of many other tech giants, they decided to reduce their costs by operating entirely online, without fees, and with no storefront offices. This is a very important and disruptive approach by Silicon Valley. The world's largest taxi firm, Uber Technologies Inc. (ticker: UBER), owns no cars. The world's most popular media company, Facebook, Inc. (ticker: FB), creates no content. The world's most valuable retailer, Alibaba Group Holding Ltd.—ADR (ticker: BABA), based in China, carries no inventory. And the world's largest accommodation provider, Airbnb, Inc., owns no property. Disruptive indeed.

The Robinhood app officially launched in March 2015 and, according to one study, 80% of the firm's customers belong to the "millennial" demographic (people born in the 1980s through mid-1990s), with the average customer being 26 years old. By March 2020, Robinhood had over 10 million user accounts. To put that in context, giant brokerage firms TD Ameritrade and The Charles Schwab Corporation (who are planning to merge) have 24 million users combined.

Robinhood makes most of its money from the interest earned on customers' cash balances, the lending capability which arises from the stocks that its users keep in their accounts, as well as from selling their order flow to high frequency traders.

Commission-free brokers such as Robinhood and TradeZero (which does not permit residents of the

United States to hold accounts) are suitable for swing trading and investing, but not for day trading. Sometimes when something is free, it is free for a reason! Although Robinhood has steadily improved its app and website platforms since its launch, as of writing (April 2020), it is still not a reliable brokerage service for day trading. The opportunity cost or loss because your broker cannot execute your order fast enough or your platform crashes can be much more expensive than the commissions that you must pay to a good and reliable broker. This has in fact been experienced several times thus far in 2020 by Robinhood's clients. In March 2020, during the unprecedented volatility of the stock market due to the COVID-19 pandemic, the Robinhood app crashed multiple times, blocking users from accessing their accounts, causing them severe losses and opportunity costs. Immediately, a frustrated Robinhood user filed a potential class-action lawsuit in federal court in Tampa, Florida that accuses the company of failing to meet contractual obligations, violating its warranty, and negligence.

Nevertheless, it is very important to note that although I do not recommend Robinhood for day trading, I credit the company with revolutionizing the stodgy trading industry. Robinhood has forced established players to either abolish or significantly reduce their commissions and it has even sparked the potential blockbuster merger of The Charles Schwab Corporation and TD Ameritrade.

While many other brokers have indeed introduced commission-free programs to attract new clients, my research has shown that most of these programs are not suitable for active day traders, as unlike swing traders and investors, day traders require fast execution of trades.

Trade for Proprietary Trading Firms

Another excellent way to trade, especially for those who are passionate about trading but may lack the sufficient funds (capital), is to trade for proprietary trading firms, also known as "prop firms". Prop firms provide traders with the capital needed for trading, and offer them the best services and tools, as well as the mentorship and training required, in order to find success in trading. They then also share the profits with their traders. Essentially, traders do not need to have any cash. If they pass the consistency criteria of the firm, they will have access to a buying power assigned by their managers. As their skills in trading improve, their buying power will be gradually increased.

In 2020, I founded Peak Capital Trading, a proprietary trading firm based in Vancouver, Canada. We have been successful in negotiating an excellent commission rate from clearing firms with advanced trading platforms. In our firm, we offer a $100,000 buying power to new traders, and then we gradually increase it as they gain experience. For example, one of our junior traders now has access to a buying power of $500,000 after his first month of trading, as he demonstrated excellent trading skills. We also share the profit with our traders on a gradual basis. Those traders who make over $10,000 a month are able to retain 85% of their profits, and our firm retains 15%. With the advancement of technology, traders do not need to be in a physical office or at a firm's trading stations. Our traders, for example, live all over the world and trade from their homes.

One of the longest standing firms which offers excellent training and coaching is SMB Capital (*www.smbcap.com*), a firm founded by my dear friend and mentor, Mike Bellafiore, and his trading partner, Steve Spencer. Another well-known prop firm is Seven Points Capital (*https://www.sevenpointscapital.com*).

I recommend considering joining a prop firm if you are really passionate about trading but do not yet have sufficient capital saved up.

TRADING PLATFORM

An electronic online trading platform is a computer software program that is used to place orders for day trading. The trading platform is different from the direct-access brokers themselves. However, I see often that traders confuse these two as one. The trading platform sends and places your order at the Exchange so the direct-access brokers can clear the order for you. Usually, direct-access brokers offer their own proprietary trading platform to their clients. The quality, charting capability, speed of the software, and many other features regarding the software, varies significantly, which also of course affects their pricing. Many brokers offer their platform for a monthly fee, but they may waive that fee if you make sufficient commissions for the broker. For example, Interactive Brokers offers a trading platform called Trader Workstation (TWS), but it also allows you to use the DAS Trader platform. Lightspeed Trading also offers its own platform called Lightspeed Trader. TD Ameritrade's own software is called thinkorswim.

The table below summarizes some of the well-known direct-access brokers for day trading. Please note that there are many more firms that are not listed below.

BROKER	TRADING PLATFORM	PDT RESTRICTION	BASED IN
Interactive Brokers	TWS or DAS Pro	Yes	USA
Lightspeed	Lightspeed Trader	Yes	USA
TD Ameritrade	thinkorswim (TOS)	Yes	USA
Alliance Trader	DAS Pro	No	Jamaica
CMEG	DAS Pro	No	Trinidad and Tobago

From the brokers listed in the table above, I personally prefer Interactive Brokers (IB) as my broker and DAS Trader (*www.dastrader.com*) as my trading platform. My broker, Interactive Brokers, offers their own platform called Trader Workstation or TWS, which I do not recommend for day trading. The DAS Trader platform is one of the nine Nasdaq Platinum Partner order entry platforms that offer the highest level of efficient execution and market functionality for online traders. As mentioned earlier, DAS Trader is not a broker, it is only a trading platform, so I linked my IB trading account to it. When I enter my order in the platform, DAS will send my orders to Nasdaq data centers and Interactive Brokers, as my clearing firm, will fill my orders. I pay my trading commissions to IB and a monthly fee to DAS Trader for using their platform and providing me with a real time data feed and Level 2, which I will explain in just a few paragraphs.

Fast trade execution is the key for day traders to be successful. You need to be able to move in and out of trades quickly. If your broker doesn't use a platform or software that has Hotkeys, you're not going to get in and out of trades fast enough. I can't tell you how many times I've been up a thousand dollars because all of a sudden the stock spiked. When the stock spikes, you want to be able to put money in your pocket and profit from it quickly. You definitely don't want to be fumbling with your orders. You need quick executions, which is why I highly recommend a good broker and also a fast order execution platform.

REAL TIME MARKET DATA

Swing traders enter and exit trades within days or weeks, therefore end-of-day data that is available on the Internet for free is sufficient for them. But day traders need real time intraday data because they enter and exit trades within a few hours and often within a few minutes. Unfortunately, real time market data is not free, and you need to pay a monthly fee to your broker or to your platform provider such as DAS Trader. Which market data you should buy depends on the market that you are trading in. If you are planning to trade in the Canadian market, you need real time Toronto Stock Exchange (TSX) data. I largely limit my trading to the U.S. markets because of its high volume (liquidity) and volatility, therefore I need the real time Nasdaq TotalView Level 2 data feed. Without real time market data, you cannot day trade properly.

NASDAQ LEVEL 2 AND BID-ASK

From my perspective, having access to Nasdaq Level 2 is virtually mandatory in order to day trade in the U.S. markets. Level 2 provides important insight into a stock's price action, including what type of traders are buying or selling a stock and where the stock is likely to head in the near term. Level 2 is known to be a "leading indicator", which means it shows activity before a trade happens. Moving averages, charts and most of the other indicators are known as "lagging indicators", meaning they provide information after the trades take place.

Level 2 is essentially the order book for Nasdaq stocks. When orders are placed, they are placed through many different market makers and other market participants. Level 2 will show you a ranked list of the best bid and ask prices from each of these participants, giving you detailed insight into the price action. Knowing exactly who has an interest in a stock can be extremely useful, especially if you are day trading.

Figure 5.1 below is what a Level 2 quote looks like:

MMID	BID	SIZE	MMID	ASK	SIZE
NYSE	157.38	2	NYSE	157.43	2
NASD	157.38	2	ACB	157.45	1
BATS	157.38	2	ARCA	157.45	1
NSDQ	157.38	2	BYX	157.46	1
ACB	157.38	1	NSDQ	157.47	1
EDGX	157.38	1	NASD	157.47	1
ARCA	157.38	1	EDGX	157.48	2
IEX	157.37	1	NSDQ	157.48	0
NSDQ	157.36	2	ACB	157.49	1
NSDQ	157.35	1	NSDQ	157.49	0
ACB	157.35	1	ACB	157.50	1
ACB	157.34	2	NSDQ	157.51	1
NSDQ	157.34	1	NSDQ	157.52	2
ACB	157.33	1	ACB	157.53	1
NSDQ	157.32	1	BATS	157.53	1

UNH 160.67 - 156.23 PCL 160.73 N
Last 157.4145 -3.315 (-2.1%) Vol 2,424,371
Lv1 157.38 157.43 VWAP: 157.45 S
Montage INET ARCA

Figure 5.1: Example of a Nasdaq Level 2 for UnitedHealth Group Inc. (ticker: UNH) in the middle of the trading day. Note that the number of shares (the "SIZE") is in hundreds (×100).

Whenever the market is open, there are always two prices for any trading stock—a bid and an ask. A bid is what people are offering to pay for that stock at that moment; an ask is what sellers are demanding in order to sell it. A bid is always lower, an ask is always higher, and the difference is called the bid–ask spreads. Bid-ask spreads vary for each stock and even for the same stock at different times of the day.

The image in Figure 5.1 above shows us (first row, right hand side) that someone is offering 200 shares (2 (the "SIZE", the number of lots of shares) x 100 shares/lot) of UNH for $157.43 on the ask side through NYSE (a market maker). On the bid side, there are various market players who are willing to buy shares of UNH at a price of $157.38. Traders who want to buy UNH at various prices are sending their bids through market makers to the bid side of the Level 2 (NYSE, NASD, BATS, NSDQ, ACB, EDGX, and ARCA are all market makers active on this stock).

The most important information you must take away from Level 2 is the bid–ask spreads. Spreads are higher in lower volume traded stocks, as the market makers who dominate such stocks demand higher fees from those who want to join their party.

The bid-ask spreads are likely to be small, perhaps only 1 cent on a quiet day in an actively traded stock. They grow wider as prices accelerate on the way up or down and may become huge - I have seen up to $2 - after a severe drop or a very sharp rally.

INDICATORS ON MY CHARTS

I keep my charts relatively clean with a minimal number of indicators displayed. In day trading, you need to process information quickly and you need to make decisions very, very quickly. Therefore, I cannot keep track of too many indicators. Here is what I have on my charts:

1. Price action in the form of candlesticks

2. Volume of shares being traded

3. 9 Exponential Moving Average (9 EMA)

4. 20 Exponential Moving Average (20 EMA)

5. 50 Simple Moving Average (50 SMA)

6. 200 Simple Moving Average (200 SMA)

7. Volume Weighted Average Price (VWAP)

8. Previous day's closing price

All of the above indicators are automatically being calculated and plotted by my DAS Trader Pro platform. I do not find, calculate or plot these manually. I'll explain these terms later on in this book.

9. Daily levels of support or resistance

For daily levels of support or resistance, my platform does not automatically find and plot them. These levels have to be identified manually by traders. I usually find and plot these levels during my pre-market screening for Stocks in Play on my watchlist or during the day when a new stock hits my scanners. I don't trade without knowing nearby significant intraday levels of support or resistance.

I keep the color of all of my moving average indicators in gray except VWAP which is colored in blue. *VWAP is the most important day trading indicator and needs to be easily and quickly distinguished from other moving averages.* I don't want to have a lot of colors on my charts and so I maintain a white background with mostly red and black coloring. Heavily colored charts are confusing and over the long term irritate your eyes and limit your vision. I avoid dark background colors on my charts because processing dark colors for any length of time makes my eyes feel achy and weak. Figure 5.2 below is a screenshot of the type of chart I use with my indicators marked on it.

Figure 5.2: Screenshot of the type of chart I use with my indicators marked on it. Only 200 SMA is not shown because it was moving outside of the zoomed price range.

BUY AND SELL ORDERS

There are three important types of orders you can use for day trading:

1. Market orders
2. Limit orders
3. Marketable limit orders

Market Orders

"Buy me at any price! Now!"

"Sell me at any price! Now!"

When you use *market orders*, you are asking your broker to immediately buy or sell the stock for you at any cost. Let me repeat that: at ANY cost. If you place a market order, it will be filled at the current price, whatever that happens to be. A limit order, on the other hand, allows you to specify the maximum or minimum price you will accept.

In market orders, essentially, you are getting filled at the bad side of bid–ask spreads. A market order buys at the ask (high side) and sells at the bid (low side). The problem with using market orders is that the market can quickly change, and so then does the bid–ask spread, and thus you may get your order filled at a very bad price. For example, if the bid–ask spread is $10.95–$10.97, market orders should buy immediately at $10.97 for you, right? When your market orders come to the Exchange, the market can quickly change to $11.10–$11.15, and therefore your buy market order will be filled at $11.15. That is a slippage of 18 cents. And that is really bad.

Market makers and many professional traders make a good living from filling market orders. I discourage traders from placing market orders at any time. A market order is like a blank check. Most of the time a market order will be filled very closely to the quoted bid or ask price, but sometimes you will get a nasty surprise.

Use limit orders whenever possible.

Limit Orders

"Buy me at this price only! Not higher!"

"Sell me at this price only! Not lower!"

A *limit order*, in contrast to a market order, limits the price you are willing to pay for the stock. You specify the number of shares you want to buy and the price you are willing to pay. For example, in the Level 2 screenshot below, marked as Figure 5.3, you will see I have two limit orders. I asked my broker to buy me 100 shares of TEVA at $34.75, and another 100 shares at $34.74. You'll recall from before, "SIZE" is the number of lots of shares, with one standard lot equaling 100 shares. As you can see, my orders are now sitting in Level 2, waiting to get filled. There is no guarantee that I will get filled at those prices. If the price moves higher, I will never get filled and my order will stay in the Level 2 until the price moves back down. Sometimes the order will come back partially filled because the price of the stock moved up too quickly.

Just as an aside, swing traders commonly use limit orders.

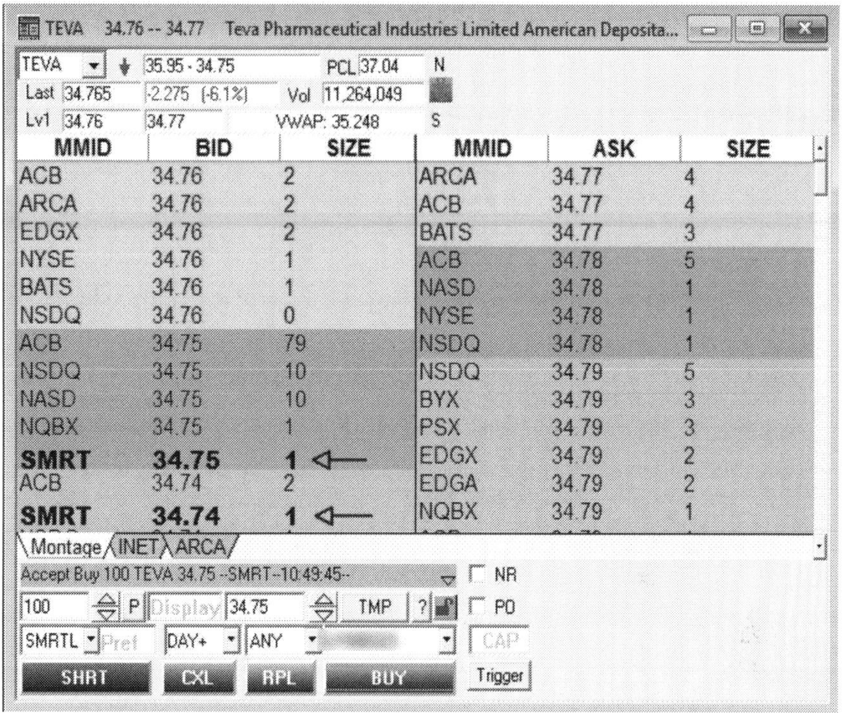

Figure 5.3: Example of a Nasdaq Level 2 for Teva Pharmaceutical Industries Limited (ticker: TEVA) in the middle of the day. I have two limit orders to buy in total 200 shares on the bid. Note that the number of shares is in hundreds (×100). SMRT is the default clearing route for my broker, IB.

Marketable Limit Orders

"Buy me now, but up to this price! Not higher!"

"Sell me now, but down to this price! Not lower!"

The most important type of order for day traders is a *marketable limit order.* Marketable limit orders, once sent, will immediately give you as many shares as possible within the price range you have set. In marketable limit orders, you ask your broker to buy or sell stock for you immediately, but you specify the highest price you are willing to pay. For example, in the above Figure 5.3, the Level 2 for TEVA, you can ask your broker to buy 100 shares at "ask price + 5 cents". Your broker will go to the ask and try to fill your order. As you can see in the top three highlighted rows on the right-hand side of Figure 5.3, there are currently 1,100 shares offered at ask ([4+4+3 = 11] ×100). Therefore, you should get filled immediately (like a market order). But, if the ask price moves up quickly before you get filled, you have already authorized your broker to buy TEVA for you at a higher price as well, up to $34.82 (ask of $34.77 + 5 cents). Therefore, your broker will try to buy 100 shares of TEVA for you at a cost of no more than $34.82.

A similar example is also true for selling or short selling on the bid. In selling on the bid, you specify the range you are willing to sell at. For example, if you ask your broker to sell at "the bid – 5 cents", it means that you are not willing to sell at a price lower than the bid minus 5 cents.

I use marketable limit orders for all of my day trades. I typically buy at the "ask+5 cents" and sell at the "bid–5 cents". In the next section, I will show you details of my order Hotkeys.

HOTKEYS

Hotkeys are key commands that can be programmed to automatically send orders with the touch of a combination of keys on your keyboard. Professional traders will use Hotkeys to enter trades, exit trades, place stop orders, and cancel orders. They don't use a mouse or any sort of manual order entry system. The use of Hotkeys eliminates the delay of manual entry. The volatility of the market, especially at the Open, can allow for huge profits if you can trade properly, but it can also result in significant losses if you fail to act quickly. Often, the proper use of Hotkeys distinguishes the losers from the winners.

Most of the day trading strategies I use require high-speed trading. In day trading, the market can move very fast, especially at the market Open. Stocks can very quickly hit your entry or exit price, often in a matter of mere seconds. In order to be able to day trade effectively, it is important to use a trading platform that offers Hotkeys. For high-speed trading, you should have all of the possible trade combinations in your Hotkeys. In my opinion, it is almost impossible to day trade profitably without using Hotkeys.

The following Figure 5.4 is the list of my Hotkeys in my DAS platform. Other platforms may use different scripts. It is best to check with your broker and trading platform support team to make sure you are familiar with how to write a proper script for your Hotkeys.

Figure 5.4: A chart showing some of my Hotkeys for my DAS Trader platform. A complete detailed Hotkeys script of my platform can be found on our website at *www.BearBullTraders.com*

FUNCTION	HOTKEY
1 MIN CHART	F1
5 MIN CHART	F2
DAILY CHART	F4
WEEKLY CHART	F5
MONTHLY CHART	F6
Buying Long	
Buy 400 shares at limit Ask+0.05	Alt+1
Buy 200 shares at limit Ask+0.05	Alt+Q
Buy 100 shares at limit Ask+0.05	Alt+A
Sell 1/2 position at limit Bid-0.05	Alt+2
Sell full position at limit Bid-0.05	Alt+3
Selling Short	
Short 400 shares at limit Bid-0.05	Alt+4
Short SSR 400 shares at limit Ask	Alt+5
Short 200 shares at limit Bid-0.05	Alt+R
Short SSR 200 shares at limit Ask	Alt+T
Short 100 shares at limit Bid-0.05	Alt+F
Short SSR 100 shares at limit Ask	Alt+G
Buy to cover 1/2 position at limit Ask+0.05	Alt+6
Buy to cover full position at limit Ask+0.05	Alt+7

For a long position (you'll recall "buying long" means you buy shares at one price and hope to sell them at a higher price), my buy orders are in blocks of 400, 200 and 100 shares. I use a marketable limit order to buy at the ask price + 5 cents. My "sell" Hotkeys are marketable limit orders to sell my half or full positions on the bid price—5 cents. When selling, I will accept the bid price and a price no more than 5 cents lower, to ensure my order gets filled immediately. The DAS platform will automatically calculate what half of my position equals in number of shares. The computer will also calculate the current bid and ask prices and place my order at the price I specify.

Similarly, for short positions (you'll recall "short" is when you borrow shares from your broker, sell them, and hope to later buy back the shares at a lower price for return to your broker), I short sell on the bid price or on a price no more than 5 cents lower. My "buy to cover shorts" Hotkeys are marketable limit orders to buy my half or full positions on the ask price + 5 cents. I am willing to pay higher prices (up to 5 cents) to asks, just to get my orders filled immediately.

You may have noticed in Figure 5.4 that I have different Hotkeys for when a stock is in Short Selling Restriction (SSR) mode. An SSR is triggered when a stock is down 10% or more from the previous day's closing price. In that case, regulators and the Exchanges restrict short selling of the stock when its price is dropping. You can only sell short on the ask, you cannot sell short directly to the buyers (on the bid). It means that the priority for selling is for the sellers who currently hold positions, not for the short sellers who are wanting to profit from the downward movement. If you want to sell short, you have to queue up on the ask side and wait for buyers to come to you. Real sellers, on the other hand, can accept bids from buyers and get rid of their positions.

The SSR is designed to give the real sellers, who own the stock, a priority to sell over the short sellers on the market. Therefore, when a stock is in SSR mode, I send my orders to sell on the ask, and then I must wait until my orders get filled. I cannot use a marketable limit order for short selling when a stock has a short selling restriction placed on it. If you are interested in reading more about SSR, an online search will direct you to a good number of resources.

The most important advantage of these Hotkeys is that when a stock suddenly moves, you can press your Hotkey to sell your full or half-position on the bid without having to type in the new bid price or your number of shares. It is impossible to consistently profit from day trading without mastering Hotkeys. Part of your education includes trading in simulators for a few months, and during these months you must master your Hotkeys. I have made many mistakes while using Hotkeys and you no doubt also will. That is part of the learning process in day trading. That is why it is extremely important to practice in real time simulators and practice with Hotkeys while you are mastering a trading strategy. Hotkeys are an amazing tool, but they must be used with caution and with sufficient practice to prevent errors. Day trading is difficult enough; don't let your Hotkeys make it even more difficult.

It is very common to make some mistakes when you are getting used to Hotkeys. When I was learning to use them, I had stickers on my keyboard to help me to keep track of the different key combinations. When I define new Hotkeys, I will ensure that I only practice with them in my simulator account. It takes some time, but eventually you will remember your Hotkeys and use them efficiently. Another important reminder is to always use a wired keyboard that is plugged into your computer. Wireless keyboards can send repeat keystrokes, errant keystrokes, or can fail to send orders at all, especially when low in battery power. This could impact and quite simply mess with your trading. I have seen traders in difficult and costly situations because their wireless mouse or keyboard was low in battery power and did not work properly. I even keep one extra keyboard in my office, ready to go, just in case something happens to the keyboard I'm using. One time I spilled water on my keyboard while trading. My keyboard stopped working. Fortunately, I did not have any open positions at that moment. I immediately purchased two new sets of keyboards and mice and I keep one set as a backup next to my trading desk.

WATCHLIST AND SCANNERS

I talk to new traders almost every single day. I talk to hundreds of traders every month. One of the common challenges that new traders mention is not knowing what to trade. Thousands of stocks are moving in the market every single day, but finding a setup that is both consistent and a good fit is really hard. I explained my scanners and watchlist building in Chapter 4 and I will explain in detail later in this book what I am looking for with my scanner as well as with my trading strategies. You will also see some pictures of my scanner in the sections that follow.

COMMUNITY OF TRADERS

Trading alone is very difficult and can be emotionally overwhelming. To whom will you ask your questions? It is beneficial to join a community of traders and ask questions, talk to them if needed, learn new methods and strategies, get some hints and alerts about the stock market, and also make your own contributions. Online trading rooms are excellent places for meeting like-minded traders, and they can be powerful learning tools.

Two long-standing educational communities are Don Kaufman's trading room, TheoTrade (*www.theot rade.com*), which emphasizes technical trading across multiple markets such as Futures and Options, and the trading room run by author John Carter and his colleagues (*www.simplertrading.com*). You should also take a look at the educational programs offered by Dr. Alexander Elder and Kerry Lovvorn (*www.spiketrade.com*) as a possible place for connecting with like-minded traders.

Another two well-known trading forums are Investors Underground (*www.investorsunderground.com*), founded by Nathan Michaud, and Warrior Trading (*www.warrior trading.com*), run by Ross Cameron. There are several good online forums also available for traders to learn and collectively improve their trading performance. These include Elite Trader (*www.elitetrader.com*) and Trade2Win (*www.trade2win.com*).

Indeed, if you have a favorite trading platform or application, connecting with traders who are using the same tools can be quite valuable. Trade Ideas (*www.trade-ideas.com*) runs educational programs and online chatrooms for their users that I've found useful.

I personally trade in our chatroom at Bear Bull Traders with some of my friends and family, in addition to a group of serious traders. We can talk to each other and everyone can view my live screen and platform and watch how I am trading. It is a fun, interactive environment, and we all learn from each other. I frequently answer questions from other traders, and if there is anything I'm not sure of, I will ask other traders. There are some experienced traders in our chatroom who I learn much from, and we tip each other off about potential good trades and setups. We would like to grow our chatroom slightly and therefore everyone who is reading this book is welcome to join with us. You will benefit from both watching me trade and hearing my responses to questions people have, including your own questions. Don't be shy to ask!

New and developing traders will absorb the knowledge of mentors and experienced traders like a sponge; this helps them establish the right trading behaviors faster and more effectively. When you share your trading results and your ups and downs with other professionals, you turn social interaction into social learning. Find experienced traders who will not hesitate to tell you when you are making a mistake. It is in interacting with other traders that you will learn to teach yourself.

If you join a chatroom, you will see that quite often even very senior traders will lose money. It is always a good feeling to see that losing money is not just limited to yourself, but that everyone, including the most experienced of traders, have to take some losses. It is part of the process.

It is extremely important to remember, however, that you should not follow the pack. You need to be an independent thinker. Don't blindly follow the crowd but do partake of the benefits inherent in being part of a trading community that fits with your personality. People often change when they join crowds. They become more unquestioning and impulsive as they follow the herd. Stressed traders in online communities nervously search for a leader whose trades they can mirror and then, when those trades don't work out, who they can blame their losses on. They react impulsively with the crowd instead of using their own common sense and reason. Chatroom members may catch a few trends together, but they will also get killed together when trends reverse. Never forget that successful traders are independent thinkers. Simply use your judgment to decide when to trade and when to not.

CHAPTER 6

INTRODUCTION TO CANDLESTICKS

To understand my strategies in the next chapter, we need to quickly review the concept of *price action* and the fundamentals of candlestick charts. The Japanese began using technical analysis and some early versions of candlesticks to trade rice in the 17th century. Much of the credit for candlestick development and charting goes to a legendary rice trader named Homma from the town of Sakata, Japan. While these early versions of technical analysis and candlestick charts were different from today's version, many of the guiding principles are very similar. Candlestick charting, as we know it today, first appeared sometime after 1850. It is likely that Homma's original ideas were modified and refined over many years of trading, eventually resulting in the system of candlestick charting that we now use.

In order to create a candlestick chart, you must have a data set that contains (1) opening price, (2) highest price in the chosen time frame, (3) lowest price in that period, and (4) closing price values for each time period you want to display. The time frame can be daily, 1-hour, 5-minute, 1-minute, or any other period you prefer. The hollow (white) or filled (red) portion of the candlestick is called "*the body*". The long thin lines above and below the body represent the high/low range and are called "*shadows*" (also referred to as "*wicks*" and "*tails*"). The high is marked by the top of the upper shadow and the low by the bottom of the lower shadow. Two examples follow in Figure 6.1. If the stock closes higher than its opening price, a hollow candlestick is drawn with the bottom of the body representing the opening price and the top of the body representing the closing price. If the stock closes lower than its opening price, a filled (usually red) candlestick is drawn with the top of the body representing the opening price and the bottom of the body representing the closing price.

Besides candlestick charting, there are other styles for representing price action including bars, lines, and point and figure. I personally however consider candlestick charts more visually appealing and easier to interpret. Each candlestick provides an easy-to-decipher picture of price action. A trader can immediately compare the relationship between the open and close as well as the high and low. The relationship between the open and close is considered vital information and forms the essence of candlesticks.

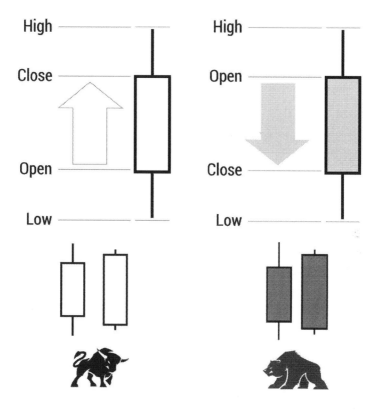

Figure 6.1: Candlestick examples.

Here is my ninth day trading rule:

RULE 9

Hollow candlesticks, where the close is greater than the open, indicate buying pressure. Filled candlesticks, where the close is less than the open, indicate selling pressure.

PRICE ACTION AND MASS PSYCHOLOGY

At every moment in the market there are basically three categories of traders: the buyers, the sellers, and the undecided traders. The actual prices of transactions are the result of the actions of all of these traders at a particular point in time: the buyers, the sellers, and the undecided.

Buyers are looking for deals and want to spend as little as possible to enter a trade. Conversely, sellers are wanting to sell their shares for as high of a price as possible. It's basic human nature. In some countries and cultures, bargaining and negotiating a price is very common when you are shopping in a store. The person selling the product wants to make as much money as possible, while the person shopping for the product wants to spend as little of their money as possible. In day trading, the difference between the two is called the *bid-ask spread* (explained in Chapter 5). The "ask" is the asking price of the merchant and, of course, the "bid" is the price the shopper offers. In both the marketplace and in day trading, there is a third factor that can also affect prices: the undecided shopper and the undecided trader. The undecided traders are the people staring patiently—and at times not so patiently— at their computer monitors to see which side will prevail.

The undecided traders are the key in pushing the price higher or lower. They're feared by all of the other traders. Let's go back to the example of a marketplace in the previous paragraph. You walk into the store, you see a product you want, and you offer a low price for it. You're the buyer. The seller isn't all that keen on your suggested price. They offer to sell you the product for a higher price than you suggested. Just as you are deciding what to make as a counter-offer, a tour bus pulls up and a whole crowd of tourists enter the store. You really want that product. Do you buy it at the higher price or do you take your chances that one of these tourists (the undecided) isn't going to buy it instead? The clock is ticking and you are under pressure.

Likewise, let's pretend you're the seller for a moment. You know that quite a few stores in this imaginary marketplace are selling the exact same product. You're a savvy merchant. You open your store thirty minutes before the others open their doors to the public. Do you take your chances that this early morning shopper (the buyer) will buy your product at your price or will they wait until all of the other stores (the other undecided sellers) open and try to strike a better deal with them for the same product? The clock is ticking and you are under pressure.

In each of these scenarios, the fear of the unknown, the fear of the undecideds, "encourage", shall we say, buying and selling.

Buyers are buying because they expect that prices will go up. Buying by bulls pushes the market up, or as I like to phrase it, "*Buyers are in control.*" The result is that buyers are willing to pay higher and higher prices and to bid on top of each other. They are apprehensive that they will end up paying higher prices if they don't buy now. Undecided traders accelerate price increases by creating a feeling of urgency among the buyers, who then buy quickly and cause prices to go higher.

Sellers are selling because they expect that prices will go down. Selling by bears pushes the market down, or as I like to express it, *"Sellers are in control."* The result is that sellers are willing to accept lower and lower prices. They are apprehensive that they may not be able to sell any higher and will end up selling at even lower prices if they miss selling now. Undecided traders make prices decrease faster by creating a sense of urgency among the sellers. They rush to sell and push the prices lower.

The goal of a successful day trader is to figure out if the sellers will end up in control or if the buyers will end up in control, and then make a calculated move, at the appropriate time, quickly and stealthily. You'll remember that I expounded upon guerrilla warfare and guerrilla trading in both Chapter 2 and in my Rule 8. This is the practical application of it. Your job is to analyze the balance of power between the buyers and sellers and bet on the winning group. Fortunately, candlestick charts reflect this fight and mass psychology in action. A successful day trader is a social psychologist with a computer and charting software. Day trading is the study of mass psychology.

Candlestick patterns tell us a great deal about the general trend of a stock and the power of the buyers or sellers in the market. Candles are always born neutral. After birth, they can grow to become either bearish, bullish or, on rare occasions, neither. When a candle is born, traders do not know what it will become. They may speculate but they do not truly know what a candle is until it dies (closes). After a candle is born, the battle begins. The bulls and the bears fight it out, and the candle displays who is winning. If buyers are in control, you will see the candle move up and form a bullish candle. If sellers are in control of the price, you will see the candle move down and become a bearish candle. You may be thinking that this is all very obvious, but many traders don't see candles as a fight between buyers and sellers. That little candle is an excellent indicator to tell you who is currently winning the battle, the bulls (buyers) or the bears (sellers).

In the following section, I'll provide you with a brief overview of the three most important candle-sticks for day trading (bullish, bearish, and indecision) and then, in the next chapter, I will explain how you can trade using these patterns in each of your trading strategies.

BULLISH CANDLESTICKS

Candles with large bodies toward the upside, as you will see in Figures 6.2 and 6.3 below, are very bullish. It means that the buyers are in control of the price action, and it is likely that they'll keep pushing the price higher.

The candle not only tells you the price, it tells you that the bulls are winning and that they have power.

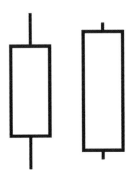

Figure 6.2: Bullish candles.

Figure 6.3: A series of bullish candles shows that bulls (buyers) are in control of the price.

BEARISH CANDLESTICKS

On the other hand, bearish candles are any candles that show a bearish body. So what does the bearish candle tell you? It tells you that the sellers are in control of the price action in the market and that buying, or a "long" position, would not be a great idea.

Filled candles that have a big filled body, such as in Figures 6.4 and 6.5 below, mean that the open was at a high and the close was at a low. This is a good indicator of a bearishness in the market.

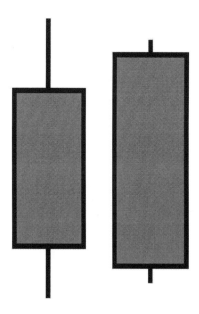

Figure 6.4: Bearish candles.

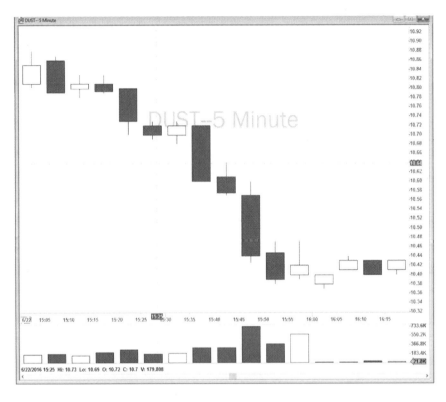

Figure 6.5: A series of bearish candles shows that bears (sellers) are in control of the price.

Just by learning to read candlesticks, you will begin to generate an opinion on the general attitude for a stock. Again, this is called the "*price action*". Understanding who is in control of the price is an extremely important skill in day trading. As I mentioned, a successful trader really is a social psychologist armed with a computer and trading software. Day trading truly is the study of mass psychology.

To summarize this section: your job as a successful day trader is to figure out if the sellers will end up in control or if the buyers will end up in control. Back in Chapter 2, I used the example of a sandbox in a school-yard. You don't want to be off in the sandbox doing your own thing. If you are, you're in the wrong place. If the buyers are strong, you want to be buying and holding. If the sellers are strong, you want to be selling or selling short. You definitely do not want to be off in the sandbox doing your own thing. You want to be where the action is. And if you can't decide what that action is, if it looks like it's a toss-up, don't do anything. Bide your time or move on to look for another potential trade. Never forget that the successful day trader is just like a guerrilla soldier, you make calculated moves, at the appropriate time, quickly and stealthily.

Stand aside if you cannot recognize who is winning the battle. Let the bulls and the bears fight with each other and then enter trades only when you are reasonably certain which side is likely to win.

You never want to be on the wrong side of the trade. It is important therefore to learn both how to read candlesticks and how to constantly interpret the price action while you are trading.

INDECISION CANDLESTICKS

I now want to review the two most important indecision candlesticks for day trading (spinning tops and
Dojis).

Spinning Tops

Spinning tops, as seen in Figures 6.6 and 6.7 below,
are candles that have similarly-sized high wicks and
low wicks that are usually larger than the body and
will often be a little bit more indecisive. Let's call them
indecision candles. In these candlesticks, the powers of
the buyers and the sellers are almost equal. Although
no one is in control of the price, the fight continues on.
Usually, the volume is lower in these candlesticks as
traders are waiting to see who wins the fight between
the sellers and the buyers. Trends in price can change
immediately after indecision candles and they therefore are important to recognize in the price action.

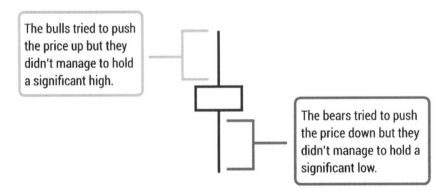

**Figure 6.6: Buying and selling pressure definition on spinning top
candlestick.**

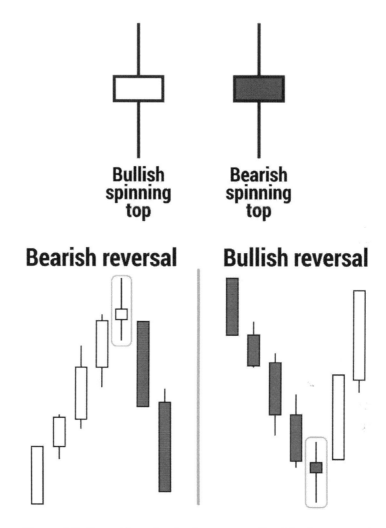

Figure 6.7: Formation of spinning top candlesticks for reversal trends.

Dojis: Simple, Shooting Star, Hammer

Dojis are another important candlestick pattern and come in different shapes and forms but are all characterized by having either no body or a very small body.

A Doji is also an indecision candlestick that is similar to a spinning top. When you see a Doji on your chart, it means there is a strong fight occurring between the bears and the bulls. Nobody has won the fight yet.

Doji
indecision

Buyers tried to push the price up,   Sellers tried to push the price down,
but did not manage to hold it   but did not manage to hold it

Shooting Star Doji   **Hammer Doji**
Indecision, Sellers may take control   *Indecision, Buyers may take control*

Figure 6.8: Examples of Doji candlesticks.

In Figure 6.8 above, a Doji tells us the same story as a spinning top does. In fact, most types of indecision (reversal) candles tell you basically the same thing. This will be discussed in greater detail in the next section.

At times, Dojis will have unequal top and bottom wicks. If the top wick is longer, it means that the buyers tried unsuccessfully to push the price higher. These types of Dojis, such as the shooting star, are still indecision candlesticks, but they may indicate that the buyers are losing power and that the sellers may take over.

If the bottom wick is longer, as in hammer Dojis, it means that the sellers were unsuccessful in trying to push the price lower. This may indicate an impending takeover of price action by the bulls.

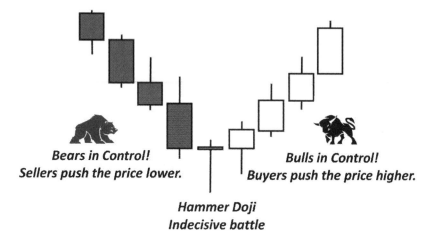

Bears in Control!
Sellers push the price lower.

Bulls in Control!
Buyers push the price higher.

Hammer Doji
Indecisive battle

Figure 6.9: Bottom Reversal Strategy with an indecision hammer candlestick formed as a sign of entry.

All Dojis indicate *indecision* and possible reversals if they form in a trend. If a Doji forms in a bullish trend, it suggests that the bulls have become exhausted and the bears are fighting back to take control of the price. Similarly, if a Doji forms in a bearish downward trend, it suggests that the bears have become exhausted and the bulls (buyers) are fighting back to take control of the price. You will see examples of these in Figures 6.9 and 6.10.

Figure 6.10: Top Reversal Strategy with an indecision shooting star candlestick formed as a sign of entry.

After learning to recognize these candlesticks, it is important that you not get too excited too quickly. Candles are not perfect. If you take a trade every time you see a Doji formed in a trend, you will end up with significant losses. Always remember that these candles only indicate indecision and not a definite reversal. To use indecision candles effectively, you must look for confirmation candles and ideally use them with other forms of analysis such as support or resistance levels, both of which are explained in the next chapter.

CANDLESTICK PATTERNS

Many traders love to identify complicated chart patterns and make trading decisions based on them. There are hundreds of imaginatively-named candlestick patterns that you will find with an online search including Abandoned Baby, Dark Cloud Cover, Downside Tasuki Gap,

Dragonfly, Morning Star, Evening Star, Falling Three Methods, Harami, Stick Sandwich, Three Black Crows, Three White Soldiers, and many more. Believe me, I did not make any of these names up. These candlestick patterns are really out there. As intriguing as their names might be, many of them, in my opinion, are useless and confusing. They're exceptionally arbitrary and fanciful. The biggest problem with fancy chart patterns is, as Dr. Alexander Elder describes it, "wishful thinking". You can find yourself identifying bullish or bearish patterns depending on whether you are in a mood to buy or sell. If you're in a mood to buy, you will find a bullish pattern, eventually, somewhere. If you feel like selling short, you'll "recognize" somewhere on your chart a bearish pattern. I am skeptical about even the most famous of these patterns. Accordingly, I won't discuss these types of patterns in this book. Instead, in the following chapter, I introduce a day trading strategy based on a simple formation: the ABCD Pattern.

CHAPTER 7

IMPORTANT DAY TRADING STRATEGIES

In this chapter, I will introduce some of my strategies, based on three elements: (1) price action, (2) technical indicators, and (3) candlesticks and chart patterns. It is important to learn and practice all three elements at the same time. Although some strategies (such as Moving Average and VWAP) require only technical indicators, it's helpful to also have an understanding of price action and chart patterns in order to become a successful day trader. This understanding, especially regarding price action, comes only with practice and experience.

As a day trader, you shouldn't care about companies and their earnings. Day traders are not concerned about what companies do or what they make. Your attention should only be on price action, technical indicators and chart patterns. I know more stock symbols than the names of actual companies. I don't mingle fundamental analysis with technical analysis while making a trade; I focus exclusively on the technical indicators.

I don't care about the fundamental aspects of companies because I'm not a long-term investor – I'm a day trader. We trade very quickly – guerrilla trading! – at times we will trade in time periods as short as ten to thirty seconds.

There are millions of traders out there and hundreds of different strategies. Every trader, however, needs their own strategy that works for them. We call that "the edge". You need to find your spot in the market where you feel comfortable. I focus on these strategies because these are what work for me.

I've come to recognize in my trading career that some of the best setups are the nine strategies that I will be explaining in this chapter. These are simple strategies in theory, but they are difficult to master and require plenty of practice, as they give signals relatively infrequently.

Another point to remember is that in the market right now, the majority of trading volume, which some say is as high as 60%, is algorithmic high frequency trading. That means you are trading against computers and machines. If you've ever played chess against a computer, you know that you're eventually going to lose. You might get lucky once or twice, but play sufficient times and you are guaranteed to be the loser. The same rule applies to algorithmic trading. You're trading stocks against computer systems. On the one hand, that represents a problem. It means that the majority of changes in stocks that you are seeing are simply the result of computers moving shares around. On the other hand, it also means that there's a small handful of stocks each day that are going to be trading on such heavy retail volume (as opposed to institutional algorithmic trading) that you will overpower the algorithmic trading and you and I, the retail traders, will control that stock. Each day, you need to focus on trading those particular stocks. These are what I call in Chapter 4 the Stocks in Play: stocks that are typically gapping up or down on earnings. You must look for the stocks that have significant retail traders' interest and significant retail volume. These will be the stocks you will trade, and together, we the people, the retail traders, will overpower the computers, just like in a storyline for the next Terminator sequel.

I personally use the candlestick charts explained in Chapter 6. Each candlestick represents a period of time (such as 1 minute, 5 minutes, etc.). As I mentioned before, you can choose any intraday time frame, depending on your personality and trading style - hourly charts, 5-minute charts, or even 1-minute charts. Although it depends somewhat on their trading style, most successful day traders monitor at least two time frames at a time. The larger time frame is the strategic one, showing the overall trend and bigger picture of the stock's price movement. The smaller time frame is the tactical time frame, allowing you to find good entries and exits. My preference is 1-minute charts, but I will also simultaneously monitor 5-minute charts.

And please, remember, my philosophy of trading is that you must master only a few solid setups to be consistently profitable. In fact, having a simple trading method will work to reduce confusion and stress and allow you to concentrate more on the psychological aspect of trading, which is what separates the winners from the losers.

TRADE MANAGEMENT AND POSITION SIZING

Before explaining my strategies, it is important to understand my order entry, exit, position sizing and trade management.

Two traders enter into a trade based on one strategy. The positions go their way and then pull back a bit. The first trader fears losing their gain and takes a quick, small profit. The second trader adds to the position on the pull back and books a large gain. Same idea, different outcomes, all as the result of two different mindsets and trade management styles.

As I've previously outlined, day trading is a business. Like any other business, success is not just about products and services but much of it will be the result of an excellent management of the business. For example, if you don't hire the right people for your business, or supervise them properly, or track your inventory, you'll fail to make money with even the best products and services.

This is also true in the day trading business. Managing trades is the key to success. By trade management, I mean something different from finding the Stocks in Play and then executing a strategy. Rather, trade management is referring to what you do with the position after you've entered it and before you've exited it.

Trade management is just as important as the quality of your initial trade plan. The proper management of trades makes all of the difference between consistently profitable traders and those who eventually fail.

Novice traders believe that when they enter the trade, they should not do anything else but patiently wait for the price to hit their profit target or stop loss level. This is the opposite of what professional traders do. The professionals know that this is not sufficient. When you plan for the trade and enter a position, you have a minimum of information regarding the market and the validity of your idea. As the market moves after your entry, you will receive new price action and data about your initial trade idea. The price action of the stock will either be supporting or not supporting your reasons for being in that trade. Therefore, you need to manage your open position.

For example, if you are expecting a break from a strong support level to the downside, and you want to profit the move to the downside with a short position, you may want to start with shorting 100 shares. Momentum scalper traders will usually start scalping when the level breaks to the downside. When those scalpers take their profit, the price often pulls back to that support level to test it as a new resistance level. If it is held below the support level (now acting as a resistance level), you can start adding to your short position on the way down. If it does not act as a resistance level and the price moves back up, you will get stopped out for a small loss because you only had 100 shares. Trade management means that you have to be actively engaged in processing information while the trade is on, not just watching your position or moving away from your computer hoping your profit target order hits. I'll discuss scalping and scalpers further in the section that follows on the Bull Flag Momentum Strategy.

Unfortunately, trade management is the most important element of learning how to be a consistently profitable trader and, at the same time, it is very difficult to teach it to new traders, especially in a book. Trade management requires experience and real time decision-making. That is why I strongly encourage you to join chatrooms, watch for a few weeks how experienced traders trade, and hear their thought process on managing their open trades.

It always intrigues me in our chatroom when two experienced traders select the same stock: one long and the other short. Often, by the end of the day, both are profitable, proving that experience in trade and risk management and proper position sizing are more important than the stock and the direction that traders pick. For example, although my friend Brian Pezim and I often trade together at the same time live in our community, we at times end up trading against each other, but we will both be profitable when we finish our day. And how does that happen? It's based on practice, discipline and controlling our emotions in the heat of the trade, even though I do like to think that I'm a better trader than him!

Position sizing refers to how large of a position that you take per trade. Some trades are so obvious that you can take a huge position or, as some call it, "*load the boat*". These setups are shouting "*grab me by the face*". Some trading opportunities are attractive enough for a "large" position. In other trades, you just want to go for a "taste" and perhaps add more later. Learning when to have the most size is a skill that new traders must acquire. Poor position sizing can lead to inconsistent results. But remember the 2% rule in Chapter 3. No matter how good of an opportunity, you may not risk more than 2% of your account in one trade. Live to trade another day.

New traders think they need to trade with huge size to make significant profits. Although I take a large position at times when the risk/reward is in my favor, I know I need to be able to handle the risk. There is plenty of money to be made trading with modest size, especially in actively traded Stocks in Play. You can make a lot of money trading in and out of an active stock with small size. Likewise, you can lose a great deal of money trading in and out of an active stock with too big of a size. For example, for low float stocks that can move 10% or 20% in a matter of seconds, I never take a large position, even though their price is typically low (in the range of

$1–$10) and I have sufficient buying power for a very large position. Develop your trading skills, build your trading account, and slowly increase your size.

My trade size depends on the price of the stock and on my account size and risk management rule (set forth in Chapter 3), but 2,000 shares is my usual size if I am trading in the $10–$50 price range.

1. I buy 1,000 shares.

2. If the trade goes in my favor, I add another 1,000 shares (note that I add into my winning position, not into a losing one).

3. I sell 400 shares at the first target, bringing my stop loss to break-even (my entry point).

4. I sell another 600 shares at the next target point.

5. I usually keep the last 1,000 shares until I am stopped out. I always retain some shares in case the price keeps moving in my favor.

For a more expensive price range ($50–$100), I reduce my total share size to 400 shares. I rarely trade stocks higher than $100. The more expensive stocks are less attractive to retail traders and are often dominated by computers and institutional traders.

As explained earlier, some experienced traders never enter the trade all at once. They scale into the trade, meaning they buy at various points. Their initial share size might be relatively small, but traders will add to their position as the price action validates their idea.

They might start with 100 shares and then add to their position in various steps. For example, for a 1,000-share trade, they enter either 500/500 or 100/200/700 shares. If done correctly, this is an excellent method of risk and trade management. However, managing the position in this system is extremely difficult and of course requires a low-commission brokerage firm. Many new traders who try to do this will end up overtrading and will lose their money in commissions, slippage and the averaging down of the losing trades.

I rarely *scale down* into a losing trade. I always *scale up*; I add to my winning position. Remember, scaling into a trade is a double-edged sword and beginners may use it incorrectly as a way to average down their losing positions, sending good money after bad. I don't recommend scaling as a method for beginners. Although they can appear similar, there is a huge difference between scaling into a trade and averaging down a losing position. Averaging down losing positions is perhaps the most common mistake a beginner will make and that will almost certainly lead to the end of their short trading career.

What is averaging down?

Imagine you buy 1,000 shares of a company at an important intraday support level of $10 in the anticipation of selling them at the next level of around $12. Instead, the stock breaks the support level and drops to $8. You have lost the trade and you should have been stopped out. As your original trade idea was to go long above the support level, you now have no reason to be in this trade since that level has been broken. But, if instead of accepting the loss and moving on, you buy another 1,000 shares at $8, you now have 2,000 shares with an average cost of $9. It is unlikely the price will hit your $12 target, but it is likely that the price will rally back to $9. At $9, you can sell all of your 2,000 shares at break-even and extricate yourself from this losing trade with no loss. Even better, if their price goes to $9.50, you can close your 2,000 shares with a $1,000 profit. It sounds very tempting, but it is wishful thinking.

For a beginner, averaging down a losing trade is a recipe for wiping out one's account. Remember, *averaging down does not work for day traders.* I have tried it. 85% of the time you will profit when you average down. But the 15% of the time you are wrong, you will blow up your account. The losses during these 15% of trades will far outweigh your gains from the 85%. As Mike Bellafiore, co-founder of SMB Capital (a proprietary trading firm in New York City), writes in his book, *One Good Trade,* "*Just forget about it. It is a waste of your mental energy ...*" Remember, it only takes ONE bad trade to blow up your account and for you to be done with your day trading career forever.

During 2015 I made good money from a bullish trend in the shares of biotech companies. In October 2015, however, biotech companies began an incredibly large sell off. When something is selling off, you really do not know if it will be a massive bear market until you see the charts. And, sadly, you cannot see the charts until it is too late, not until after the sell off is finished. I thought the sell off must be a normal pull back. During that time, the Direxion Daily S&P Biotech Bull 3x Shares (ticker: LABU) started to sell off too, and its share price dropped from $148 to below $60. I purchased 100 shares at $120 with the hope that it would go back to $148. It did not. It went below $100. I added an additional 100 shares. My average was now $110. It plunged further to $80. I added 200 more. My average became $95. It went further to $60. I added 400 shares more (and I was almost out of money). My average became $77.50 and I held a huge 800 share position on LABU. It dropped further to $58. I was just long, and I was so very wrong. I got a margin call from my broker. I could not add further money because I did not have any. My broker froze my account and sold my position. It was the most devastating loss in my trading career to that date. Two days later LABU rebounded to over $100.

I said to myself, if I only had a bigger account...

If you think that my severe loss on LABU was because of my account size and not my overtrading and improper risk management, let me share with you the story of a Canadian trader whose gamble on the natural gas Futures market went bad. You can do an online search of Brian Hunter yourself and read further about him.

Brian Hunter was a superstar trader with an impressive track record at Amaranth Advisors, a massive hedge fund with over $9 billion in assets in 2006. This 32-year-old trader from Calgary, Alberta, Canada was up $2 billion from trading in natural gas earlier in 2006. That summer though, natural gas dropped to below $4 in a terrible, unusually steep down move. With a deep billion–dollar pocket, Mr. Hunter ignored the market and repeatedly averaged down on a risky, volatile bullish position on natural gas. JPMorgan, his broker, kept calling for more collateral to support his enormous positions, and when the collateral didn't arrive, he was forced to liquidate his positions. Amaranth Advisors went from $10 billion in managed assets to $4.5 billion, accepting a $6.6 billion loss which led to the company being dissolved entirely.

Just a few weeks after that, natural gas prices rebounded and actually went higher. *"If only Brian Hunter had a bigger account..."* Apparently an account with $10 billion in it was not big enough.

For the trader at home with many dollars less than billions, you cannot withstand such draw downs. Brian Hunter believed that the price had to go up and not down. He was wrong at that time. I don't know why, but traders such as Brian Hunter will at times stubbornly put being right about their decision over making money. These are the types of traders who conveniently forget that the market can remain irrational longer than they can survive in the game. You cannot let your pride get the best of you. If you've made a bad decision, take a loss and get out early. Predictions and speculations have their place, but the price action of the stock is the most important indicator for traders like us. If you believe in an irrefutable trading opinion and the price action does not confirm your bias, then simply do not make the trade. Predictions without validation from the price action are not advisable if you wish to enjoy a long trading career. Your job is not prediction and anticipation, but the *identification* of trends and then the taking of a successful ride on them.

Now that I have warned you about day trading, let's review some important day trading strategies.

STRATEGY 1: ABCD PATTERN

The ABCD Pattern is one of the most basic and easiest patterns to trade, and it is an excellent choice for beginner and intermediate traders. Although it is simple and has been known for a long time, it still works effectively because so many traders are still trading it. You should do whatever all of the other traders are doing because a trend is your friend. A trend may very well be your only friend in the market.

Let's take a look at this pattern in Figure 7.1:

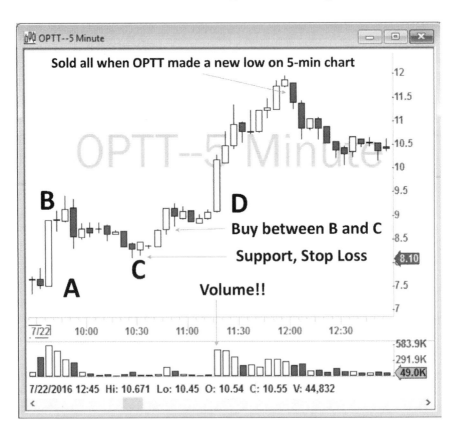

Figure 7.1: Example of an ABCD Pattern.

ABCD Patterns start with a strong upward move. Buyers are aggressively buying a stock from point A and making constantly new highs of the day (point B). You want to enter the trade, but you should not chase the trade, because at point B it is very extended and already at a high price. In addition, you cannot say where your stop loss should be. You must never enter a trade without knowing where your stop is.

At point B, traders who bought the stock earlier start slowly selling it for profit and the price comes down. You should still not enter the trade because you do not know where the bottom of this pull back will be. However, if you see that the price does not come down from a certain level, such as point C, it means that the stock has found a potential support. Therefore, you can plan your trade and set up stops and a profit taking point.

The above screenshot, marked as Figure 7.1, is of Ocean Power Technologies Inc. (ticker: OPTT) at July 22, 2016, when they announced a public offering of shares and warrants (warrants are a tool used to purchase shares in the future at a set price) which was expected to bring in gross revenue of some $4 million. (There's a fundamental catalyst! Remember Chapter 2?)

The stock surged up from $7.70 (A) to $9.40 (B) at around 9:40 a.m. I, along with many other traders who missed the first push higher, waited for point B and then a confirmation that the stock wasn't going to go lower than a certain price (point C). When I saw that point C was holding as a support and that buyers would not let the stock price go any lower than $8.10 (C), I bought 1,000 shares of OPTT near C, with my stop being a break below point C. I knew that when the price went higher, closer to B, buyers would jump on massively. As I mentioned before, the ABCD Pattern is a very classic strategy and many retail traders look for it. Close to point D, the volume suddenly spiked, which meant that many more traders were jumping into the trade.

My profit target was when the stock made a new low on a 5-minute chart, which was a sign of weakness. As you can see in Figure 7.1, OPTT had a nice run up to around $12 and then showed weakness by making a new low on a 5-minute chart at around $11.60. That is when I sold all of my position.

Figure 7.2 is another example, this time for SPU on August 29, 2016. There are actually two ABCD Patterns in this example. I marked the second one as *abcd pattern*. Usually, as the trading day progresses, volumes become lower and therefore the second pattern is smaller in size. Please note that you will always have high volumes at points B and D (and in this instance also at points b and d).

Figure 7.2: Example of ABCD Pattern and abcd pattern.

For this 2020 edition of my book, I wanted to ensure that the ABCD Pattern is still a valid strategy. As part of my investigations, I asked one of our most senior traders in the community, Aiman, to provide me charts of some of his recent trades. Aiman is a medical student in Russia who trades the U.S. market in the evening. He is known to be a genius in the ABCD Pattern Strategy! He provided me with two examples as shown below in Figures 7.3 and 7.4.

Figure 7.3 below shows Aiman's trade on PG&E Corporation (ticker: PCG) on April 8, 2020, as marked on its 1-minute chart. I did not mark the ABCD points on this chart, but if you want to test your knowledge, please send your answer to me at *andrew@bearbulltraders.com* or to Aiman himself at *aiman@bearbulltraders.com*. Do include your:

- Entry price and time
- Stop loss price

We will let you know if your response is correct or not!

Figure 7.3: Example of an ABCD Pattern trade on PCG on April 8, 2020. What should be the entry price, time of entry, and stop loss price? Email your answer to *andrew@bearbulltraders.com* or to Aiman at *aiman@bearbulltraders.com*

Another example is a trade Aiman had on American Airlines Group Inc. (ticker: AAL) on June 15, 2020. The airline and cruise line sector was very volatile during the first months of the COVID-19 pandemic as the future of travel was quite unclear. American Airlines was one of our favorite stocks to trade. Figure 7.4 below is AAL's 5-minute chart and you will see that I marked three ABCD Patterns in it for you to review. Interestingly, point C fell on VWAP, which acted as a strong support during Aiman's trades.

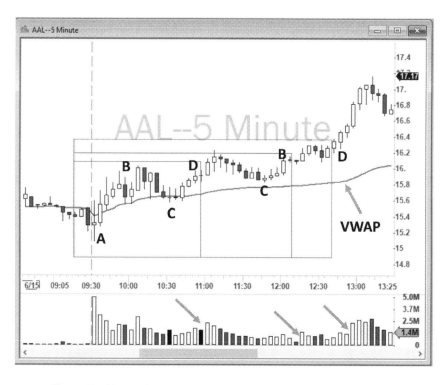

Figure 7.4: Example of ABCD Patterns on AAL on June 15, 2020.

To summarize my trading strategy for the ABCD Pattern:

1. When I observe with my scanner or I'm advised by someone in our chatroom that a stock is surging up from point A and reaching a significant new high for the day (point B), I wait to see if the price makes a support higher than point A. I call this point C. I do not jump into the trade right away.

2. I watch the stock during its consolidation period (I'll explain this term in the next strategy). I choose my share size and stop and exit strategy.

3. When I see that the price is holding support at level C, I enter the trade close to the price of point C in anticipation of moving forward to point D or higher.

4. My stop is the loss of point C. If the price goes lower than point C, I sell and accept the loss. Therefore, it is important to buy the stock close to point C to minimize the loss. Some traders wait and buy only at point D to ensure that the ABCD Pattern is really working. In my opinion, that approach basically reduces your reward while at the same time increasing your risk.

5. If the price moves higher, I sell half of my position at point D, and bring my stop higher to my entry point (break-even).

6. I sell the remaining position as soon as my target hits or I sense that the price is losing

steam or that the sellers are acquiring control of the price action. When the price makes a new low on my 5-minute chart, it is a good indicator that the buyers are almost exhausted.

STRATEGY 2: BULL FLAG MOMENTUM

In day trading, Bull Flag is a Momentum Strategy that usually works very effectively on low float stocks under $10 (described in Chapter 4). This trading strategy is difficult to manage the risk in and requires a fast execution platform.

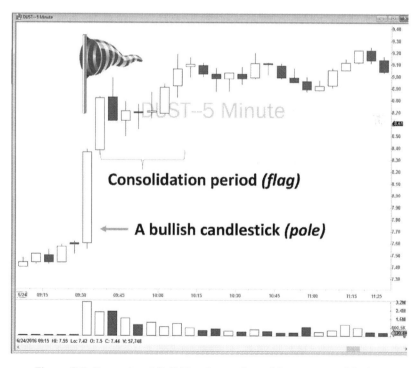

Figure 7.5: Example of Bull Flag formation with one consolidation period.

This pattern, shown above in Figure 7.5, is named Bull Flag because it resembles a flag on a pole. In Bull Flag, you have several large candles going up (like a pole), and you also have a series of small candles moving sideways (like a flag), or, as we day traders say, "consolidating". Consolidation means that the traders who bought stocks at a lower price are now selling and taking their profits. Although that is happening, the price does not decrease sharply because the buyers are still entering into trades and the sellers are not yet in control of the price. Many traders who missed buying the stock before the Bull Flag started, will now be looking for an opportunity to take a trade. Wise traders know that it is risky to buy a stock when the price is increasing significantly. That's called "*chasing the stock*". Professional traders aim to enter the trade during quiet times and take their profits during the volatile times. That is the total opposite of how amateurs trade. They jump in or out when stocks begin to run, but grow bored and lose interest when the prices are, shall I say, sleepy.

Chasing the stocks is an account killer for beginners. You must wait until the stock finds its high point, and then you must wait for the consolidation. As soon as the price starts breaking up in the consolidation area, you can begin purchasing stocks. Patience truly is a virtue.

Usually a Bull Flag will show several consolidation periods. I enter in only during the first and second consolidation periods. Third and higher consolidation periods are risky because the price has probably been very extended in a way that indicates that the buyers will soon be losing their control. Let's study an example in Figure 7.6 below of a Bull Flag on RIGL on August 30, 2016.

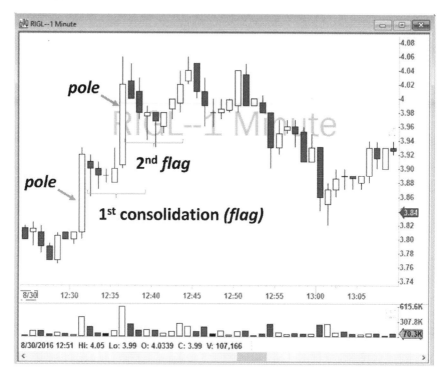

Figure 7.6: Example of Bull Flag formation with two consolidation periods on RIGL.

This is an example of two Bull Flag Patterns. It is normally hard to catch the first Bull Flag, and you will probably miss it, but your scanner should alert you to it so that you can be ready for the next Bull Flag. Figure 7.7 that follows is an example from my scanner in this time period:

Time	Symbol	Price ($)	Vol Today	Rel Vol	Flt (Shr)	Vol 5 Min	Strategy Name
12:45:00 PM	CELP	8.68	53,491	2.70	4.26M	4,059	Strong Low-Float Bull Flag Momentum
12:38:51 PM	RESN	5.66	88,841	3.78	5.63M	2,168	Strong Low-Float Bull Flag Momentum
12:36:15 PM	RIGL	3.94	42.49M	120.83	89.1M	4,111	Medium-Float Bull Flag Momentum
12:34:59 PM	ITEK	7.16	659,979	7.18	13.2M	19.3K	Medium-Float Bull Flag Momentum
12:31:52 PM	RIGL	3.91	41.87M	120.97	89.1M	3,994	Medium-Float Bull Flag Momentum
12:29:30 PM	KPTI	9.42	1.47M	22.72	3.93M	1,450	Low-Float Bull Flag Momentum
12:29:30 PM	KPTI	9.39	1.47M	22.72	3.93M	1,445	Low-Float Bull Flag Momentum
12:12:37 PM	AMID	12.08	2.62M	28.09	20.7M	55.5K	+$10 Strong Bull Flag Momentum
11:57:44 AM	LNTH	9.96	604,695	4.84	11.3M	543.7	Medium-Float Bull Flag Momentum
11:56:42 AM	LNTH	9.95	599,426	4.83	11.3M	569.0	Medium-Float Bull Flag Momentum
11:51:04 AM	BIOL	1.81	224,633	6.43	32.4M	2,353	Medium-Float Bull Flag Momentum

History: Intraday Bull Flag Momentum Scalping Strategy

Figure 7.7: Example of my intraday Bull Flag Strategy scanner.

As you can see, my scanner showed RIGL at both 12:31:52 p.m. and 12:36:15 p.m. As soon as I saw that, I realized that there was also a very high relative volume of trading (120 times the normal trading volume), which made this a perfect setup for day trading. I waited for the first consolidation period to finish and, as soon as the stock started to move toward its high for the day, I jumped into the trade. My stop loss was the breakdown of the consolidation period. I marked my exit and entry in Figure 7.8 below.

Figure 7.8: Entry, stop and exit of a Bull Flag Strategy on RIGL.

You can see the Bull Flag Pattern on any short time frame: 1-minute, 2-minute and 5-minute charts. Now let's take a look at Figure 7.9, a 2-minute chart for OPTT on June 1, 2016. As you can see, the stock had a powerful Bull Flag right at the Open, followed by a consolidation period. As soon as the first consolidation period was completed, another small Bull Flag formed. The volume of shares traded is significantly higher after consolidation, which is a confirmation for a long entry.

You can also see another Bull Flag on the OPTT 2-minute chart followed by another consolidation period. As shown below in Figure 7.9, after the second consolidation period, the volume of shares traded was significantly higher, a confirmation for another long entry. I don't trade more than two Bull Flags in a stock and, as you can see on this chart, the stock started to sell off after the third Bull Flag (at around $7). Aside from the strategy, did you notice that OPTT moved from $1.50 to almost $7 in just 35 minutes? This kind of move can be expected from low float under $10 stocks.

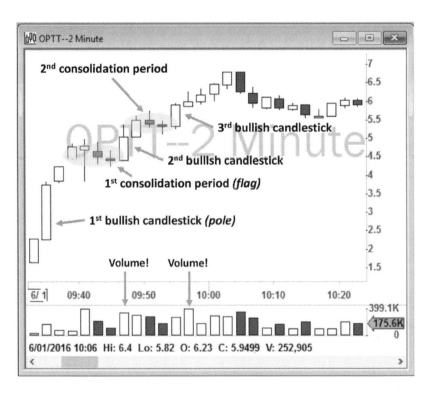

Figure 7.9: Screenshot showing three consolidation periods in OPTT. Note the volume increases after each consolidation period.

To summarize my trading strategy:

1. When I see a stock surging up (either on my scanner or when advised by someone in our chatroom), I patiently wait until the consolidation period. I do not jump into the trade right away (you will recall that is the dangerous act of "chasing the stock").

2. I watch the stock during the consolidation period. I choose my share size and stop and exit strategy.

3. As soon as prices are moving over the high of the consolidation candlesticks, I enter the trade. My stop loss is the break below the consolidation periods.

4. I sell half of my position and take a profit on the way up. I bring my stop loss from the low of the consolidation to my entry price (break-even).

5. I sell my remaining positions as soon as my target hits or I sense that the price is losing steam and the sellers are gaining control of the price action.

The Bull Flag is essentially an ABCD Pattern that will happen more often on low float stocks. However, in a Bull Flag Strategy for stocks under $10, many traders buy only at or near the breakout (opposite to the ABCD Pattern for medium float stocks). The reason for this is because moves in low float stocks are fast and they will fade away very quickly. Therefore, Bull Flag is more or less a *Momentum and Scalping Strategy*. Scalpers buy when a stock is running. They rarely like to buy during consolidation (during that waiting and holding phase). These types of stocks usually drop quickly and brutally so it is important to jump in only when there is a confirmation of breakout. Waiting for the stock to break the top of a consolidation area is a way of reducing your risk and exposure time in low float stocks. Instead of buying and holding and waiting, which increases exposure time, scalpers just wait for the breakout and then send their order. Get in, scalp, and get out quickly. That's the philosophy of momentum scalpers:

- Get in at the breakout
- Take your profit
- Get out of the way

The Bull Flag Pattern is found within an uptrend in a stock. The Bull Flag is a long-based strategy. You should not short a Bull Flag. I personally don't trade much momentum. It is a risky strategy and beginners should be very careful trading these. If you choose to, trade only in a small size and only after sufficient practice in simulators. You will also need a super-fast execution system for scalping.

STRATEGIES 3 AND 4: REVERSAL TRADING

Top and Bottom Reversals are two other trading strategies that day traders love using because they have very defined entry and exit points. In this section, I'm going to explain how to find reversal setups using scanners, how to use indecision or Doji candlesticks to take an entry, how to understand where to set your stops and your profit targets, and how to trail your winners.

Members of our chatroom will hear me say time and time again that what goes up, must come down. *Don't chase the trade if it is too extended.* The inverse is also true. What goes down will definitely come back up to some extent. When a stock starts to sell off significantly, there are two reasons behind it:

1. Institutional traders and hedge funds have started selling their large position to the public market and the stock price is tanking.

2. Traders have started short selling a stock because of some bad fundamental news, but they will have to cover their shorts sooner or later. That is where you wait for an entry. When short sellers are trying to cover their shorts, the stock will reverse quickly. That is called a "short squeeze". You want to ride that.

I'm going to illustrate this strategy with a few examples so that you can see exactly what to look for. Figure 7.10 below is an example of what it looks like to find a stock that has sold off really hard after the market opens. Moves like this are extremely hard to catch for the short side, because when you find the stock, it is already too late to enter the short selling trade. But please, remember the mantra: *what goes up, must come down.* Therefore, you have the option of waiting for a reversal opportunity.

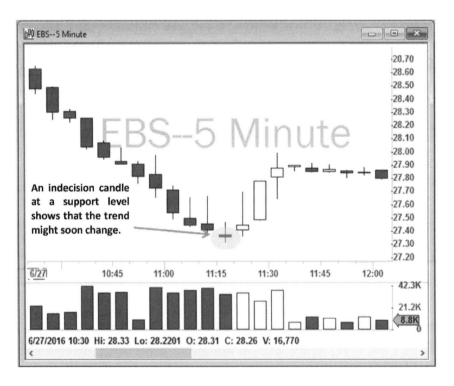

An indecision candle at a support level shows that the trend might soon change.

Figure 7.10: Example of a Reversal Strategy on EBS.

Each Reversal Strategy has four important elements:

1. At least five candlesticks on a 5–minute chart moving upward or downward.

2. The stock will have an extreme 5-minute RSI indicator (Relative Strength Index). An RSI above 90 or below 10 will pique my interest. The RSI, developed initially by famous technical analyst Welles Wilder, Jr., is an indicator that compares the magnitude of recent gains and losses in price over a period of time to measure the speed and change of price movement. The RSI values range from 0 to 100. Traders in Reversal Strategies use RSI values to identify overbought or oversold conditions and to find buy or sell signals. For example, RSI readings above 90 indicate overbought conditions and RSI readings below 10 indicate oversold conditions. Your trading platform or scanner software calculates the RSI automatically for you. If you are interested, an online search will bring up quite a bit more information about the RSI.

These two elements demonstrate that a stock is really stretched out, and you must pay close attention to your scanner for all of these data points. I have configured my scanner to highlight RSIs lower than 20 and higher than 80 so I can very quickly recognize them. You must simultaneously look for a certain RSI level and a certain number of consecutive candles.

3. The stock is being traded at or near an important intraday support or resistance level. For details on how to find support or resistance levels, please read my commentary that

follows for support or resistance trading. I only take reversal trades when the price is near a significant support level (for Bottom Reversal) or a significant resistance level (for Top Reversal).

4. When the trend is coming to an end, usually indecision candles, such as a spinning top or Doji, form. That is when you need to be ready.

In reversal trading, you are looking for one of the indecision candlesticks that we reviewed in Chapter 6. They are an indication that the trend may soon change. A Doji is a candle that has a wick longer than its body. You can see a picture of a bearish Doji in Figure 7.11 below. It has that long upper wick that some would call a top tail and that others would call a shooting star. This candle tells you four things: the open price, the close price, the high of that period and the low of that period. So, when you have a candle with a top tail, you know that at some point during that candle period the price moved up, was unable to hold at that level, and was then sold off. It depicts a bit of a battle taking place between the buyers and the sellers in which the buyers lost their push up. It is a good indication that the sellers may soon control the price and will push that price down.

The same is true about a bullish Doji. You can see a picture of a bullish Doji in Figure 7.12 below. It has that long lower wick that some would call a bottom tail and others would call a hammer. When you have a hammer candle with a bottom tail, you know that at some point during that candle period the price moved down, was unable to hold at those low levels, and was bought up. This indicates a battle between the buyers and the sellers in which the sellers lost their push down. It is a good indication that the buyers may now gain control of the price and push that price up.

Figure 7.11: Top Reversal Strategy with an indecision shooting star candlestick formed as a sign of entry.

In reversal trading, you look for either Doji or indecision candlesticks. They are an indication that the trend may soon change. In Reversal Strategies, you are looking for a clear confirmation that the pattern is beginning to reverse. What you definitely don't want is to be on the wrong side of a reversal trade, or, as we call it, "*catching a falling knife*". It means that when a stock is selling off badly (the falling knife), you don't want to buy on the assumption that it should bounce. If the stocks are dropping, you want to wait for the confirmation of the reversal. This will usually be (1) the formation of a Doji or indecision candle and (2) the first 1-minute or the first 5-minute candle to reach a new high near an important intraday support level. That is my entry point. I set my stop at the low of the previous candlestick or at the loss of the support level.

In reversal trading, it is best that the RSI be at the extremes (above 90, below 10). Once you find that, you must then look for an actual entry near a strong intraday support (for Bottom Reversal) or resistance level (for Top Reversal). As mentioned, an entry for me is going to be either the first 1-minute or the first 5-minute candle to reach a new high (for Bottom Reversal) or to make a new low (for Top Reversal) and only when the price is being traded near an important intraday support or resistance level.

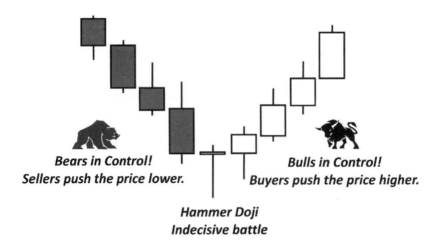

Bears in Control!
Sellers push the price lower.

Bulls in Control!
Buyers push the price higher.

Hammer Doji
Indecisive battle

Figure 7.12: Bottom Reversal Strategy with an indecision hammer candlestick formed as a sign of entry.

In a Bottom Reversal, when you've had a long run of consecutive candles making new lows, the first candle that makes the new high near an important support level is very significant. That's my entry point. There are times when I'll use the 1-minute chart, but typically I'll wait for the 5-minute chart because it is a much better confirmation. The 5-minute chart is cleaner. The first 5-minute candle to make a new high near an intraday support level is the point at which I enter the reversal, with a stop at the low of the day.

Once you're in one of these trades, your exit indicators are quite simple. I take profit when the price reaches a moving average (either 9 EMA, 20 EMA or VWAP) or reaches another important intraday level.

In a Bottom Reversal, if the stock pops up and then suddenly moves back down, I stop out for a loss. If I jump in long, buying stock and hoping the price will go higher, and instead the price ends up just going sideways, it's a sign that I am probably going to see a consolidation for another move down, and that is an indication that the price is probably going to continue to drop. If I get in and I hold for a few minutes and the price stays flat, I get out, no matter what happens after that. I may be wrong, but I don't like to expose my account to the unknown. I need to be in the right setup, and if it is not ready yet, I'm out. If I get into the profit zone, I can start adjusting my stop, first to break–even, and then to the low of the last 5-minute candle. I will then keep adjusting my stop as I move up.

In Reversal Strategies, one of the main tasks of a trader is to watch stocks that are running up or down, while simultaneously identifying possible support or resistance levels and areas that could provide a good reversal opportunity on daily charts. This allows you to resist being impulsive and rushing into the trade. Instead, you wait for the areas of stagnation. You take your time and watch the trade develop and wait for the reversal to begin.

Bottom Reversal

This beautiful illustration that follows in Figure 7.13 is on Emergent BioSolutions Inc. (ticker: EBS) and shows a perfect reversal that I found using my stock scanners. An indecision candlestick at the bottom of the down-trend signifies a potential reversal, and, as you can see, right after that is a big swing back up. I took this trade right after seeing an indecision Doji, and kept my stop at the low of that indecision candlestick. When EBS hit my scanner, I quickly changed my chart to a daily one and found important nearby support and resistance levels of $27.36 and $28. As mentioned previously, to learn how to find support and resistance levels, please read further along in this chapter.

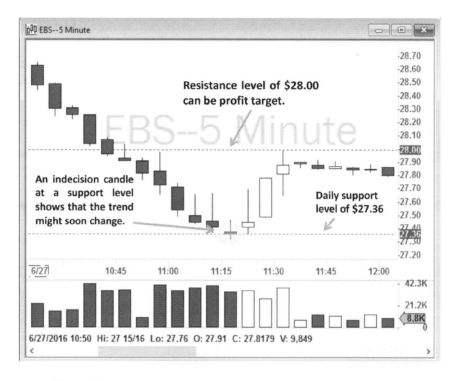

Figure 7.13: Example of a Bottom Reversal Strategy on EBS.

The most significant advantage to Reversal Strategies is that they overcome the difficulty of anticipating when stocks will make major moves. You will probably miss the moment when the stock starts to sell off, and you won't have time to sell short the stock for profit, but you can always prepare for the reversal trade.

Another example of a Bottom Reversal Strategy is in Figure 7.14 that follows:

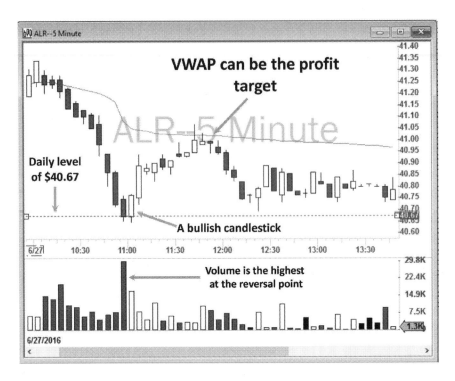

Figure 7.14: Example of a Bottom Reversal Strategy on ALR.

I found Alere Inc. (ticker: ALR) on June 27, 2016 at 10:57 a.m. using my Trade Ideas real time Bottom Reversal scanner. See the image below in Figure 7.15:

Symbol	Time	Consec Cndls	Price ($)	Flt (Shr)	Avg True	Vol 10 Min	Rel Vol
GWRE	10:57	-6	57.49	72.45M	1.50	48.7	2.35
PHG	10:57	-8	23.04	912.49M	0.66	163.9	3.18
BXP	10:57	-10	125.53	152.55M	1.91	82.6	1.68
ALR	10:57	-7	40.70	82.21M	0.77	142.9	1.21
BOFI	10:57	-7	15.51	57.57M	0.65	105.6	1.63
IMAX	10:57	-6	27.62	58.75M	0.90	77.6	1.02
DIS	10:57	-6	94.19	1.49B	1.41	141.8	1.45
COP	10:57	-10	41.29	1.24B	1.47	84.4	1.65
YELP	10:57	-9	26.57	54.92M	1.09	138.0	1.61
P	10:57	-4	11.25	188.46M	0.48	245.0	1.23
UHS	10:57	-11	129.57	87.99M	2.75	99.0	1.29
AYI	10:57	-8	234.47	43.02M	5.03	172.2	1.73
RNG	10:57	-6	19.04	56.45M	0.60	60.7	1.98
YNDX	10:57	-10	19.78	264.00M	0.81	496.1	2.02
CAB	10:57	-6	46.42	45.13M	0.99	112.5	1.46
ETN	10:57	-8	54.36	456.47M	1.33	485.9	5.74
FSIC	10:57	-5	8.55		0.17	89.7	0.83
EZPW	10:56	-5	6.77	45.20M	0.34	106.3	1.50
ZOES	10:56	-6	34.60	17.22M	1.18	733.1	2.85

Figure 7.15: Example of my Trade Ideas real time Bottom Reversal scanner showing ALR with seven consecutive downward candlesticks.

My scanner, at 10:57 a.m., showed me that ALR had seven consecutive candles to the downside, a relatively medium float (80 million shares) and a relative volume of 1.21, which meant it was trading higher than usual. I actually did not take this trade because I missed my entry, but I wanted to show you what overall trading strategies look like for Bottom Reversals. If you look again at the above Figure 7.14, the screenshot of ALR's 5-minute chart, you will see a significant intraday level of support at $40.67. The price reversed at that level with higher than usual trading volume. Please note that no indecision candlestick formed in this reversal. Instead, the reversal was indicated by a strong bullish candlestick (marked in the above Figure 7.14). At times, a reversal happens so fast that indecision candlesticks will not form. Therefore, it is important to observe the price action near significant intraday levels, and to of course confirm the reversal with an indication of higher than usual trading volume.

When you're looking at reversals, you want to ensure that you only trade in the extremes. The example you just saw was a stock that had made an extreme move to the downside before that move was reversed. A stock that has been selling off slowly all day long is usually not suitable for a reversal. That stock may be a good candidate for a Moving Average Trend trade (explained in the pages to come). You want to find stocks that are really stretched out to the downside or, for short selling, really stretched out to the upside, in a short period of time, and with high volume at the reversal point.

You want to see that large extension, which means that you should look for considerable volume at the reversal point (such as the ALR Bottom Reversal in the above example from my scanner that is marked as Figure 7.15). Once you find that, you then must look for a couple of key indicators that will suggest that the price may be about to turn, and that is when you then take the position. I've said it many times: what goes up, must come down. Oftentimes these stocks will give up days' and weeks' or years' worth of price gain in just a matter of minutes. It is very critical to be able to correctly time the reversal.

Again, the key to your success with Top and Bottom Reversals is trading the extremes at or near a significant daily support or resistance level. How do I quantify these extremes? These are a few of the things that I look for:

1. An extreme RSI above 90 or below 10 will pique my interest.

2. A very high volume of shares being traded. Volume is usually increasing with the direction of price action and is at its maximum at the point of reversal.

3. Finally, more than five consecutive candles ending with an indecision candle or a Doji is definitely going to catch my attention. These candles usually demonstrate that some sort of a battle has taken place between the sellers and the buyers, and that the one which had been more powerful is no longer. As you

saw in the previous ALR example (Figures 7.14 and 7.15), sometimes reversals happen without an indecision candlestick. In those cases, you should look for strong reversal candlesticks – a bullish body for Bottom Reversals and a bearish body for Top Reversals.

I will add a caveat to this final point: there will be times when you will have between five and ten consecutive candles without much price action. They may be drifting down slowly, but not quickly enough for you to sense that it is a good reversal. You must look for a combination of these indicators all occurring at the same time. Never try to go short just because the prices are too high. You should never argue with the crowd's decision or the market, even if it doesn't make sense to you. You do not have to run with the crowd – but you should not run against it.

Utilizing all of these different factors will recreate the strategy that has been successful for me because of its attractive profit-to-loss ratio. Your profit-to-loss ratio is your average winners versus your average losers. Many new traders end up trading with a very poor profit-to-loss ratio because they sell their winners too soon and they hold their losers too long. This is an extremely common habit among new traders. The Reversal Strategy, however, lends itself to having a larger profit-to-loss ratio for new traders.

To summarize my trading strategy for the Bottom Reversal Strategy:

1. I set up a scanner to flag stocks with four or more consecutive candlesticks going downward in an extreme manner. When I see a stock hit my scanner, I quickly review the volume and daily levels of support or resistance near the stock to see if it will be a good candidate for a reversal trade or not.

2. I wait for confirmation of a Bottom Reversal Strategy: (1) formation of a bullish Doji or indecision candle or, instead, a very bullish candlestick, (2) the stock is being traded at or near a significant intraday support level, and (3) the RSI must be lower than 10.

3. When I see the stock make a new 1-minute or 5-minute high, I buy the stock.

4. My stop loss is the low of the previous red candlestick or the low of the day.

5. My profit target is either (1) the next level of support, or (2) VWAP (Volume Weighted Average Price, described later in this chapter) or 9 EMA or 20 EMA moving averages (whichever is closer), or (3) the stock makes a new 5-minute low, which means that the buyers are exhausted and the sellers are once again gaining control.

Top Reversal

As discussed before, a Top Reversal is similar to a Bottom Reversal, but on a short selling side. Let's take a look at Bed Bath & Beyond Inc. (ticker: BBBY) as it traded on June 23, 2016. My scanner, displayed in Figure 7.16 below, showed BBBY going up at 10:18 a.m. with six consecutive candles. It had a relative volume of around 21.60, which meant it was trading significantly higher than usual (remember, we retail traders look for unusual trading volumes).

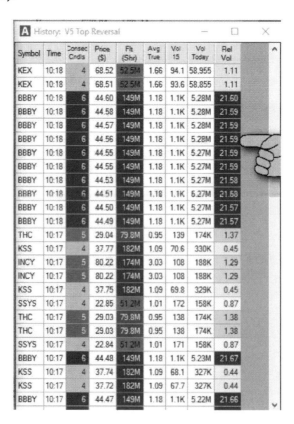

Symbol	Time	Consec Cndls	Price ($)	Flt (Shr)	Avg True	Vol 15	Vol Today	Rel Vol
KEX	10:18	4	68.52	52.5M	1.66	94.1	58.955	1.11
KEX	10:18	4	68.51	52.5M	1.66	93.6	58.855	1.11
BBBY	10:18	6	44.60	149M	1.18	1.1K	5.28M	21.60
BBBY	10:18	6	44.58	149M	1.18	1.1K	5.28M	21.59
BBBY	10:18	6	44.57	149M	1.18	1.1K	5.28M	21.59
BBBY	10:18	6	44.56	149M	1.18	1.1K	5.28M	21.59
BBBY	10:18	6	44.55	149M	1.18	1.1K	5.27M	21.59
BBBY	10:18	6	44.55	149M	1.18	1.1K	5.27M	21.59
BBBY	10:18	6	44.53	149M	1.18	1.1K	5.27M	21.58
BBBY	10:18	6	44.51	149M	1.18	1.1K	5.27M	21.58
BBBY	10:18	6	44.50	149M	1.18	1.1K	5.27M	21.57
BBBY	10:18	6	44.49	149M	1.18	1.1K	5.27M	21.57
THC	10:17	5	29.04	79.8M	0.95	139	174K	1.37
KSS	10:17	4	37.77	182M	1.09	70.6	330K	0.45
INCY	10:17	5	80.22	174M	3.03	108	188K	1.29
INCY	10:17	5	80.22	174M	3.03	108	188K	1.29
KSS	10:17	4	37.75	182M	1.09	69.8	329K	0.45
SSYS	10:17	4	22.85	51.2M	1.01	172	158K	0.87
THC	10:17	5	29.03	79.8M	0.95	138	174K	1.38
THC	10:17	5	29.03	79.8M	0.95	138	174K	1.38
SSYS	10:17	4	22.84	51.2M	1.01	171	158K	0.87
BBBY	10:17	6	44.48	149M	1.18	1.1K	5.23M	21.67
KSS	10:17	4	37.74	182M	1.09	68.1	327K	0.44
KSS	10:17	4	37.72	182M	1.09	67.7	327K	0.44
BBBY	10:17	6	44.47	149M	1.18	1.1K	5.22M	21.66

Figure 7.16: Example of my real time Top Reversal scanner alerting me to BBBY.

I took this trade and made a good profit on it. I quickly reviewed the daily chart and found a significant resistance level at $44.40. I decided to see if I could get a good short entry near that level. A nice Doji around that level formed so I decided to take the trade. I shorted 800 shares at $44.10 when a new 5-minute candlestick was made, with my stop being the break of the high of the last 5-minute candlestick, which was also a new high of the day, as I have marked in Figure 7.17 below. I covered my shorts at VWAP near $43.10 for an $800 profit when the stock reached VWAP.

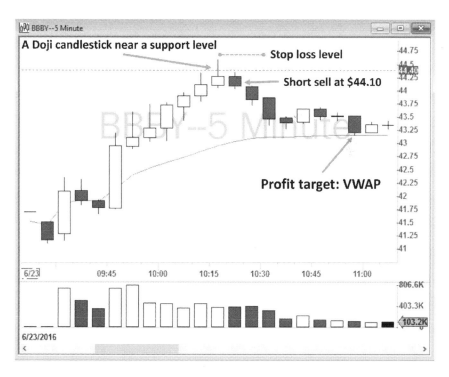

Figure 7.17: Example of a Top Reversal Strategy on BBBY.

To summarize my trading strategy for the Top Reversal Strategy:

1. I set up a scanner to highlight stocks with four or more consecutive candlesticks moving upward. When I see the stock hit my scanner, I quickly review the volume and daily level of support or resistance near the stock to see if it will be a good trade or not.

2. I wait for confirmation of a Top Reversal Strategy: (1) formation of a bearish Doji or indecision candle or, instead, a very bearish candlestick, (2) the stock is being traded at or near a significant resistance level at high volume, and (3) the RSI must be higher than 90.

3. When I see the stock make a new 5-minute low, I consider this as a sign of weakness. I start short selling the stock if I have shares available to short.

4. My stop will be the high of the previous candlestick or simply the high of the day.

5. My profit target is either (1) the next level of support, or (2) VWAP or 9 EMA or 20 EMA moving averages (whichever is closer), or (3) when the stock makes a new 5-minute high, which means the buyers are once again gaining control and the sellers are exhausted.

Some day traders focus exclusively on reversal trades and in fact base their entire careers on them.

Reversal trades are certainly the most classic of the various strategies with a very good risk/reward ratio and, interestingly, virtually every trading day you will find stocks that are good candidates for reversal trades. I myself am trading more and more reversal trades these days, especially during Late-Morning and afternoon trading. However, reversal trading is not yet the cornerstone of my trading strategies. Until recently, I was more of a VWAP and Support or Resistance trader, but 1-minute Opening Range Breakouts have now become one of the main strategies that I use. All of these strategies will be explained later on in this chapter.

STRATEGY 5: MOVING AVERAGE TREND TRADING

Some traders use moving averages as potential entry and exit points for day trading. Many stocks will start an upside or downside trend around 11 a.m. New York time and you will see their moving averages on 1-minute and 5-minute charts as a type of moving support or resistance line. Traders can benefit from this behavior and ride the trend along the moving average (on top of the moving average for going long or below the moving average for short selling).

As I explained in Chapter 5 about my indicators, I use 9 and 20 Exponential Moving Averages (EMA) and 50 and 200 Simple Moving Averages (SMA). For the sake of keeping this book short, I won't go into the details of what moving averages are and the differences between simple and exponential. You can, however, do an online search and find much more detailed information about these moving averages. I've also included very brief definitions in the glossary at the back of this book. Your charting software will have most of the moving averages built in. They are ready to be used and there is no need to change the default setting in them.

Let's take a look at the chart below, marked as Figure 7.18, for Direxion Daily Gold Miners Bull 3x Shrs ETF (ticker: NUGT) to see how you could trade based on 9 EMA on a 1-minute chart.

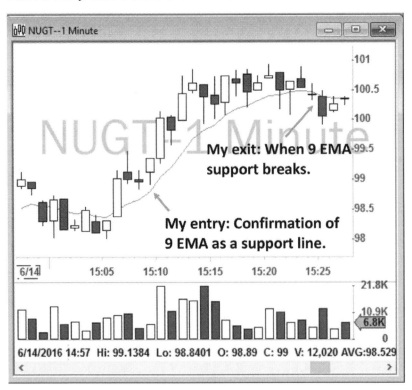

Figure 7.18: Example of a long Moving Average Trend Strategy on NUGT on a 1-minute chart.

As you can see, at 15:06 p.m. I noticed NUGT had formed a Bull Flag. I saw that a consolidation period was happening on top of 9 EMA. As soon as I saw that 9 EMA was holding as the support, I jumped on the trade and rode the trend until the price broke the moving average at 15:21 p.m. I've marked my entry and exit points on the chart.

Moving Average Trends can happen in any intraday time frame. I monitor prices on both 1-minute and 5-minute charts and make my trades based only on these two time frames.

Let's take a look now at Figure 7.19, which is another Moving Average Trend on NUGT, this time on June 16, 2016 and on a 5-minute chart.

Figure 7.19: Example of a short Moving Average Trend Strategy on NUGT on a 5-minute chart.

As you can see, NUGT sold off on a very steep down-trend from $116 to around $100: about a 14% drop in only some 2.5 hours. I sold short in the morning at around $115 with a stop loss at the break of 9 EMA on a 5-minute chart. I got stopped out at around 14:20 p.m. when the price broke the 9 EMA and closed above it at $104.

Let's take a look at another example, Celgene Corporation (CELG), on June 23, 2016. On the chart below, Figure 7.20, I've marked my entry and exit points and you will see how you can trade based on 9 EMA on a 5-minute chart. I entered the long position when 9 EMA held as a powerful support at around $99.90, and I then rode the upward move until 9 EMA broke at $100.40, for a profit of about 50 cents per share.

Figure 7.20: Example of a Moving Average Trend Strategy on CELG.

Another example of a 9 EMA Moving Average Trend Strategy is Figure 7.21 below, a 5-minute chart for Exact Sciences Corp. (ticker: EXAS) on July 28, 2016.

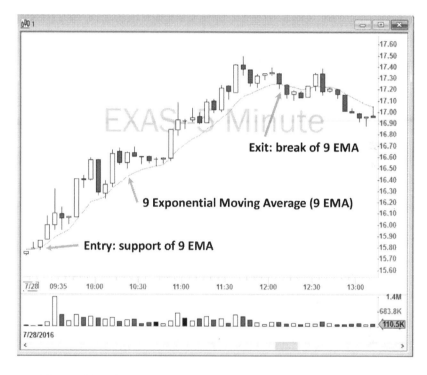

Figure 7.21: Example of a Moving Average Trend Strategy on EXAS.

Another fantastic example of a 9 EMA Moving Average Trend Strategy is set out below in Figure 7.22 for AMAG Pharmaceuticals, Inc. (ticker: AMAG). On January 9, 2017 its stock sold off from $31 to $23 in only a few hours. The 9 EMA held as a strong resistance. A great trade would have been a short sell on AMAG with a stop loss of the break of 9 EMA. In three areas marked on the chart, the price broke the 9 EMA and went slightly higher, but a 5-minute candlestick did not actually close above 9 EMA. These false breakouts usually happen with low volume. Experienced traders wait for a 5-minute candlestick to "close" above 9 EMA before they get out. A sudden break of 9 EMA with low volume may not be a good indicator of a trend coming to an end.

Figure 7.22: Example of a Moving Average Trend Strategy on AMAG.

A more recent example is Uber Technologies Inc. (ticker: UBER) on April 6, 2020. As you can see in Figure 7.23 below, as soon as UBER came above VWAP and held 20 EMA on the 1-minute chart, you could go long and ride the trend from \$24.70 toward \$25.60, and then exit when the moving average trend line is broken at around 12:40 p.m.

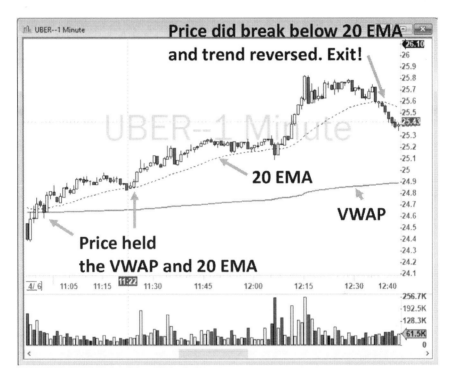

Figure 7.23: Example of a Moving Average Trend Strategy on UBER on April 6, 2020.

To summarize my trading strategy for Moving Average Trend trading:

1. When I am monitoring a Stock in Play and notice a trend is establishing around a moving average (usually 9 EMA), I consider trend trading. I quickly look at the previous days' trading data (on a 1-minute or 5-minute

chart) to see if the stock is responding to these moving averages.

2. Once I learn which moving average is more suitable to the behavior of the trade, I buy the stock after confirmation of moving averages as a support, and I buy as close as possible to the moving average line (in order to have a small stop). My stop will usually be 5 to 10 cents below the moving average line or, if a candlestick, a close below the moving average line (for long positions). For short positions, a close above the moving average line would stop me out.

3. I ride the trend until the break of moving average.

4. I usually do not use trailing stops and I constantly monitor the trend with my eyes.

5. If the stock is moving really high away from the moving average, offering me an equally really nice unrealized profit, I may take some profit, usually at half-position. I do not always wait until the break of moving average for my exit. Traders say: you can never go broke by taking good profits. If the price pulls back to the moving average, I may add again to my position and continue the trend trade.

I personally don't trade very often based on moving averages. I look at them to see potential levels of support or resistance, but I rarely make any trade based upon a trend because, in a trend trade strategy, you are usually left exposed in the market for a considerable length of time. Some trend trades can last as long as several hours and that is too long for my personality. I would like to take my profit in a matter of minutes. I rarely will wait even an hour. Another reason that I do not often trade these strategies is that they usually best work during Mid-day and the Close. At the Open (in the morning session), when volatility is high, it's hard to identify a Moving Average Trend play. These slow trends are best identified during the Late-Morning and Mid-day, when there is lower volatility, and they usually end near the Close (around 3 p.m. New York time) when the professional traders on Wall Street start to dominate the trading.

Having said that, a Moving Average Trend Strategy is an excellent trading strategy, because it usually does not require a very fast decision-making process and trade execution. It also often does not require the use of Hotkeys. You can enter the trades manually and still be successful. In addition, entry points and your stop loss can be clearly recognized from the moving averages on the charts. This is especially important for traders who pay high retail commissions (sometimes as high as $4.95/trade) and cannot scale in and out of trades without a high fee. The Moving Average Trend Strategy has clear entry and exit points and usually a good profit can be made by only two orders, one for the entry and one for the exit.

As I have discussed, strategies depend on your account size, personality, psychology of trading and risk tolerance, as well as on your software and the tools and brokers that you have. However, I want to emphasize that trading strategies are not something that you can imitate just from reading a book, speaking with a mentor, or attending a class. You have to slowly and methodically develop your preferred method and then stick with it. There is nothing wrong with any strategy if it works for you. There is no good and bad in any of these strategies; it truly is a matter of personal choice.

STRATEGY 6: VWAP TRADING

Volume Weighted Average Price, or VWAP, is the most important technical indicator for day traders. Definitions of VWAP can be found in many online resources. I will skip explaining it in detail for the sake of keeping this guide short, but essentially, VWAP is a moving average that takes into account the volumes of the shares being traded at any price. Other moving averages are calculated based only on the price of the stock on the chart, but VWAP also considers the number of shares in that stock that are being traded on every price. Your trading platform should have VWAP built into it and you can use it without changing any of its default settings.

VWAP is an indicator of who is in control of the price action - the buyers or the sellers. When stock is traded above VWAP, it means that the buyers are in overall control of the price and there is a buying demand on the stock. When a stock price breaks below VWAP, it is safe to assume that the sellers are gaining control over the price action.

VWAP is often used to measure the trading efficiency of institutional traders. Professional traders working for investment banks or hedge funds need to trade large amounts of shares each day. They cannot enter or exit the market by just one single order though because the market is not liquid enough to enter a 1 million share buy order in. Therefore, they need to liquidate their orders slowly during the day. After buying or selling a large position in a stock during the day, institutional traders compare their price to VWAP values. A buy order executed below VWAP would be considered a good fill for them because the stock was bought at a below average price (meaning that the trader has bought their large position at a relatively discounted price compared to the market). Conversely, a sell order executed above VWAP would be deemed a good fill because it was sold at an above average price. Therefore, VWAP is used by institutional traders to identify good entry and exit points. Institu-tional traders with large orders try to buy or sell large positions around VWAP. The performance of institutional traders is often evaluated based on what price they fill their large orders at. Traders who buy significantly higher than VWAP may be penalized because they cost the institution money for taking that large position. Institutional traders therefore try to buy below or as close to VWAP as possible. Conversely, when a professional trader has to get rid of a large position, they try to sell at VWAP or higher. Day traders who are aware of these tendencies may benefit from this market activity.

After the market opens, the Stock in Play will trade heavily in the first five minutes. If the Stock in Play has gapped up, some individual shareholders, hedge funds or investment banks may want to as soon as possible sell their shares for a profit, before the price drops. At the same time, some investors wanting to take positions in the stock will want to buy as soon as possible, before the price goes even higher. Therefore, in the first five minutes, an unknown heavy trading is happening between the overnight shareholders and the new investors. Scalpers usually ride the momentum right at the Open. After volatility decreases around ten to fifteen minutes into the Open, the stock will move toward or away from VWAP. This is a test to see if there is a large investment bank waiting to buy or sell. If there is a large institutional trader aiming to buy a significant position, the stock will pop over VWAP and move even higher. This is a good opportunity for us day traders to go long.

Conversely, if there are large shareholders wanting to get rid of their shares, then this is a good point for them to liquidate their positions. They start selling their shares at VWAP. The price will reject VWAP and start to move down. This is an excellent short selling opportunity for day traders. If there is no interest in the stock from market makers or institutions, the price may trade sideways near VWAP. Wise traders will then stay away from that stock.

Let's have a look now at Figure 7.24, which documents a trade that I took on SolarCity Corporation (ticker: SCTY) on June 24, 2016.

Figure 7.24: Example of a long VWAP Strategy on SCTY.

At around 10:30 a.m. on June 24, 2016, I noticed that SCTY had found a support above VWAP at around $21. I purchased 1,000 shares of the stock with the anticipation of moving toward $22 with VWAP as a support. My stop was a 5-minute candlestick close below VWAP. I first sold a half-size position at $21.50, and then moved my stop to break-even. I sold another position at $22 because I know half-dollars (such as $1.50, $2.50, $3.50) and whole dollars ($1, $2, $3) usually act as a support or resistance level.

VWAP also works well when you want to short stocks. Let's have a look at Figure 7.25, which documents another trade that I took on SCTY, this time on June 22, 2016, and this time on the short side.

Figure 7.25: Example of a short VWAP Strategy on SCTY.

At around 11 a.m., I noticed that VWAP was acting as a resistance level. I shorted the stock with the anticipation of losing VWAP at around $23.25. At around

12 p.m., the buyers gave up and the sellers took control of the price action. I had a nice run down to $22 and covered my shorts at $22 for a good $1,000 profit.

To summarize my trading strategy for VWAP trading:

1. When I make my watchlist for the day, I monitor the price action around VWAP at the Open. If a stock shows respect toward VWAP, then I wait until a confirmation of VWAP break (for short selling) or VWAP support (for going long).

2. I usually buy as close as possible to VWAP to minimize my risk. My stop will be a break and a close 5-minute close below VWAP. For short selling, I short near VWAP with a stop loss of a close above VWAP.

3. I keep the trade until I hit my profit target or until I reach a new support or resistance level.

4. I usually sell half-positions near the profit target or support or resistance level and move my stop up to my entry point or break-even.

STRATEGY 7: SUPPORT OR RESISTANCE TRADING

Many traders love to draw diagonal trend lines. I'm not one of them. As far as I am concerned, they're the exact opposite of objective. There's a very good chance that two traders looking at the same chart will draw trend lines with very different slopes. A person in a mood to buy will be apt to draw a trend line in a way that shows a steep upward movement. On the other hand, if a person feels like shorting, they'll be apt to draw a downward trend line.

The market only remembers price levels, which is why horizontal support or resistance lines on previous price levels make sense, but diagonal trend lines don't. Accordingly, horizontal support or resistance trading is my favorite style of trading.

Support is a price level where buying is strong enough to interrupt or reverse a downtrend. When a downtrend hits a support level, it bounces. Support is represented on a chart by a horizontal line connecting two or more bottoms (see Figure 7.26 below).

Resistance is a price level where selling is strong enough to interrupt or reverse an uptrend. Resistance is represented on a chart by a horizontal line connecting two or more tops (as also set out in Figure 7.26 below).

Minor support or resistance causes trends to pause, while major support or resistance causes them to reverse.

Traders buy at support and sell at resistance, making their effectiveness a self-fulfilling prophecy.

Using this method, every morning I shortlist the stocks that I would like to trade based on the criteria I set forth in Chapter 4. As potential stocks hit my scanner, I look for significant news events that may explain their price swings, such as an extreme earnings report or a new drug approval. You'll recall that these are called fundamental catalysts and the shortlisted stocks are what we call Stocks in Play. They're the ones that I'll be monitoring carefully and planning to trade.

With these Stocks in Play identified, and before the market opens, I go back to their daily charts and find price levels that have been shown in the past to be critical. Finding price support or resistance levels is tricky and requires trading experience.

For example, let's take a look at Figure 7.26, an SCTY daily chart without support or resistance lines and another including the lines.

Figure 7.26: Example of a Support or Resistance Strategy on SCTY daily chart.

Support or resistance lines on daily charts are not always easy to find, and at times you will not be able to draw anything clear. If I cannot see anything clear, I don't have to draw anything. There is a good chance that other traders who have shortlisted the same stock will also not see those lines clearly and therefore there is no point in forcing myself to draw support or resistance lines. In that case, I will plan my trades based on VWAP or Moving Averages or other chart patterns that I earlier discussed.

Here are some hints for drawing support or resistance lines on daily charts:

1. You will usually see indecision candles in the area of support or resistance because that is where buyers and sellers are closely fighting each other.

2. Half-dollars and whole dollars usually act as a support or resistance level, especially in lower than $10 stocks. If you don't find a support or resistance line around these numbers on daily charts, remember that in day trading these numbers can act as an invisible support or resistance line.

3. You should always look at the recent data to draw lines.

4. The more of a line that is touching extreme price lines, the more that the line is a better support or resistance and has more value. Give that line more emphasis.

5. Only the support or resistance lines in the current price range are important. If the price of the stock is currently $20, there is no point in finding support or resistance lines in the region when it was $40. It is unlikely that the stock will move and reach that area. Find only the support or resistance area that is close to your day trading range.

6. Support or resistance lines are actually an "area" and not exact numbers. For example, when you find an area around $19.69 as a support line, you must expect price action movement around that number but not at exactly $19.69. Depending on the price of the stock, an area of 5 to 10 cents is safe to assume. In the example with a support line of $19.69, the real support area might perhaps range from $19.62 to $19.72.

7. The price must have a clear bounce from that level. If you are not certain if the price has bounced in that level, then it is probably not a support or resistance level. Important support or resistance levels on daily charts stand out. They shout at you: "*grab me by the face*".

8. For day trading, it is better to draw support or resistance lines across the extreme prices or wicks on daily levels rather than across areas where the bulk of the bars stopped. This is the complete opposite of swing trading.

For swing trading, you need to draw support or resistance lines across the edges of congested areas where the bulk of the bars stopped rather than across the extreme prices. This is because the close price is more important for swing trading than the extreme wicks in daily bars are. The close price of a stock on a daily chart is the price that the market makers and professional traders have agreed on. Previous extreme high and low wicks have been made by day traders, so you should look at those.

Placing support or resistance lines, although difficult when you are first learning how to trade, is actually quite simple once you get the hang of it. For the sake of keeping this book more understandable for the novice trader, I deliberately limited my commentary on how to locate important support and resistance levels. You will find considerably more detailed information and criteria in my other book, *Advanced Techniques in Day Trading.*

Let's review a trade that I took based on these lines. Please see Figures 7.27 to 7.29 below. On June 21, 2016, CarMax Inc. (ticker: KMX), the United States' largest used-car retailer, had extreme earnings and its stock gapped down over 3%. That was a perfect opportunity for retail traders like us to find a good trade plan. I quickly found the support or resistance area levels on a daily chart and watched the price action around those levels.

Trade-Ideas Pro

File New Tools Windows Help Account

17ms

Up Gappers: 9:20:00 - 9:24:59 6/21/2016

Symbol	Price ($)	Gap ($)	Gap (%)	Vol Today (Shr)	Flt (Shr)	Avg True	Company
UAL	45.00	1.60	3.7	63,191	336M	1.53	UNITED CONTINE
LEN	48.30	1.64	3.5	59,372	189M	0.94	LENNAR
TM	107.60	1.80	1.7	51,698	1.36B	1.62	TOYOTA MOTOR
BUD	128.53	2.08	1.6	99,945	784M	2.52	ANHEUSER-BUSC
BTI	124.60	1.39	1.1	120,962	894M	2.24	BRITISH AMERICA
KMX	49.05	-1.58	-3.1	265,779	193M	1.53	CARMAX
CSAL	26.85	-1.31	-4.7	1,984,509	136M	0.64	COMMUNICATI LEASING
WERN	22.12	-2.56	-10.4	315,191	44.6M	0.70	WERNER ENTER

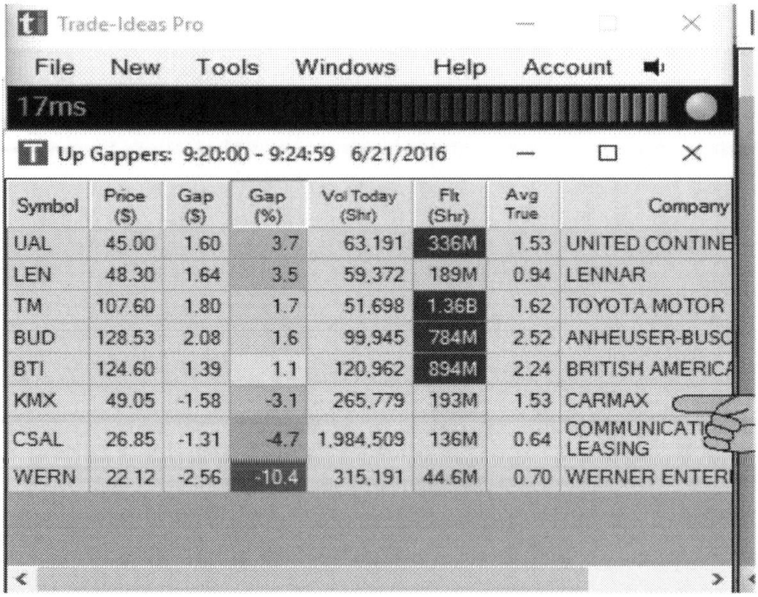

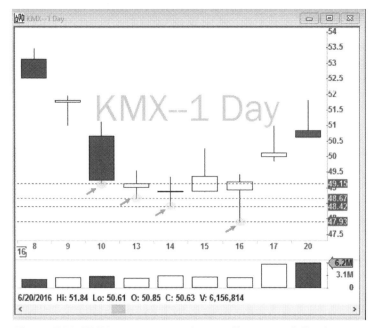

Figure 7.27: My Gappers watchlist on June 21, 2016 at 9:20 a.m. showing KMX may be a Stock in Play for that day.

Figure 7.28: KMX support or resistance lines on a daily chart up to June 20, 2016.

After reviewing the daily charts up to June 20, 2016, I found four levels of $47.93, $48.42, $48.67, and $49.15. As you can see in Figure 7.28 above, all of these levels are extreme price levels for the previous days and, as I explained, I give more attention to wicks and extreme prices than I do to the open or close prices.

Now, let's take a look at Figure 7.29, which is the next day intraday chart for June 21, 2016, and see what happened to the price action at those levels. I marked the areas where they acted as support or resistance. Do ensure that you give special attention to the volume of shares traded at or near those levels. Do you see that the volume is considerably higher? A high volume confirms that these levels are significant and day traders should therefore pay attention to them.

Figure 7.29: Example of a Support or Resistance Strategy on KMX on a 5-minute chart with my trades for that day marked.

When the market opened, I watched the stock and realized that the area of around $48.67 was acting as a resistance level. Later, the stock sold off to $47.93 with high volume. I bought 1,000 shares at that support, with a stop loss below $47.93. If the price closed below that, I would be out with a loss, but it didn't. The price instead quickly bounced back. I sold 500 shares at $48.42. I sold the other 500 shares at the next resistance level of $48.67. I kept monitoring the price action and, in the afternoon, when the price rejected the $49.15 level with high volume, I went short with a stop loss of a new high of the day or a close above $49.15. I covered half of my shares at the level of $48.67 and the other half at $48.42, both for another nice profit.

To summarize my trading strategy for support or resistance trading:

1. Each morning, after I make my watchlist for the day, I quickly look at the daily charts for that watchlist and find the areas of support or resistance.

2. I monitor the price action around those areas on a 5-minute chart. If an indecision candle forms around one of those areas, that is the confirmation of that level and I enter the trade. I usually buy as close as possible to the support level to minimize my risk. Stop will be a break and a close of a 5-minute candlestick under the support level.

3. I will take profit near the next support or resistance level.

4. I keep the trade open until I hit my profit target or I reach a new support or resistance level.

5. I usually sell half-positions near the profit target or support or resistance level and move my stop up to my entry point for break-even.

6. If there are no next obvious support or resistance levels, I will consider closing my trade at or near half-dollar or round-dollar levels.

A similar approach will also work when you sell short a stock below a resistance level.

STRATEGY 8: RED-TO-GREEN TRADING

Red-to-Green is another easy to recognize trading strategy. As I mentioned in Chapter 5, one of the indicators I have on my chart is the *previous day close* level. The previous day close is a powerful level of support or resistance and traders should trade toward it when there is rising volume.

If the current price of a stock is higher than the previous day close (for Stocks in Play that gapped up), the market is moving from a Green day to a Red day (meaning that the percentage that the price has changed will now be negative, which will be shown as red in most of the Exchanges and platforms). This is a Green-to-Red move.

If the price is lower than the previous day close (for stocks that gapped down), the market is moving from a Red day to a Green day (meaning that the percentage that the price has changed will now be positive, which will be shown as green in most of the Exchanges and platforms). This is a Red-to-Green move.

The strategy is almost identical for both Red-to-Green and Green-to-Red except for the direction of the trade (short or long). So, for the sake of simplicity, I will use the term Red-to-Green Strategy for both directions, but depending on the trade, I may be referring to a Green-to-Red trade.

For example, take a look at Figure 7.30, the 5-minute chart for Mallinckrodt Public Limited Company (ticker: MNK), which was a Stock in Play on January 19, 2017. After a weak Open, the price held below VWAP. I went short, but there was no nearby support or resistance level except the previous day close at $46.52 (the dashed line on my chart). Therefore, I decided to go short from VWAP at around $47.80 for the profit target of the previous day close at $46.52, a nice $1.20 per share profit.

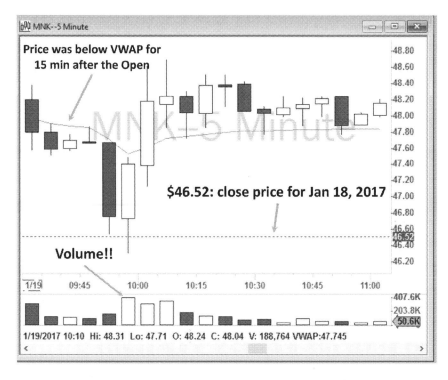

Figure 7.30: Example of a short sell Red-to-Green Strategy on MNK.

For another example, let's take a look at Figure 7.31, the 5-minute chart for Barracuda Networks, Inc. (ticker: CUDA) on January 10, 2017. The same price action can be seen at the Open. CUDA gapped up in the pre-market because of a good earnings report. At the Open, it was sold off heavily, perhaps because over-night shareholders and long-term investors started to sell their shares for a profit. The stock tested VWAP for about twenty minutes and then sold off in a high volume toward the previous day close of $23.81. Its price bounced back later, during Mid-day, toward VWAP, after it could not break the previous day close.

Later, in the early afternoon, the price sold off again toward the previous day close for another Red-to-Green trade before it bounced back yet again.

In this example too, the previous day close level of $23.81 acted as a strong support level. In both morning and afternoon trading, a short sell opportunity was possible from VWAP at around $24.40 to $23.81. I did not take this trade as I was trading another stock around the same time that day.

Figure 7.31: Example of a short Red-to-Green Strategy on CUDA.

To summarize my trading strategy for Red-to-Green trading:

1. When I make my watchlist for the day, I monitor the price action around the previous day close.

2. If a stock moves toward the previous day close with high volume, I consider going long with the profit target of the previous day close.

3. My stop loss is the nearest technical level. If I buy near VWAP, my stop loss will be the break of VWAP. If I buy near a moving average or an important support level, my stop loss will be the break of moving average or support level.

4. I usually sell all at the profit target. If the price moves in my favor, I bring my stop loss to the break-even and do not let the price turn against me. Red-to-Green moves should work immediately.

A similar approach will work equally as well when you short a stock for a Green-to-Red Strategy (see the MNK and CUDA examples in Figures 7.30 and 7.31 above).

STRATEGY 9:
OPENING RANGE BREAKOUTS

Another well-known trading strategy is the so-called Opening Range Breakout (ORB). This strategy signals an entry point, but does not determine the profit target. You should define the best profit target based on the other technical levels you learn from this book. Later on, you will notice that I list further possible profit targets. The ORB is an entry signal only, but remember, a full trading strategy must define the proper entry, exit and stop loss.

Right at the market Open (9:30 a.m. New York time), Stocks in Play usually experience violent price action that arises from heavy buy and sell orders that come into the market. This heavy trading in the first five minutes is the result of the profit or loss taking of the overnight position holders as well as new investors and traders. If a stock has gapped up, some overnight traders start selling their position for a profit. At the same time, some new investors might jump in to buy the stock before the price goes higher. If a stock gaps down, on the other hand, some investors might panic and dump their shares right at the Open, before it drops any lower. On the other side, some institutions might think this drop could be a good buying opportunity and they will start buying large positions at a discounted price.

Therefore, there is a complicated mass psychology unfolding at the Open for the Stocks in Play. Novice traders sit on their hands and watch for the opening ranges to develop and allow the more experienced traders to fight against each other until one side wins.

Typically, a new trader should give the opening range at least five minutes (if not more). This is called the 5-minute ORB. Some traders will wait even longer, such as for thirty minutes or even for one hour, to identify the balance of power between the buyers and sellers. They then develop a trade plan in the direction of the 30-minute or 60-minute breakout. The longer the time frame, the less volatility you can expect. As with most setups, the ORB Strategy tends to work best with mid to large cap stocks, which do not show wild price swings intraday. I do not recommend trading this strategy with low float or penny stocks that have gapped up or down. Ideally, the stock should trade within a range which is smaller than the Average True Range of the stock (ATR). The upper and lower bound-aries of the range can be identified by the high and low of the 5-, 15-, 30- or 60- minute candlesticks.

To gain a better understanding of this strategy, let's take a look at Figures 7.32 and 7.33 for e.l.f. Beauty Inc. (ticker: ELF) on March 9, 2017. ELF was on my Gappers watchlist that day, and had gapped up over 19% for good results. I decided to watch it closely to see if I could trade it on the short side. There was a strong chance that many overnight investors and traders would try to sell their positions for profit. An overnight profit of 19% is very tempting for many investors. Why not take the profit?

Pre-Market Movers up or down $1: 9:00:00 - 9:04:59 3/09/2017							
Symbol	$	T	C $	C %	Float	I, I S Float	Sector
ELF	30.30	186,010	5.00	19.8	3,556,310	0.90	7.49 Retail Trade
HZN	14.00	59,961	-3.02	-17.7	18.08M	0.58	6.54 Manufacturing
TLRD	16.70	437,617	-6.67	-28.5	48.34M	0.91	26.12 Retail Trade

Figure 7.32: My Gappers watchlist on March 9, 2017 at 9 a.m. showing ELF may be a Stock in Play for that day.

As you can see in Figure 7.33 below, the stock opened at $31 and sold off heavily to below $30 in the first five minutes. That was the sign that investors were selling for profit after it had gapped up over 19%. I waited for the first 5-minute battle of buyers and sellers to settle down. As soon as I saw that the price broke the 5-minute opening range, I went short below VWAP. As I mentioned before, ORB is a buy or sell signal, and you must define the proper exit and stop loss for it. For me, stop loss is always a close above VWAP for short positions, and a close below VWAP for long positions. Profit target point is the next important technical level.

As you can also see in Figure 7.33 below, I rode the wave down to the next daily level of $28.62 and covered my shorts at around that level.

Figure 7.33: Example of the ORB Strategy on ELF 5-minute chart.

Another example could be Procter & Gamble Co. (ticker: PG) on February 15, 2017. The stock hit my Gappers scanner, see Figure 7.34 below, and I had it on my watchlist at the Open.

Symbol	$	T	C $	C %	Float	I	SFloat	Sector
SODA	50.70	107,445	3.35	7.1	20.93M	1.04	5.78	Manufacturing
PG	89.44	449,389	1.58	1.8	2.56B	0.79	1.37	Manufacturing
AIG	63.10	552,600	-3.79	-5.7	1.03B	0.81	1.45	Finance and Insurance
FOSL	18.71	702,161	-4.16	-18.2	33.89M	1.11	35.88	Wholesale Trade

Pre-Market Movers up or down $1: 9:00:00 - 9:04:59 2/15/2017

Figure 7.34: My Gappers watchlist on February 15, 2017 at 9 a.m. showing PG may be a Stock in Play for that day.

As you can see below in Figure 7.35, in only the first five minutes more than 2.6 million shares were traded, but PG's price only moved from $89.89 to $89.94. That was a range of only 5 cents while the Average True Range (ATR) of PG was $0.79. As I have mentioned, you need the opening range to be smaller than the daily ATR. If a stock moves near or higher than its ATR at the Open, it is not a good candidate for the ORB Strategy. It means that the stock is too volatile and without a catchable move. It is worth mentioning again, Stocks in Play move, and those moves are directional and catchable. If a stock constantly moves up and down $2 with high volume, but without any directional signal, you want to stay away from it. Those stocks are usually being heavily traded by computers.

In the PG example, as soon as I saw that it broke the opening range to the upside, I went long and rode the wave up toward the next resistance level of $91.01. If there was no obvious technical level for the exit and profit target, you can exit when a stock shows signs of weakness. For example, if its price makes a new 5-minute low, that means weakness, and you should consider selling if you are long. If you are short and the stock makes a new 5-minute high, then it could be a sign of strength and you may want to cover your short position. In this PG example, if you did not previously identify the $91.01 level, you could exit when PG made a new 5-minute low just below $91. I marked it for you in Figure 7.35 below.

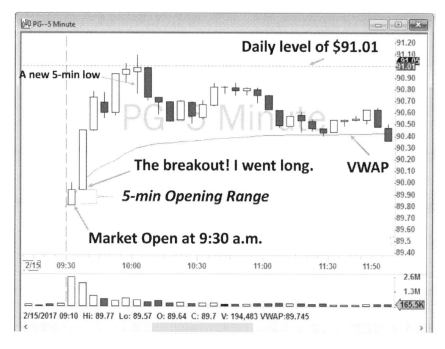

Figure 7.35: Example of the ORB Strategy on PG 5-minute chart.

I personally avoided trading in the first five minutes for years, but as I am now more confident in my trading and risk management, I often implement 1-minute Opening Range Breakups or 1-minute Opening Range Breakdowns. I recommend if you are a new trader that you avoid the first volatile five minutes of the market Open (9:30 a.m. to 9:35 a.m.) but then, as you become more confident in your trading, you can gradually implement more volatile trading strategies. 1-minute ORBs have become one of the main trading strategies that I do almost every single day. Let's review some recent examples from trades I took in June 2020:

Figure 7.36 shows a 1-minute ORB up on Carnival Corp. (ticker: CCL). As mentioned earlier, during the first months of COVID-19, the stock of airlines and cruise lines had been extremely volatile. On June 9, 2020, CCL was gapping down over 10% and at the first minute sold off heavily below VWAP. I decided to wait for the first one minute of trading to see the initial result of the battle between buyers and sellers. Buyers were weak, and I therefore took a 2,000-share trade to the short side at $23.10, and covered my shorts at the break of the candlestick toward $22.50, for a $0.60 per share profit (or $1,200) in a matter of one minute.

Figure 7.36: Example of the 1-minute ORB Strategy on the 1-minute chart of CCL for June 9, 2020.

During the first months of the COVID-19 pandemic, some of the airline and cruise line stocks were our best friends! The volatility of these stocks created amazing opportunities for me and many of our traders. My friend and colleague at Bear Bull Traders, Thor Young, traded Norwegian Cruise Line Holdings Ltd. (ticker: NCLH) almost every single day. He was in love with that ticker!

Figure 7.37 shows a 1-minute ORB up on Advanced Micro Devices, Inc. (ticker: AMD), the famous semiconductor company, on June 9, 2020. As you can see, the stock opened strong in the first minute, and an opportunity to go long presented right after the first 1-minute candlestick closed at around $52.90. The stock moved up to about $53.80 in less than ten minutes!

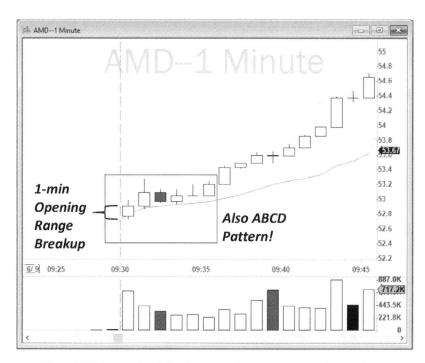

Figure 7.37: Example of the 1-minute ORB Strategy on the 1-minute chart of AMD for June 9, 2020.

If you look closely at the above Figure 7.37, you can also see the 1-minute candlesticks form into an ABCD Pattern. If you miss one strategy on a stock, you can often find another pattern to trade! Even if you did not trade a 1-minute Opening Range Breakup on AMD, you could still trade it on a 5-minute ORB as shown below in Figure 7.38.

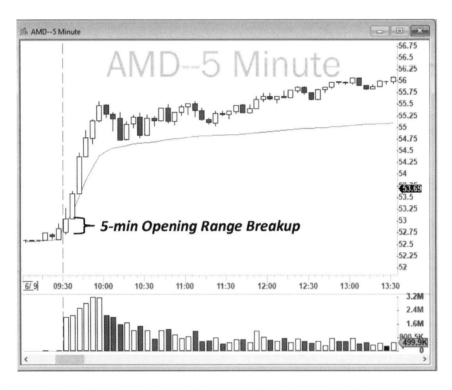

Figure 7.38: Example of the 5-minute ORB Strategy on the 5-minute chart of AMD for June 9, 2020.

To summarize my ORB Strategy:

1. After I build my watchlist in the morning, I closely monitor the shortlisted stocks in the first five minutes. I identify their opening range and their price action. How many shares are being traded? Is the stock jumping up and down or does it have a directional upward or downward movement? Is it high volume with large orders only, or are there many orders going through? I prefer stocks that have high volume, but also with numerous different orders being traded. A stock that has traded 1 million shares, but those shares were only ten orders of 100,000 shares each, is not a liquid stock to trade. Volume alone does not show the liquidity; the number of orders being sent to the Exchange is as important.

2. The opening range must be significantly smaller than the stock's Average True Range (ATR). I have ATR as a column in my Trade Ideas scanner.

3. After the close of the first five minutes of trading, the stock may continue to be traded in that opening range in the next five minutes. But, if I see the stock is breaking the opening range, I enter the trade according to the direction of the breakout: long for an upward breakout and short for a downward move.

4. My stop loss is a close below VWAP for long positions and a close above VWAP for short positions.

5. My profit target is the next important technical level, such as: (1) important intraday daily levels that I identify in the pre-market, (2) moving averages on a daily chart, and/or (3) previous day close.

6. If there was no obvious technical level for the exit and profit target, I exit when a stock shows signs of weakness (if I am long) or strength (if I am short). For example, if the price makes a new 5-minute low, that means weakness and I consider selling my position if I am long. If I am short and the stock makes a new 5-minute high, then it could be a sign of strength and I consider covering my short position.

My strategy summarized above was for a 5-minute ORB, but the same process will also work well for 15-minute or 30-minute ORBs. I recommend you avoid the 1-minute ORB at the beginning of your trading journey, as price movements right at the Open can be wild and, if the stock runs against you, it can result in a sudden loss, which will happen much more quickly than you will be able to stop out. As you grow as a trader, you can slowly implement faster paced ORBs. These days, I mostly trade 1-minute ORBs (up or down).

OTHER TRADING STRATEGIES

You have now read a summary of some of my favorite trading strategies. You may be wondering what other traders do. As I mentioned before, there is an unlimited number of trading strategies that individuals have developed for themselves. Traders often choose and modify their strategies based on personal factors such as account size, amount of time that can be dedicated to trading, trading experience, personality and risk tolerance.

You should develop your own strategy. A trading strategy is very personalized to each individual. My risk tolerance and psychology are most likely different from yours and from those of other traders. I might not be comfortable with a $500 loss, but someone who has a large account can easily hold onto the loss and eventually make profit out of a losing trade. You cannot mirror-trade anyone else; you must develop your own risk management method and strategy.

Some traders focus heavily on technical indicators like the RSI, the moving average convergence divergence (also known as the MACD), or the moving average crossover. There are hundreds, if not thousands, of sophisticated technical indicators out there. Some traders believe they have found the Holy Grail of technical indicators, and it might be a combination of the RSI or the moving average crossover. I don't believe having a large number of technical indicators will automatically make you a successful day trader. Day trading is not mechanical and automated, it is discretionary, and traders need to make real time decisions. The success of each strategy is based on judgment and the proper execution of it by the trader.

I am also skeptical of the strategies that have many indicators. I don't think that having more indicators on your chart helps you in day trading, especially since you need to be able to process information very quickly, at times in just a matter of seconds. I have found that often indicators' signals will also contradict each other and that will lead to confusion.

That is why my day trading indicators are limited to VWAP and a few other moving averages. For my swing trading, I use more complicated indicators such as MACD because I do not have to make quick decisions. I usually review my swing trading after the market closes, with proper due diligence and evaluation. You can easily find more information about the indicators I've mentioned in this section, along with many others, by doing a simple online search.

Some of my day trader colleagues may disagree with me, but as I mentioned above, my personal experience is that you cannot enter a trade with a mechanical and systematic approach and then let the indicators dictate your entry and exit.

Computers are trading all of the time. When you set up a system for trading that has no input or requires no decisions by the trader, then you are entering the world of algorithmic trading, and you will lose trades to investment banks that have million-dollar algorithms and billions of dollars in cash for trading.

Of course, I use the RSI in my scanner for some of my trading strategies, and in particular for reversal trading. Obviously, I have scanners that rely on a high or low RSI, but those are more conditioned to find stocks at extremes. They are by no means a buy or sell indicator.

DEVELOP YOUR OWN STRATEGY

You must still find your own place in the market. I may be a 1-minute or a 5-minute trader; you may be a 60-minute trader. Some may be daily or weekly traders (swing traders). There's a place in the market for everyone. Consider what you are learning in this book as pieces of a puzzle that together make up the bigger picture of your trading career. You're going to acquire some information here in this book, you're going to pick up some other information or knowledge from your other reading and research, and, overall, you will create a puzzle that will develop into your own unique trading strategy: "your edge". In addition, for every strategy you develop for yourself, make sure you give it a "name". If it is a new strategy, coin a name for it! Having a name for a strategy gives it an identity, and that helps to prevent you from trading without a plan. If you cannot identify why you are in a trade, and which strategy the trade belongs to, very likely you should not be in that trade.

In our chatroom, whenever I enter a trade live in front of our traders, I say out loud the name of the strategy I am planning it on. This is important to me as it ensures I am not jumping into a "strategy-less" gamble without any plan. You will hear me all of the time say out loud things such as: *"I am going long CCL for a 1-minute Opening Range Breakup with a stop loss of below $11.50 below VWAP."* I may get stopped out, and the trade may not work for me, but at least I know when I enter a trade that I have a viable strategy set forth, and so should you for each and every one of your trades.

I don't expect everything I do to work exactly the same for you. But my goal in writing this book is to help you develop a strategy that is going to work for you, your personality, your account size and your risk tolerance. Please contact me in our chatroom at *www.BearBullTraders.com* or email me directly at *andrew@bearbulltraders.com* if you think I can be of any help. I try to respond to all emails in a timely manner, especially if I am not traveling or climbing!

Later, in Chapter 9, we will examine the case of a recently successful trader who was also a reader of an earlier edition of this book. What is fascinating about this case study is that the trader learned the basics from my books, but he found his own edge in the market by working hard and putting the requisite time and effort in. He trades completely differently from me. He has his own set of rules and has defined his own strategy, and they are not what I myself trade or teach. He has developed one very different strategy for himself.

I hope you find this case study useful, even inspiring, as you grow as a trader. In your early days of trading, the key is to master one strategy. You can start casting out later, but first you need to master just one strategy. It can be the ABCD Pattern, it can be the Opening Range Breakout Strategy, or you can create a strategy of your own.

It is absolutely critical for every trader to be trading a strategy. Plan a trade, and trade the plan. I wish someone had said to me when I first started training, *"Andrew, you need to trade a strategy. If you're trading with real money, you must be trading a written strategy, and it must have historical data to verify that it's worth trading with real money."* You cannot change your plan once you have already entered the trade and have an open position. As I just mentioned, you also need to have a name for your strategy. Give it a name! When you name a strategy, it means you are able to identify it and you know its criteria.

The truth about traders is that they fail. They lose money, and a large percentage of those traders are not gaining the education that you are receiving from reading this book. They're going to be using live trading strategies that are not tested or do not have proper criteria, they will just be randomly trading a little of this and a little of that until their account is gone, and then they will wonder what happened. You don't want to live trade a new strategy until you've proven that it's worth investing in. You may practice three months in a simulator, and then trade small size with real money for one month, and then go back to the simulator to work on your mistakes or practice new strategies for another three months. There is no shame in going back to a simulator at any stage of your day trading career. Even experienced and professional traders, when they want to develop a new strategy, test it out in a live simulator first.

Your focus while reading this book and practicing in simulated accounts should be to develop a strategy worth trading. Remember, the market is always here, and it's only getting more volatile and more liquid. You don't need to rush day trading. A day trading career is a marathon and not a sprint. It's not about making $50,000 by the end of next week. It's about developing a set of skills that will last a lifetime.

TRADING BASED ON THE TIME OF DAY

I categorize day trading sessions based upon the time of day: the Open, Late-Morning, Mid-day, and the Close. Each time period should be treated differently, and you have to be careful because not all strategies are effective in every time period. Good traders make note of what time of day their most profitable trades occur and adjust their trading and strategies to fit such times.

The Open tends to last about thirty to sixty minutes (from 9:30 a.m. up to 10:30 a.m. New York time). I trade with the most size, and most frequency, during the Open, which statistically is my most profitable time period. As such, I increase my size during this time and make more trades.

- **Opening Range Breakouts (my favorite), Bull Flag Momentum and VWAP trades tend to be the best strategies for the Open.**

During the Late-Morning (10:30 a.m. to 12 p.m.), the market is slower but there is still good volatility in the Stocks in Play. This is one of the easiest times of the day for new traders. There is less volume compared to the Open but also less unexpected volatility. A review of our new traders' trades indicates that they do the worst during the Open and best during the Late-Morning session. Especially excellent risk/reward trades can be expected during this period. I explain VWAP Reversal and VWAP False Breakout (the two strategies that tend to be the best strategies for the Late-Morning) in my second book, *Advanced Techniques in Day Trading*. I rarely trade Bull Flag in the Late-Morning, Mid-day or at the Close.

During the Mid-day (12 p.m. to 3 p.m.) the market is slower. This is the most dangerous time of the day. There is less volume and liquidity. A small order can cause a stock to move much more than you would anticipate. Strange and unexpected moves will stop you out more frequently during the Mid-day. A review of my trades indicates that I do the worst during the Mid-day. Accordingly, should I decide to trade during the Mid-day, I lower my share size and keep my stops tight. I will only make trades that offer the best risk/

reward during this period. New traders tend to overtrade at Mid-day. At times, good trading, and smart trading, is to not be trading at all. It is best to gather information during the Mid-day in preparation for the Close. Watch the stocks, prepare for the Close, and be very, very careful with any trading you do.

- **Reversal, VWAP, Moving Average, and Support or Resistance trades tend to be the best strategies for the Mid-day.**

Into the Close (3 p.m. to 4 p.m.), stocks are more directional, so I stick with those that are trending up or down in the last hour of the trading day. I raise my tier size from the Mid-day, but not as high as it is at the Open. The daily closing prices tend to reflect the opinion of Wall Street traders on the value of stocks. They watch the markets throughout the day and tend to dominate the last hour of trading. Many of the market professionals take profits at that time to avoid carrying trades overnight. If the stock is moving higher in the last hour, it means the professionals are probably bullish on that stock. If the stock is moving lower in the last hour, the market professionals are probably bearish. It is thus a good idea to trade with the professionals and not against them.

- **VWAP, Support or Resistance, and Moving Average trades tend to be the best strategies for the Close.**

Many traders lose during the day what they have profited in the Open. Don't be one of them. I created a rule for myself. I am not allowed to lose more than 30% of what I have made in the Open during the Late-Morning, Mid-day and the Close. If I lose more than the allowed 30%, then I either stop trading or start trading in a simulator.

CHAPTER 8

STEP BY STEP TO A SUCCESSFUL TRADE

Now that we have reviewed important trading strategies, building a watchlist and price action analysis, let's take a look at two of my trades. Later, I'll explain in detail how I did them.

BUILDING A WATCHLIST

On the morning of June 2, 2016, before the market Open, Sarepta Therapeutics Inc. (ticker: SRPT) hit my watchlist scanner. Please see Figure 8.1 below. It was gapping down 14.5%, had a relatively medium float (only 36 million shares, which meant the stock had the potential for good movement intraday) and a high Average True Range of $1.86 (which meant the stock on average moved in a range as large as $1.86 during the day). Higher ATRs are desirable for day trading.

Symbol	Price ($)	Gap ($)	Gap (%)	Vol Today	Flt (Shr)	Avg True	Avg Vol	Company Name
SRPT	18.30	-3.11	-14.5	77,117	36.0M	1.86	9.48M	SAREPTA THERAPEUTICS
CXRX	32.58	1.53	4.9	60,106	39.2M	2.25	609K	CONCORDIA HEALTH CARE
BOX	11.75	-1.06	-8.3	135,063	42.4M	0.33	1.15M	BOX INC
QLIK	30.25	1.28	4.4	1.22M	86.6M	1.06	2.17M	QLIK TECHNOLOGIES
CIEN	19.56	1.80	10.1	536,084	134M	0.46	2.73M	CIENA CORP
ORCL	39.03	-1.23	-3.1	97,831	3.03B	0.53	9.12M	ORACLE CORP

Up Gappers: 9:15:00 - 9:19:59 6/02/2016

Figure 8.1: My watchlist at 6:15 a.m. (9:15 a.m. New York time) - SRPT is on my watchlist.

TRADING PLAN (ENTRY, EXIT, AND STOP LOSS)

I looked at the chart and decided to wait and see the price action for the first ten minutes of trading. You can follow along with my commentary in Figure 8.2. When the market opened, I saw that the buyers could not push the price any higher. There was no interest in buying back the stock. Therefore, I decided to do a VWAP trade. I monitored VWAP and the price action around VWAP for two 5-minute candlesticks. I realized that the sellers were in control and that the buyers could not push the price higher than VWAP and hold it. I knew it must be a good short with a stop above VWAP.

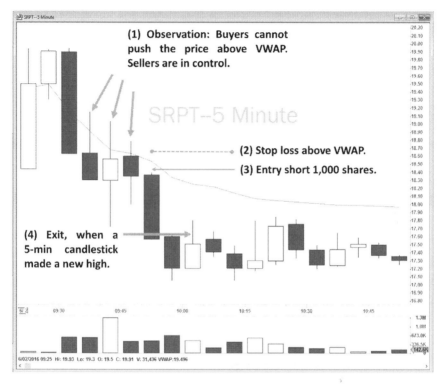

(1) Observation: Buyers cannot push the price above VWAP. Sellers are in control.

SRPT–5 Minute

(2) Stop loss above VWAP.

(3) Entry short 1,000 shares.

(4) Exit, when a 5-min candlestick made a new high.

6/02/2016 09:25 Hi: 19.93 Lo: 19.3 O: 19.5 C: 19.91 V: 31,436 VWAP:19.496

Figure 8.2: 5-minute chart on June 2, 2016. Market opened at 9:30 **a.m.** New York time.

EXECUTION

After ten minutes, when SRPT closed below VWAP, I entered the trade by shorting stock around $18.20 with a stop loss in mind just above VWAP. As expected, the sellers took control, and the stock price tanked to $17. I exited when a 5–minute candlestick made a new high, as that meant that the buyers were gaining control. I covered my shorts at around $17.40 and locked in a $650 profit, as you can see in Figure 8.3 below.

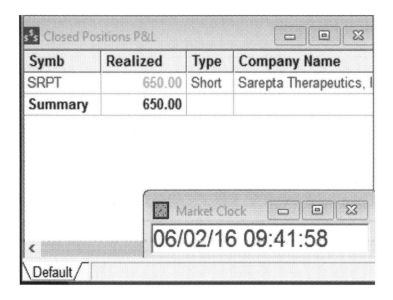

Symb	Realized	Type	Company Name
SRPT	650.00	Short	Sarepta Therapeutics, I
Summary	650.00		

Market Clock

06/02/16 09:41:58

Default

Figure 8.3: My profit on June 2, 2016 (only twelve minutes into my trading day).

Now let's take a look at one of my recent 2020 trades.

On the morning of June 12, 2020, the stock market gapped up 2%. Due to the pandemic, the stock market had been weak for months, but some signs of recovery were slowly appearing. Oil prices had dropped significantly as the demand for oil went down because of the economic slowdown. As you read these words, you may recall that the price of oil dropped in April 2020, and some people in the States could fill a tank of gas for less than $30. In addition to oil and energy companies, several sectors were hit hard in the first months of the pandemic, including airline, cruise line, and hotel/motel/resort companies.

One of the stocks we day traded very often in our community during the pandemic was Occidental Petroleum Corporation (ticker: OXY), an American company engaged in oil exploration in the United States, South America and the Middle East. As you can see in Figure 8.4, OXY was gapping up by over 7%, and by 9 a.m. (New York time) was being traded in the pre-market at $18.76, with volume at almost 1.2 million shares. This is a very good volume and liquidity for the pre-market. Only Stocks in Play can show good trading volume in the pre-market. OXY's Average True Range (ATR) was $1.92, meaning the stock's price on average moves around $1.90 in a day! That is basically 10% intraday volatility for an $18/$19 stock. We day traders love this: volatility and liquidity!

Gappers Watch List (Pre-Market Movers): 9:00:00 - 9:04:59 6/12/2020 — ☐ ✕

Symbol	Price ($)	Vol Today	Chg Close	Chg Close	Flt (Shr)	Avg True	Shrt Flt (%)	Sector
SPR	28.69	182,946	2.52	9.6	104M	3.24	8.37	Manufacturing
AMC	5.66	109,955	0.49	9.5	52.5M	0.69		Information
CLDX	9.58	868,551	0.83	9.4	17.6M	0.83	1.59	Manufacturing
M	7.34	1.38M	0.58	8.6	309M	0.98	46.12	Retail Trade
MGM	19.33	555,554	1.49	8.4	469M	1.77	8.16	Accommodation and Food Services
APA	13.85	159,774	1.06	8.3	376M	1.42		Mining, Quarrying, and Oil and Gas Extraction
MT	10.80	205,757	0.81	8.1	1.01B	0.57		Manufacturing
MIK	5.98	122,503	0.44	7.9	147M	0.96	37.86	Retail Trade
OXY	18.76	1.19M	1.35	7.8	899M	1.92	7.85	Mining, Quarrying, and Oil and Gas Extraction
BA	183.15	2.14M	13.15	7.7	564M	16.11	2.66	Manufacturing
MRO	6.73	368,350	0.47	7.5	789M	0.54	8.20	Mining, Quarrying, and Oil and Gas Extraction
SPG	77.14	125,765	5.22	7.3	303M	7.45	10.34	Finance and Insurance

Figure 8.4: My watchlist at 6 a.m. (9 a.m. New York time) - OXY is on my watchlist.

OXY's float was around 900 million shares, which placed it in a range that I am comfortable trading. I find low float stocks too difficult to trade (primarily) because they can be very difficult to manage risk in. I looked at the price action in the pre-market (see Figure 8.5 below) and found two important levels of $19.13 (high of pre-market and also the previous day's high) and $18.49 (low of pre-market). I also noted that the stock had already gapped up by more than 7%. I decided that if OXY stayed above VWAP, then I would look for either a 1-minute or 5-minute Opening Range Breakup.

Figure 8.5: OXY price action in the pre-market before market Open at 9:30 a.m. (New York time).

As the market opened, OXY made a nice hammer Doji above VWAP on its 5-minute chart. A hammer Doji is an indecision candlestick leaning toward buyers. Having developed a trading plan pre-market, I knew in advance what I would be looking for (as set out in the previous paragraph). The stock was gapping up (see Figure 8.6 below), the overall market was in fact gapping up, and OXY was above VWAP.

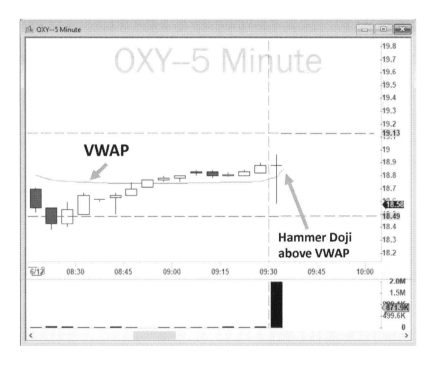

Figure 8.6: OXY price action at the market Open at 9:30 a.m. (New York time).

I decided to take the trade to the long side at $18.85 for a 5-minute ORB. I also looked at my 1-minute chart and saw that OXY had claimed VWAP (closed above VWAP) at 9:36 a.m. This made a perfect 5-minute ORB up! You will see this plotted on the two charts comprising Figure 8.7 below.

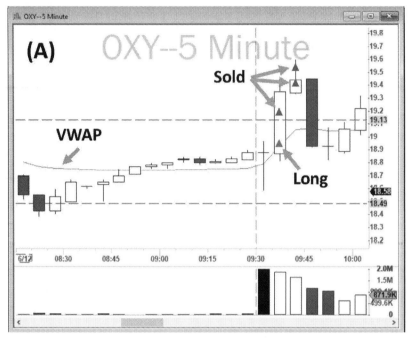

Figure 8.7: (A) 5-minute and (B) 1-minute charts plotting my ORB trades on OXY on June 12, 2020.

I sold my long positions toward $19.40 in three steps for a profit of $2,421.81 (before commissions and fees). One good trade and I was done for my day at 9:39 a.m., as shown below in Figure 8.8. I saw OXY even went higher to $19.60 before selling off below VWAP later in the morning.

Symb	Realized	Type	Company Name	Account
OXY	2421.81	Margin	Occidental Petroleum Corp.	U1588
IWM	0.00	Margin	iShares Russel 2000 ETF	U4079
Summary	2421.81			

Closed Positions P&L

06/12/20 09:39:38

Figure 8.8: My profit on June 12, 2020 (only nine minutes into my trading day).

HOW DID I DO THEM?

My philosophy in trading is that you need to master only a few solid setups to be consistently profitable. In fact, having a simple trading method consisting of a few minimal setups will help to reduce confusion and stress and allow you to concentrate more on the psychological aspect of trading, which is truly what separates the winners from the losers.

Now that you have learned the basics of a few trading strategies, let's review the actual process of planning and making a trade. You now understand the setup you want to trade, but as a beginner trader, you will have a hard time planning and initiating a trade beforehand. It is very common to have a good setup but then enter or exit a trade at the wrong time and lose money while everyone else is making money. I believe the solution lies in developing a process for your trading. Plan a trade, and trade a plan.

I have a Ph.D. in chemical engineering, and my university studies have led me to firmly believe in the process approach to trading. I can safely and confidently say that this is a major reason for my success. My trading process looks like this:

- Morning routine
- Develop my watchlist
- Organize a trade plan
- Initiate the trade according to plan
- Execute the trade according to plan
- Journaling and reflection

You must remember that what makes a trade profitable is the correct execution of all of the steps in the above process. Write down your reasons for entering and exiting every trade. Anyone can read this book or dozens of other books, but only a few people have the discipline to execute correctly. You might have a good setup but select a wrong stock to trade, such as a stock that is being manipulated by computers and institutional traders. Perhaps you will find a proper stock to trade, but you will enter the trade at the wrong time. A bad entry will make a mess of your plan and you will eventually lose your money. You can find a good stock to trade and enter a trade correctly, but if you don't exit properly, you will turn a winning trade into a losing one. All of the steps of the process are important.

Think about something significant that you do frequently in your life, and then think of how it can best be done. Now, consider how you do it currently. This is a great thought process for traders to have. When you take a trade, you need to ensure that you are focused on the right things both prior to entering it as well as during the trade. Creating a system for this thought process will take away most of the emotional hang-ups traders experience when looking to enter into a trade as well as managing it while they are in it.

This brings you to my final rule:

RULE 10	**Profitable trading does not involve emotion. If you are an emotional trader, you will lose your money.**

Education and practice give you a perspective on what matters most in trading, how you trade, and how you can grow and develop your skills. Once you have a perspective on what matters, you can proceed to identify the specific processes on which to focus. The key to success is knowing your exact processes.

Often you will learn them the hard way - by losing money.

I have found that trading, sticking to my plan and the discipline inherent in my trading methodology have had a snowball effect of positive habits in my life in general, and these habits have contributed to even more trading success. For example, I start my trading process by following the same routine when I get up each morning. I always go for a morning run before the trading session starts. As I mentioned before, I live in Vancouver, Canada, and the market opens at 6:30 a.m. my time. I wake up at 4:30 a.m. every morning. I go for a 45- to 60-minute run (usually between seven and ten kilometers (some four to six miles)). I come home, take a shower, and at 6 a.m. start developing my plan.

When my body has not been active prior to trading, I will make poor decisions. There are scientific studies showing that aerobic exercise has a positive effect on the decision-making process. People who regularly participate in an aerobic exercise (such as running for at least thirty minutes) have higher scores on neuropsychological functioning and performance tests that measure such cognitive functions as attentional control, inhibitory control, cognitive flexibility, working memory updating and capacity, and information processing speed. You can easily read about these topics on the Internet. Very often, our moods are influenced by our physical state, even by factors as delicate as what and how much we eat. Keep a record of your daily trading results as a function of your physical condition and you will see these relationships for yourself. Begin preventive maintenance by keeping body, and thus mind, in their peak operating condition. I stopped drinking coffee and alcohol, and I have stopped eating animal-based food, and my performance levels have increased significantly. Not eating meat and fish (any living beings that are marked with blood), and not using alcohol, coffee and tobacco lifts you above the curse and accelerates you forward in every facet of life. Likewise, in trading, your focus should be about being better than your current state, in all aspects of your life.

In 2014, I was visiting New York City and decided to go for a walk along Wall Street during lunchtime on a working day and perhaps take a selfie with Charging Bull, the famous 3.5-ton bronze sculpture of a bull located near Wall Street that symbolizes New York's financial industry.

I assumed that most of the people walking around in that area on a weekday must either be traders or working in the financial sector. I knew there was a good chance that the person sitting next to me in a coffee shop was taking home a $2 million bonus at the end of the year. I tried to observe people's attitudes, how they walked, how they dressed and how they treated themselves. I rarely saw anyone who was not well-dressed, without confidence and without being in excellent physical shape. I wondered to myself, are these people well-dressed, confident, in great physical shape and disciplined because they are rich and successful or did they become rich and successful because they were disciplined, confident and ambitious? This is possibly a "chicken and egg" problem with no real answer, but I personally believe it is the latter. Based on what I saw, successful traders have often succeeded in almost everything they have done. They are ambitious and they expect a lot from themselves and they expect it at an early age. They expect to be the best. Success has been their history, so why should trading be any different?

Research has shown that the winners in any endeavor think, feel, and act differently than those who lose. If you want to know if you have the self-discipline of a winner, try right now, starting today, to stop a habit that has challenged you in the past. If you have always wanted to be in better physical shape, try adding exercises such as running into your routine, and also take control of your salt and sugar intake. If you drink too much alcohol or coffee, try to see if for one month you can stay away from them. These are excellent tests to see if you are emotionally and intellectually strong enough or not to discipline yourself in the face of a losing trade. I am not saying that if you drink coffee or alcohol, or that if you are not a regular runner, you cannot become a successful trader, but if you make a try at these types of improvements and fail, then you should know that exercising self-control in trading will not be any easier to accomplish. Change is hard, but if you wish to be a successful trader, you need to work on changing and developing your personality at every level. Working hard at it is the only way to sustain the changes you need to make. The measure of intelligence is not in IQ tests or how to make money, but it is in the ability to change. As Oprah Winfrey, the American talk show host and philanthropist once said, the greatest discovery of all time is that a person can change their future by merely changing their attitude.

Traders who fail to make money in trading often get frustrated and go out and study more about the market to learn new strategies and additional technical indicators. They don't realize that their lack of self-discipline, impulsive behavior and their bad life habits are the main cause of their failure, not their technical knowledge.

As discussed previously, trading cannot be looked at as a hobby. You must approach trading seriously. As such, I wake up at 4:30 a.m., go for a 45- to 60-minute run, take a shower, get dressed, and eat oatmeal for breakfast, all prior to firing up my trading station at 6 a.m. I am awake, alert, and motivated when I sit down and start building my watchlist. This morning routine has tremendously helped my mental preparation for coming into the market. So, whatever you do, starting the morning out in a similar fashion will pay invaluable dividends. Rolling out of bed and throwing water on your face fifteen minutes in advance just does not give you sufficient time to be prepared for the market's opening. Sitting at your computer in your pajamas or underwear does not put you in the right mindset to attack the market. I know, because I have experienced all of these scenarios.

My watchlist comes from a specific scan that I use every morning. I will not look anywhere else because I am confident that the stocks on that scanner will have the best opportunity to set up for me to trade. I will vet each stock in the same way, using a checklist to determine if it is actually tradeable for me. My watchlist is built by 6:15 a.m., and I will not add anything to it afterward because there won't be enough time to review new stocks and plan for a trade. This allows me to watch the tickers on my watchlist for the fifteen minutes prior to opening.

During these fifteen minutes prior to opening, I watch the tickers on my watchlist and develop trade plans for them based on the price action I am seeing. This is the most difficult part, and it requires experience, knowledge and education. Many traders fail at this step. When the bell rings at 6:30 a.m. (9:30 a.m. New York time), I'll have my plans in place, written on note cards because it is too easy to forget what I've seen on each ticker coming into the Open. What is my plan if it sets up to the long side? What is my plan if it sets up to the short side? What setup do I want to see? What are my profit targets? Where will my stop be? Is the profit window large enough for the trade to make sense? Just asking yourself questions like these when you are planning your trades will give you a significant advantage because you can then go in with a battle plan and stick to it. If my trade plan is written down close to my face, I can easily refer to it, and that eliminates the anxiety that I used to feel when the opening bell rang. All I am doing at the opening is looking for my signal and trigger to enter the trade.

In the earlier example, I saw that Sarepta Therapeutics Inc. (ticker: SRPT) had gapped down 14.5% (please see the above Figure 8.1). I knew that there wasn't much interest in buying the stock because it had gapped down almost 15% overnight and was now trading below VWAP. I could not find any support or resistance nearby, therefore I decided to watch VWAP and I chose a VWAP short trade, as outlined in Figure 8.2. A similar thought process occurred during my trade on Occidental Petroleum Corporation (ticker: OXY) that I also outlined earlier in this chapter. The market was strong, the stock had gapped up, there was heavy volume, and the first 5-minute candle had closed as a hammer Doji (explained in Chapter 6). Its setup was ready for an Opening Range Breakup and I was ready for the signal (see Figures 8.4 to 8.8 above).

Once the stock I am monitoring sets up, signals, and triggers an entry, I will enter without question (well, that's the plan anyway). Sometimes I may second-guess myself, but not too often. I have my profit targets written out on my trade plan, as well as the technical level that I am basing my stops on, so after entry I am just concentrating on hitting my marks and booking profit. There are some who say that knowing when to exit is the hardest part of the trade. It can be extremely tough not to exit the trade too early if you do not have a pre-set plan. If you have a plan ahead of time and you stick to it, you will have a much better chance of letting your winning trades work and cutting your losses off quickly instead of the other way around. This will also help with managing your emotions while in the trade. One of my students has spoken to me about the need to filter out the noise. This strategy goes a long way to help do that so you can focus on the trade.

Once the trade is done, I will reflect on how well my plan worked and how well I stuck to what I had written. Most of the reflection on my trades will come in the evening when I review and recap my trades from the day. I believe one of the key steps forgotten by many is reflection. *"What did I do right?"*, *"What did I do wrong?"* and *"Should I have sold earlier?"* are all extremely important questions for the development of your trading strategies. Just because you made a good profit does not mean you are a perfect trader. How you play both sides of the table is extremely important. Write down or do a video recap of the trade and everything that comes to mind lesson-wise, and then file it away with other past lessons, and use them all as a reference for the future. Some lessons hit harder than others, but be confident that with time you will only get better. It only takes one incident of getting your hand slammed in a door to figure out that you must be more careful, but it may take two or three times to learn to turn on the lights before walking around your house at night.

Why is this process in trading important? This process is important because it describes how things are done to prepare for a trade and then provides the focus for executing them. It helps to filter out the emotional social noise and gives you a better chance for a more successful winning trade. It provides you with a tool to go back to and reflect on your trades and makes you a better trader. If you focus on the right processes, in the right way, you can design your way to trading success

CHAPTER 9

━━━━━

CASE STUDY OF
A NEWLY
SUCCESSFUL TRADER

As it has been quite a number of years since I started trading, I recognize I may not properly remember how difficult it was in the beginning. I still try to teach and explain trading in simple language, but it's hard to recall all of the ups and downs of a truly novice trader. I've been wondering lately how I can best deliver a sense of those early challenges to my readers and students. A good teacher should always consider how their students learn and what it takes for them to get through the learning curve. It does not really matter how much the teacher themself knows.

For this 2020 edition of *How to Day Trade for a Living*, I decided to include as an additional chapter a case study of a new day trader who had read this book and then implemented the knowledge gained as a starting point for their day trading career. I reached out to John, a member of our community who had recently presented his story in one of our weekly webinars, and he agreed to kindly and generously share his trading journey with you, the readers of this book. In his webinar to our traders, John's story was both amazing and inspiring. When John began day trading live, he experienced a horrible first two months (October and November 2019) but, subsequently, he had been on a very promising streak, as set out in Figure 9.1 below.

John's journey into trading started like everyone else's does. He had an interest in the market and casually followed it. He opened an account but did not know what exactly he wanted to do as a trader nor what he was supposed to do. He had some initial success (in swing trading) but then experienced some heavy losses (in day trading) as a result of his lack of education and planning. Thus far, John's story was like many others who begin trading. However, what made John's story different from most is that he actually realized his inability to day trade properly and he then went about fixing it. Most people are too proud to accept that they do not know what they are doing. Self-confidence is great, but self-awareness is more important.

What is fascinating about John is that he learned the basics from our trading community and my books, but he then found his own edge in the market. As I wrote earlier, John trades completely differently from me. He has his own set of rules and has defined his own strategy, and they are not something that I myself trade or teach.

INSIGHT FROM A
NEWLY SUCCESSFUL TRADER

By John Hiltz (with edits by Andrew Aziz)

About the Author of this Chapter

John retired as a Lieutenant Colonel in the United States Army after 21 years of service. Five years of his career were spent as an instructor at the United States Military Academy, which is where he developed a passion for educating others. While in the Army he also became fascinated with day trading and began to consume any information he could find on the topic. However, on his own he was unable to turn that knowledge into consistent trading profits. The turning points in his trading career were reading Andrew Aziz's "How to Day Trade For a Living" and then joining the Bear Bull Traders community upon his military retirement. With the education provided by the BBT moderators, months of simulated trading, and months of small risk trading, John was able to find consistent profitability within his first year.

John has been married for 20 years and is the father of two teenage boys. In his spare time, he enjoys playing mediocre guitar, mountain biking, and watching his sons play hockey.

I (John) recently have found consistent profitability in day trading and Andrew asked me to share some insight into my trading journey. However, I only realized this profitability after making all of the common new trader mistakes and then finally adopting the advice of other successful traders. The advice that turned around my trading career was:

- Risk the same amount of money per trade
- Risk a small amount of money per trade until you are consistent
- Use hard stops to exit trades
- Focus on a single strategy until you master it

EARLY TRADING EDUCATION

My journey into day trading actually took place over several years. In 2010, I began to watch the stock market (such as the Dow Jones Industrial Average) on a daily basis just for fun and was intrigued by the patterns the intraday charts would form. Some days it would pop up and then maintain a somewhat constant level. Other days it would do the opposite. Or on many days it might move in a kind of wave pattern. It was the repeatability of these patterns that interested me. It seemed like some days looked just like other days and I wondered if there was a way to profit off this repetition. In 2014, I began a three-year period of consuming every day trading book that I could find, but I never traded a single stock. I was still too timid to put actual money on the line. However, in 2017 I opened my first brokerage account and tried my hand at swing trading (i.e., trading stocks over the course of days). I only traded stocks that were trending up in a "wave" pattern and I would enter as they bounced off their 20-day moving average. The results were on the profitable side, but it was a bullish year, so maybe it was a biased experiment. But, I was exposed to two very important lessons, lessons I would have to relearn as a day trader:

- Focusing on a single strategy made trading easier and more consistent
- Use hard stops or be prepared to tie up capital or take large losses

BEGINNING TO DAY TRADE

In early 2019, I did some casual day trading at work and the results were disastrous. I simply was not ready for the psychological aspect of gaining and losing money so quickly and I broke every rule in the book:

- Trying to use mental stops and not hard stops
- Risking too much money
- Not calculating risk versus reward
- Jumping from strategy to strategy

I was also treating day trading as something I could do during convenient blocks of time within my actual job. If I had twenty minutes of free time, I would desperately try to find a trade worth taking, even if the reality of the situation was that there were no good setups. I was being completely impatient.

Luckily, about this same time I read Andrew Aziz' book, *How To Day Trade For a Living*, and it really resonated with me. Andrew described strategy price patterns that I had also seen over the years. He also stressed the importance of key support and resistance levels such as daily highs and lows, things I had noticed way back in my stock market watching days back in 2010.

HITTING MY LOW POINT

Inspired by his trading insights, I joined the Bear Bull Traders community in mid-2019, but at the beginning I continued to make the same dumb mistakes as before. I knew the tenets from Andrew's book and I now had live assistance from Andrew and other experienced Bear Bull Traders moderators. Yet, I still was not really listening. I was trying to mimic Andrew's trades in the morning, taking way too many trades all day, risking too much, and being completely unfocused in terms of strategy.

Then, a few months after joining Bear Bull Traders, I had the day that every book and every trader had warned me about. I had my "hulk" day. I was profitable early on, but then suddenly went "red" for the day. Angry about this turn of events, I then began a series of revenge trades, trying to get myself back to "green". My profit/loss column began to fluctuate wildly. Sometimes coming close to green, but then snapping back into the red. The harder I tried to mitigate the day's losses, the more I incurred greater defeat. This pattern continued for an hour until I had lost about $2,600, or 7% of my trading account. This moment was a turning point for me. I realized that if I had a few more days like this, my trading account would drop below $25,000 in value. If this happened, I would no longer enjoy Pattern Day Trader status and I would therefore have my number of trades restricted. I had to make a change and I began to truly focus on adhering to the following four ideas that would eventually turn things around for me.

RISK THE SAME AMOUNT OF MONEY PER TRADE

Traders often refer to the amount of money risked in a trade as "R". A trade where you lose this risked money is called a –1R trade. That is, you lose 1R when the trade hits your stop. A trade where you make twice as much as you risk would be a 2R trade. When I began day trading, I found myself starting my days rather responsibly, risking perhaps $50 per trade. However, when my first trade would stop out, I would inevitably risk more to try to make up the loss more easily and get back to "green" on the day. When that trade didn't work out, I might be down $150 and I would risk even more. It was the classic gambler error of making bigger bets to get out of a hole. To make matters worse, I often became impatient with these larger bets. In my mind I would think, *"I just need to get this trade to work out, I'll get back to profitability, and then I will reduce risk again."* It was really a recipe for psychological disaster. Eventually, I took the advice of a Bear Bull Traders moderator and began to think in terms of "R" and risk the same amount of money per trade. By doing so, I could better conceptualize what a -1R loss meant for my trading day and could become accustomed to losing it. For example, a losing trade is *always* a $50 loss. Two bad trades to start the day are a $100 loss and I need a good setup 2R trade to get back to break-even. I began to think in terms of these "R" steps and it had an immense impact on my trading maturity and patience.

RISK A SMALL AMOUNT OF MONEY PER TRADE UNTIL YOU ARE CONSISTENT

This next piece of advice also came from an experienced trader in our community. When coupled with using consistent "R", it provided the means to slow the bleeding of my account until I could develop a more consistent winning strategy. That experienced trader actually said he risked $10 per trade when he started, so that a very good 3R trade would yield only $30. In fact, he said that even on technically "green" days he might still only break-even or even lose money due to commissions.

Nevertheless, he focused on being "green" according to R and then increased his risk amount *slowly* as he gained consistency. So, I applied nearly the same strategy and began risking $20 per trade for five months with a goal of achieving 20R per month. As shown in Figure 9.1 below, I lost money in the first two months but had achieved my 20R goal by the fourth month. The key takeaway is that my account was able to survive a combined –28R in those first two months. At a $20 risk per trade, I lost about $560. And in fact, due to an increase in consistency, I was able to increase my risk per trade to $40 in months six and seven.

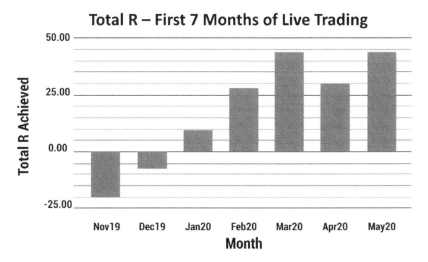

Figure 9.1: John's monthly returns from November 2019 to May 2020. "R" stands for risk per trade.

USE HARD STOPS TO EXIT TRADES

This is perhaps the easiest piece of advice to explain and the most difficult to follow. A hard stop is an automatically executed trade (whether limit or market order) that will exit your position at –1R. Every trading book I ever read said to use hard stops. Every successful trader I ever encountered said to use hard stops. It seems like a completely rational and logical step. And yet, you will constantly find traders either not using hard stops or removing them when they are about to get stopped out. I was no different when I started trading. There are many situations that can cloud your better judgment:

- Your first trade of the day and you do not want to start out "red"
- The trade that will take you to your maximum allowable daily loss
- A trade in which you are highly biased ("I know AAPL will hit $350 today")
- You are about to be stopped out by a seemingly temporary market induced pull back

Personally, I was more often guilty of placing the stop and then removing it because I did not want to take the loss. And –1R would become –1.5R and then –2R and so on. In these situations, an almost decision-making paralysis would overtake me. If it got really bad, I would begin to conjure up alternate strategies.

"I'll see where it gets by the end of the day." "Maybe I'll swing trade it until tomorrow." Whatever my original strategy had been was now co-opted by desperation. And, in some cases, I ended up taking some very bad losses. This was just a psychological battle within myself that I had to win and I eventually found the discipline. I had to learn that a –1R loss is actually a *really great* outcome. –1R can be overcome with one trade while –3R might take several "green" trades to erase the loss. It also allows you to discard a losing, distracting trade and begin the patient hunt for the next good setup.

FOCUS ON A SINGLE STRATEGY UNTIL YOU MASTER IT

All of the steps above were incredibly important because they slowed the atrophy of my account while I tried to find a winning trading strategy. In fact, I would say these steps got me to about break-even, or maybe even slightly profitable overall. However, I had to find my "edge" in the market if this day trading idea was going to work in the long run. Simply by trying different things over time I began to get a feel for what kind of trading suited my personality. Market Open trades felt like coin flips to me. Price reversal trades never seemed to work out. But I felt like I was a decent scalper and that I could recognize opportunities where a stock might make a bit of a run. In particular, I began to focus on stocks that were breaking their high of day or low of day price. Over time, I focused almost solely on "Break of High of Day" trades, or BHOD trades.

I really liked BHOD trades because there was almost no ambiguity about the setup. If a stock breaks its high of day, *then it breaks its high of the day.* For example, this is unlike a price reversal trade. When does a reversal actually start? How do you define it? I defined a BHOD as when the BID on the Level 2 broke the previous high of day sale [please refer back to Chapter 5 if you don't recall what bids on Level 2 are]. This is the moment a buyer says, *"I will pay more than anyone else has paid all day."* I believe there is often power in that statement. Show me a decent pull back in price and then a confident climb toward that high of day backed up by increasing volume. Generally, I also want a stock with a news catalyst and high relative volume. I trade BHODs aggressively and exit my position in 50% increments. Early on, these exits will be at price pauses, and then, if the price continues to climb, I will attempt to exit more shares at important levels (half-dollar, whole dollar, yesterday's high, pre-market high, etc.).

One of the most important advantages of focusing on a single, well-defined strategy is that it forces patience. Early on, I averaged over nine trades per day, but trading nearly only BHOD trades reduced that to five trades per day. I also became pickier, even among BHOD trades. I could recognize a strong one from a weak one and, as time went on, my consistency and profitability increased (as set forth in the table below).

**Statistics for John's utilizing of the
Break of High of Day Strategy for three consecutive months
(based on an average of five trades a day).**

MONTH	STRATEGY SUCCESS RATE	AVERAGE R PER TRADE
March 2020	78%	0.28
April 2020	79%	0.24
May 2020	84%	0.63

I also found that BHOD trades exist every single day. They will be more prolific on days when the market is strong, but some of the most profitable opportunities exist on a weak market day when an individual stock is performing in a contrarian manner. Many traders have been surprised by my discipline in waiting for BHOD trades. That being said, I don't necessarily recommend this specific BHOD Strategy. Remember, strategies are personality driven. But, I highly recommend aggressively focusing on a single strategy if you are struggling to find your footing in the world of day trading. This is an endeavor that can take years to find success in. It is not a stretch of the imagination that you may need to spend months on a single strategy to verify if it has potential. But it may well be worth your time to find your edge in the market.

LISTEN TO EXPERIENCED TRADERS

I can say with a high degree of confidence that I would have failed as a trader without having a supportive community. I genuinely believe that I had to have my crazy "hulk" day (a day that I lost control and traded like a gambler, with no plan, aggressively and anxiously and mindlessly), but then I needed somewhere to turn when it was over. A serious community or mastermind group is a place to be in and to share your feelings. Usually, more experienced traders enforce the tenets of responsible trading, and I needed to hear it from those who I look up to. It took a while to fully open my ears, but when I did, the positive results began to reveal them–selves. In a similar manner, I hope the advice that I have provided also shifts new traders into a path of success. It is possible to consistently succeed in day trading. Just listen to the experienced voices around you.

STEP-BY-STEP EXAMINATION OF A TRADE

BHOD Trade Example

This is a great illustration of a very typical BHOD trade. It is not the most profitable example, but it does offer insight into how you can expect many of these trades to perform. As discussed above, I find the BHOD trade to offer a high probability of success with a somewhat low average profit. You have to become accustomed with getting an initial move, taking some profit, and then often seeing the price stop out the rest of your shares at break-even. That is exactly what happened here.

June 15, 2020 was an interesting day in the market. The SPDR S&P 500 ETF Trust (ticker: SPY) opened down -3.3%, but ultimately finished the day up 1.3% on a steady climb from Open to Close. Obviously, a market trending up all day is probably going to offer many opportunities for stocks to break their high of day. The Walt Disney Company (ticker: DIS) was not a news catalyst stock on this day. However, it was often in play during this period because of the COVID-19 pandemic and its effect on Disney's theme parks. Daily relative volume was a bit low at about 70%. I prefer 90% or higher, but it is not a hard rule for a BHOD trade. It's only something to consider.

What made Disney an intriguing trade is that it had an "ideal" high of day. That is, a high of day that shares a price with some other level. In this case, the high of day and the pre-market high were both exactly $113.50. That high of day had been hit twice to the penny. A third "touch" at an exact high of day is often a great entry point. [Please refer to Figure 9.2 below to follow along with John's commentary on this trade.]

I entered the trade at $113.53 as soon as I saw the BID break the high of day. I wanted to see a single buyer say they'd pay more than anyone else had paid all day. These trades can often "pop" when they break and how far you can enter from the high of day is a matter of judgment. You have to make an assessment based on the enthusiasm of the price movement. I consider anything within 10 cents of the high of day on a $100+ stock to be very good.

I tend to prefer stocks in the $100–$400 range. They seem to make cleaner breaks of their high of day. These stocks also often offer very obvious places to take partial exits at their half-dollar and dollar levels. My goal is to get those partials within 5 cents of a half-dollar level and within 10 cents of a dollar level. I also take 50% partials due to the nature of these trades to often make an initial "pop" and then fall back to break-even. My first 50% partial was at $113.95 in case the price failed at $114.00. At this time, I also moved my stop *near* break-even at $113.53. I actually placed the stop at $113.49 in case the price pulled back and held at that previous high of day/half-dollar level. I was willing to accept this 4 cent loss on the chance that level saved me from being stopped out.

My next partial goal was $114.45 or better, but Disney began to struggle around $114.20 as SPY struggled with its own pre-market high around $301. Stocks that break their high of day will often exhibit a brief period of near complete SPY non-correlation. However, as the trade continues, SPY can start to exert a more correlated effect on the stock's price. I took the next 50% partial at $114.16 as Disney failed to break $114.20 and SPY began to pull back. My plan to place my stop at $113.49 almost worked, but I was stopped out on a pull back to $113.47.

Disney then slowly found its legs again and never looked back, making an eventual run over the day to $118.12.

Many new traders might be upset at missing this $4.62 move on Disney [$4.62 is the difference between the pre-market high of $113.50 and the high of day price of $118.12]. I have learned over time to look at the positive aspects of the trade. This was a very easy, high probability high of day trade and a $0.66 move [$0.66 is the difference between the pre-market high of $113.50 and $114.16, the price point where John took his second and final partial at]. After one easy partial, I was able to move my stop to near break-even and enjoy a risk-free trade. I competently and profession-ally added to my daily P/L and then I started looking for the next opportunity. I took four other trades on this day for a total of 2.2R.

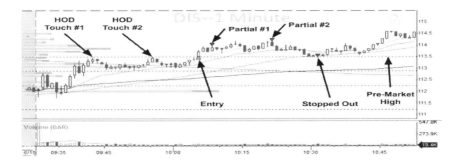

Figure 9.2: Example of one of John's Break of High of Day trades.

CONCLUSION

John Hiltz' case study was very encouraging to me and to many of our newer traders who participated in his webinar. The most important lesson of his case study is that you need to develop yourself as a trader. You must adopt your own set of rules and create your own hours, strategy and process for trading. John's Break of High of Day (BHOD) Strategy was not discussed at all in the earlier versions of this book. It is fairly similar to an ABCD Pattern or a Bull Flag, but it is different. John coined a new name for it and now "owns" this new strategy. That is excellent. You create a new strategy for yourself, and you then find a name for it. You now have a "PlayBook" on it. You can consistently trade it as well as keep track of how it performs. This is *How to Day Trade for a Living!*

CHAPTER 10

NEXT STEPS FOR BEGINNER TRADERS

I appreciate you taking the time to read thus far in this book. I hope you've found lots of valuable information and ideas to help you move forward in your day trading career. The one key message I desire that you will take away from this book is that under no circumstances can you be an emotional trader. Somehow, you have to find inside of yourself the ability to resist making emotional decisions in the midst of a trade.

You also need to learn some technical skills. You have to find one strategy that suits your personality and practice it in your simulator, and then practice it some more. And then you have to stick to it. Like glue. You also have to be able to make decisive, but reasoned, decisions based on your well-thought-out in advance trading plan. You also have to have settled in your mind, again, in advance, how much you can afford to risk on any one trade. Don't forget my rule: no more than 2%! And in many ways, that is just the beginning. Successful day trading is based on three important skills.

1. You need to constantly analyze the balance of power between buyers and sellers and bet on the winning group (discussed in Chapter 6).

2. You need to practice excellent money and trade management (discussed in Chapter 3).

3. And you need sufficient self-discipline to follow your trading plan, to avoid getting overexcited or depressed in the markets, and to resist the temptation to make emotional decisions.

THE SEVEN ESSENTIALS FOR DAY TRADING

In order to become a consistently profitable trader, I also believe that you need to follow these seven essential and fundamental steps before entering into the world of trading with your real money. Some of these steps you should do before and after each and every single trade you make:

1. Education and simulated trading

2. Preparation

3. Determination and hard work

4. Patience

5. Discipline

6. Mentorship and a community of traders

7. Reflection and review

Education and Simulated Trading

Now that you have read this book, you should be in a better position to make a decision on whether or not day trading is right for you. Day trading requires a certain mindset, as well as a discipline and a set of skills that not everyone possesses. Interestingly, most of the traders I know are also poker players. They enjoy speculation and the stimulation that comes from it. Although poker is a type of gambling, day trading is not. Day trading is a science, a skill, and a career, and has nothing to do with gambling. It is the serious business of selling and buying stocks, at times in a matter of seconds. You should be able to make decisions fast, with no emotion or hesitation. Doing otherwise results in losing real money.

After you've made up your mind and decided that you want to start day trading, the next step is to get a proper education. This book equips you with the basic knowledge essential for day trading, but you still have a long way to go before you will be a consistently profitable trader. Can you be a mechanic by just reading a book? Can you perform surgery after reading a book or taking First Aid 101? No. This book develops a foundation that you can build upon. This book introduces straight-forward trading setups to simply show what day trading looks like. It is not meant by any means to be a stand-alone book. You are not a trader yet, not even close.

I encourage you to read more books and find online or in-person courses on day trading. New traders often search for the best traders on the Internet. They think that learning from the most experienced traders is the best way to learn. On the contrary, I think new traders should look for the best "teacher". There is a difference. Sometimes the best trader has no personality, or poor people skills, while a consistently profitable, but not one of the top ten traders, can emerge as a premier lecturer, communicator, and mentor. New traders need to find the best teacher. You don't need to learn from the best traders to become a proficient trader yourself. Think about who some of the best professional sports coaches are. Often they were not superstar players. They knew the sport, but their passion was for teaching and developing players. The skills needed to become a great trader are different from those required to be an effective trading coach. Being a star trader requires superior pattern recognition and discipline. On the other hand, effective trading coaches are often obsessed with finding better ways to teach, are patient, and communicate clearly and effectively in a simple and easy-to-understand language. They can explain their methodology coherently. Often great traders lack the monetary incentive to create the best training program.

Trading in a Simulator

You should never start your day trading career with real money. Sign up with one of the brokers that provides you with simulated accounts with real market data. Some brokers give you access to delayed market data, but don't use those. You need to make decisions real time. Most of the simulated data software is a paid service, so you need to save some money for that expense. Many trading rooms and trading educators offer simulator accounts. DAS Trader offers the best simulated accounts for as low as $120 per month (at the time of writing) with higher prices for more features such as replay practice during off-market hours for those want to practice when the market is closed. Check out their website (*www.dastrader.com*) or contact them at *support@dastrader. com* for more information. This completes my unpaid and unsolicited advertisement for them!

If you use it for six months, and trade only with simulated money, it will probably cost you less than $1,000. This is the cost of a proper education. If you are seriously considering day trading as a career, it's a small expenditure compared to the cost of an education for a new profession. For example, imagine that you want to go to school to get an MBA – it will easily cost you over $50,000. Likewise, many other diploma or post-graduate programs cost significantly more than the education required for day trading.

Once you have a simulated account, you will need to develop your strategy. Try the strategies that I have discussed in this book, and master one or two of them that fit with your personality, available time, and trading platform. There is no best strategy among them, just like there is no best automobile in the market. There might, however, be a best car for you. The VWAP, Support or Resistance, and the Opening Range Breakout Strategies are my favorites. You need to only master a few of them to always be profitable in the market. Keep your strategy simple. When you have a solid strategy that you've mastered, make sure there is no emotion attached to it. Keep practicing it, and then start practicing a second strategy, and learn to incrementally add size in those strategies.

Practice with the amounts of money that you will be trading in real life. It is easy to buy a position worth $100,000 in a simulated account and watch it lose half of its value in a matter of seconds. But could you tolerate this loss in a real account? No. You will probably become an emotional trader and make a decision quickly, usually resulting in a major loss. Always trade in the simulator with the size and position that you will be using in the real account. Otherwise, there is no point in trading in a simulated account. Move to a real account only after at least three months of training with a simulated account and then, start small, with real money. Trade small while you're learning or when you are feeling stressed.

New traders often try to skip steps in the process, lose their money, and then give up their day trading career forever and tell themselves that it is impossible to make money by day trading. Remember, baby steps. Success in day trading is one foot forward and then the next. Master one topic, and then and only then move on to the next.

Most traders struggle when they first begin, and many do not have sufficient time when the markets are open to practice in real time. Those who can give trading more time when they start have a better chance to succeed. How long does it take to be a consistently profitable trader? I don't think anyone can become a consistently profitable trader in less than six to eight months. After three months of paper trading, you need at least another three months of trading in small share size to master your emotions and practice self-discipline while trading with your real money. After six months, you may become a seasoned trader. Eight months is probably better than six months, and twelve months is perhaps better than both. Are you patient enough for this learning curve? Do you really want this career? Then you should be patient enough. Do you have this much time to learn the day trading profession?

It always amuses me when I see books or online courses and websites that offer trading education that will make a person money starting on day one! I wonder who would believe such advertisements.

You must define a sensible process oriented goal for yourself, such as: *I want to learn how to day trade. I do not want to make a living out of it for now.* Do not set an absolute income for yourself in day trading, not at least for the first two years. This is very important. Many traders think of inspiring goals such as making a million dollars or being able to trade for a living from a beach house in the Caribbean. These goals may be motivating, and they definitely have their place, but they distract you from focusing on what you need to do today and tomorrow to become better. What you as a new trader can control is the process of trading: how to make and execute sound trading decisions. Many think a profitable day is a good trading day. They're wrong. A good trading day is a day when you are disciplined and you trade sound strategies. Your daily goal should be to trade well, not to make money. The normal uncertainty of the market will result in some days or weeks being in the red.

Often new traders email and ask me how they can become full-time traders while they are working at a different job from 9 a.m. to 5 p.m. New York time. I really don't have any answer for that. They probably cannot become a full-time trader if they cannot trade in a simulator real time between 9:30 a.m. and 11:30 a.m. New York time. You do not need to have the whole day available for trading, but you at least need the first two hours that the market is open. If you insist, I would say the first one hour that the market is open (9:30 a.m. to 10:30 a.m. New York time) is the absolute minimum time you should be available for trading and practice, in addition to any time you need for preparation before the market opens at 9:30 a.m. New York time. Sometimes I am done with trading and hit my daily goal by 9:45 a.m., but sometimes I need to watch the market longer to find trading opportunities. Do you have this flexibility in your work-life schedule?

When I started day trading, I was unemployed. Then I had to find a job to pay the bills because I was losing my savings on day trading. I am lucky I live in the Pacific time zone because I could trade and practice between 6:30 a.m. and 8:30 a.m. and then be at work for 9 a.m. Pacific time. If you don't have this luxury, maybe swing trading is better for you, but making a living out of swing trading is more difficult. The best swing traders can expect an annual return of 15–20% on their account size. Day traders, on the other hand, look to profit between 0.5–1% of their account size daily. The currency market (Forex) is open 24 hours/5 days per week, and perhaps you could consider trading currencies and commodities if you do not have sufficient free time to practice day trading or swing trading. This book though is not a useful guide for swing trading or for the Forex market. They are both different from day trading in so many ways.

You must always be continuing your education and reflecting upon your trading strategy. Never stop learning about the stock market. The market is a dynamic environment and it's constantly changing. Day trading is different than it was ten years ago, and it will be different in another ten years. So keep reading and discussing your progress and performance with your mentors and other traders. Always think ahead and maintain a progressive and winning attitude.

Learn as much as you can, but keep a degree of healthy skepticism about everything, including this book. Ask questions, and do not accept experts at their word. Consistently profitable traders constantly evaluate their trading system. They make adjustments every month, every day, and even intraday. Every day is new. It is about developing trading skills, discipline, and controlling emotions, and then making adjustments continually. That is *How to Day Trade for a Living*.

Traders who are consistently profitable have studied the fundamentals of trading and have learned how to make well-thought-out and intelligent trades. Their focus is on the rationale for their actions rather than on making money. Amateurs, on the other hand, are focused on making money every single day. That kind of thinking can be their worst enemy. I am not consciously trying to make money as a trader. My focus is on "doing the right thing". I am looking for excellent risk/reward opportunities, and then I trade them. Being good at trading is the result of mastering the skills of trading and recognizing the fundamentals of a good trade. Money is just the by-product of executing fundamentally solid trades.

As a new trader, you will be constantly looking at your profit and loss (P&L). P&L is the most emotionally distracting column in my trading platform. Plus $250, negative $475, plus $1,100. I tend to make irrational decisions by looking at it. I used to panic and sell my position when my P&L became negative although my trade was still valid according to my plan. Or, quite often, I became greedy and sold my winning position too early while my profit target had yet to be reached according to my plan. I did myself a favor and I hid my P&L column. I trade based on technical levels and the plan I make. I don't look at how much I am up or down in real time.

P&L is not important when novices first begin trading with real money, especially when smaller share sizes are involved. Most trading platforms include an option to hide real time P&L. When this is not available, a strategically placed strip of ever-versatile duct tape or dark-colored masking tape will conceal that information. Your goal is to develop trading skills and not to make money. You must focus on getting better every single day, one trade after another. That is *How to Day Trade for a Living.* Push your comfort zone to find greater success.

Preparation

John Wooden (or as some call him, the Wizard of Westwood), the famous American basketball player and coach, once said, "*By failing to prepare, you are preparing to fail.*" Indeed.

There are two aspects to the preparation process for day traders:

1. the preparation necessary before the market opens (usually the night before or between 8 a.m. and 9:30 a.m. New York time), and

2. the specific trading information you must obtain before you can make a trade.

Wake up on time and get in front of your PC early.

Review your scanners and shortlist your choices of stocks for the day. Review *www.finviz.com* or *www.brief ing.com* and read about the fundamental catalysts that caused the stock to gap up or down. Compile information such as daily volume, intraday range (the Average True Range), and short interest. Review daily charts and identify important levels of support or resistance. I do not make a trade unless I know the average volume, Average True Range, important technical levels, short interest, and fresh news for the Stocks in Play.

Shortlist your watchlist down to two or three stocks. During earnings season, there are many Stocks in Play to choose from. Each day, traders shouldn't choose more than two or three of these stocks to focus on. You can make considerably more money trading one or two stocks well instead of watching and trading many stocks poorly.

The earlier you start your morning, the more time you will have to go through the news and find the best Stocks in Play. Sometimes in those extra minutes you find the stock of the day that you wouldn't have if you had spent less time researching. Moreover, you have extra time to ask members of your community about their choices of stocks and obtain their feedback. Most professional traders do not arrive later than 7:30 a.m. New York time. Experienced traders with a strong community and powerful scanners can certainly stroll in later, but 9 a.m. is the latest that most serious traders would ever consider arriving at their desk. Prepare physically. Drink enough water to hydrate during the morning stretch and do not become over-caffeinated.

Being present in the pre-market is important. Every once in a while there will be an opportunity during pre-market trading to make quick money on a breaking news story. In addition, valuable information can be obtained by watching how stocks are being traded in the pre-market. Monitor the ranges of the stocks that are on your watchlist, identify intraday support or resistance levels, and confirm how much volume is being traded.

New traders will often think that trading strategies can be reduced to a few rules that they must follow in order to be profitable: *always do this or always do that.* Wrong. Trading isn't about "always" at all; it is about each single trade, and each situation. Every trade is a new puzzle that you must solve. There is no universal answer to all of the puzzles in the market. Therefore, you need to make a plan for each trade as early as when you are doing your pre-market scanning. Before making a trade, you must create a plan for your trades or a series of *"if-then"* statements. Develop some plans as to when you might take a position in one of the stocks on your watchlist: if you see *x* scenario, then you will buy at *y* price. Continue creating "if-then" scenarios for each outcome.

For an example, let's take a look at Figures 10.1 and 10.2. Imagine you plan to trade DICK'S Sporting Goods, Inc. (ticker: DKS) on March 7, 2017. The stock had gapped down because of disappointing earnings reports and was being traded at around $50.50 in the pre-market. You think it might be a Stock in Play.

Symbol	$	T	C $	C %	Float		S Float	Sector
MOMO	28.96	1,208,247	2.35	8.8	113.45M	1.07		Management of Companies and Enterprise
DISH	64.25	386,878	3.02	4.9	201.27M	1.08	7.80	Information
FRC	95.65	102,409	-1.31	-1.4	153.09M	1.44		Finance and Insurance
DKS	50.45	455,668	-2.16	-4.1	87.89M	1.63	7.73	Retail Trade
SNAP	22.53	1,625,320	-1.24	-5.2	775.61M	4.72		Information

Pre-Market Movers up or down $1: 9:00:00 - 9:04:59 3/07/2017

Figure 10.1: My watchlist at 6 a.m. (9 a.m. New York time) on
March 7, 2017 - DKS is on my watchlist.

Consider the different ways the stocks you have
picked might trade and develop a series of **if-then**
scenarios such as I've marked in Figure 10.2 below:

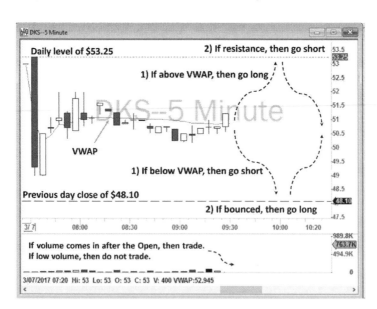

Figure 10.2: Pre-market 5-minute chart of DKS on March 7, 2017
with my if-then statements noted. Market will open at 9:30 a.m.
New York time.

If the price cannot push higher than VWAP in the first fifteen minutes of the market Open, **then** I will go short until the previous day close of $48.10.

If the price does sell off to the previous day close of $48.10, **then** I will go long and ride the reversal to VWAP.

If the price pushes over VWAP with high volume, **then** I will go long and ride the momentum to sell at the next resistance level of $53.25.

If the price breaks over the daily level of $53.25, **then** I will go long again until the daily level of $55.50 (which is not shown in the above Figure 10.2).

On the other hand, **if** the price goes to $53.25, and that level acts as a strong resistance, **then** I will go short with the stock until it goes back down to VWAP.

You can write down your statements at the beginning of your trading career to make sure you stick to them, but after a few months of simulated trading you will learn how to quickly develop and review these statements in your mind. You may find that with time, some notes are all you will need. That is one of the most important outcomes of trading in a simulator: to practice and master if-then scenarios for your strategies and to process that information quickly. That is why at least three months of live simulated trading is essential as you begin your day trading career. As intraday traders, we develop theories daily.

In case you are wondering about DKS in the above example, it actually opened weak (below VWAP) and it was a good short trade toward the previous day close of $48.10 as you can see in Figure 10.3 below. I then caught a smaller bounce from the previous day close to VWAP with a long position.

Figure 10.3: 5-minute chart of DKS on March 7, 2017 and my profit for that day (I also traded MEET, MOMO and MYL but they are not shown here and are not relevant to this example).

Determination and Hard Work

Hard work in day trading is different from what you might originally assume. A trader should not work 100 hours a week like investment bankers or corporate attorneys or other highly paid professionals do because, for us day traders, there are no end of the year bonuses. More than anything else, day trading is perhaps most similar to being a professional athlete because it is judged by one's daily performance. Having said that, day traders should work hard, consistently and productively, each and every day. Watching your trading screens intently and gathering important market information is how we define hard work in day trading. You must ask the following questions constantly and at a rapid pace for several hours every day:

- Who is in control of the price: the buyers or the sellers?
- What technical levels are most important?
- Is this stock stronger or weaker than the market?
- Where is most of the volume being traded? At VWAP? Or the first five minutes? Or near moving averages?
- How much volume at a price causes the stock to move up or down?
- What is the bid–ask spread? Is it tradeable?
- How quickly does the stock move? Is it being traded smoothly or is it choppy, jumping up and down with every trade?

- Is the stock trading in a particular pattern on a 5-minute chart? How is the stock being traded on a 1-minute chart?

These are some of the questions that I ask myself and then answer before trading a stock. All of this information should be gathered before you make any trade. This is what we mean by hard work. As you can see, day trading is an intense intellectual pursuit which requires hard work. Remember Rule 2?

It is essential to develop the routine of showing up every day to trade, whether it is in your real account or in a simulator. Searching for support and resistance levels each day, including before the market opens, will benefit your trading in the long run. Turning off the PC early after a few bad trades is a strategy that should be reserved for the rare occasions when it is absolutely essential to give your brain a break. Usually, spending some time in a simulator after some losses will clear your mind sufficiently. Novice traders using a simulator should keep on trading and practicing until the Close. After all, trading in the simulator is not nearly as stressful as real trading with real money. Using a simulator with no commission and no P&L is still no excuse for overtrading. At all times the focus must be on sound strategies with excellent risk/reward opportunities.

I am often asked, "*In your first months of trading, did you ever feel like you couldn't do it?*" The answer is "*Yes, and often!*" I still, at least once a month, get really frustrated after a few bad losses and consider quitting day trading. Frequently in my trading career I have wanted to quit, and at times I have actually believed the myth that day trading is impossible. But I did not quit. I really wanted to be a successful trader and to have the lifestyle and the freedom that come with it. So I paid the price for my mistakes, focused on my education, and eventually survived the very difficult learning curve of trading.

Patience

Becoming a consistently profitable trader requires hard work, extensive preparation, and considerable patience.

Successful trades usually look easy after they're done, but actually finding them is far from easy and requires more patience and hard work than you might imagine if you have not day traded before.

You need to watch, watch some more, and then keep watching. If a stock you're watching isn't offering excellent risk/reward opportunities, it's time to move on. Check out other stocks on your watchlist, and then monitor them closely. Consistently profitable traders often spend their trading days searching and watching for excellent risk/reward opportunities.

Successful traders are patient and resist the temptation to be involved in every move. Traders need to wait for opportunities where they feel comfortable and confident. It is not enough just to buy a strong stock, or sell short a weak one. Entry price is also very important.

You have to open your positions at a price that offers the best risk/reward opportunity and not trade a strong stock that has moved away from a good risk/reward entry. That, as I described earlier, is called *chasing the stock*.

For example, if a stock is trading near a support and then breaks out downward, and you see a short selling opportunity but miss it, well, that is your first mistake. But if, out of frustration, you sell short that same stock well below that level, you have chased it. Now you have made a bigger mistake. Chasing stocks is a deadly and unforgivable sin in day trading. Missing the opportunity will not lose you any money (just an opportunity cost), but chasing the stock will. Do not let one mistake cause you to lose money with another one.

Discipline

Success in trading comes with skill development and self-discipline. Trading principles are easy, and day trading strategies are very simple. I have a Ph.D. in chemical engineering and I have worked as a research scientist at a world-class facility. I have published numerous scholarly publications in high impact and respected scientific journals on my nanotechnology and complicated molecular level research. Believe me, I had to study and understand extremely more difficult concepts, so I can assure you that day trading, in theory at least, is easy.

What makes day trading, or any type of trading for that matter, difficult is the discipline and self-control that you need. You have no chance to make money as a trader without discipline, no matter your style, the time you commit to trading, the country you live in, or the market you are trading in.

As I wrote in Chapter 3, novice traders who fail to make money in the markets will sometimes try to improve themselves by learning more about how the markets work, studying new strategies, adopting additional technical indicators, following new traders, and joining other chatrooms. What they don't realize is that the main cause of their failure is often not their lack of technical knowledge but their lack of self-discipline, their impulsive decisions, and their sloppy risk and money management.

Professional institutional traders often perform significantly better than private retail traders. Most private traders are university-educated, literate people. They are often business owners or professionals. In contrast, typical institutional traders are loud twenty-something-year-old cowboys who used to play rugby in college and haven't read a book in years. Why do these "youngsters" outperform private traders year after year? It's not because they are younger or sharper or faster. And it's not because of their training or platforms, because most retail traders have almost the same gear as they do. The answer is the strictly enforced discipline of trading firms.

Some successful institutional traders go out on their own after asking themselves, *"Why am I sharing my profits with the firm when I know how to trade and*

could be keeping all of the profits for myself?" Most of them
end up losing money as private traders. Even though they
work with the same software and platforms, trade the
same systems, and stay in touch with their contacts,
they still fail. After a few months, most of them are
back at a recruiting office, looking for a trading job.
Why could those traders make money for their firms,
but not for themselves?

The answer is self-discipline.

When institutional traders quit their firm, they leave
behind their manager and all of the strictly enforced risk
control rules. A trader who violates risk limits is fired
immediately. Traders who leave institutions may know
how to trade, but their discipline is often external, not
internal. They quickly lose money without their managers
because they have developed no self-discipline.

We private retail traders can break any rule and
change our plan in the middle of a trade. We can average
down to a losing position, we can constantly break the
rules, and no one will notice. Managers in trading firms
though are quick to get rid of impulsive people who break
any trading rule for a second time. This creates a serious
discipline for institutional traders. Strict external discipline saves institutional traders from heavy losses and
deadly sins (such as the averaging down of a losing position), which quite often will destroy many private
accounts.

Discipline means you execute your plan and honor
your stop loss as you set it out, without altering it in the

middle of a trade. Discipline is executing your detailed plan every single time. If your plan is to buy a stock at VWAP and your stop loss is if it fails to hold VWAP, then you must accept the loss immediately and get out of the trade if the stock fails to hold VWAP.

Do not be stubborn about your decision if you are wrong. The market does not reward stubbornness. The market is not interested in how you wish stocks would trade. Traders must adapt to the market and do what the market demands. And that is the way day trading works and that is how it will always work.

There are going to be many days when you follow your plan, like in the above example, and then the stock will go back up and trade above VWAP after you were stopped out. In fact, there will be many times such as this in your trading career. But consider these two points: (1) Do not judge your trading strategy based upon one trade. Executing your plan, and being disciplined, will lead to long-term success. Many times your plan will be fine and solid but a hedge fund manager out of nowhere will decide to liquidate a position in a stock that you are trading, the price will drop suddenly, and you will get stopped out. You did not do anything wrong; it is the nature of the market that is unpredictable. At times, the uncertainty of the market will leave you in the red. (2) A professional trader accepts the loss and gets out of the trade. You then re-evaluate and plan another if-then scenario. You can always get back into the stock. Commissions are cheap (for most of the brokers), and professionals often take several quick stabs at a trade before it will start running in their favor.

Trading teaches you a great deal about yourself, about your mental weaknesses and about your strengths. This alone ensures that trading is a valuable life experience.

Mentorship and a Community of Traders

Dr. Brett Steenbarger, the author of great books such as *The Psychology of Trading* and *The Daily Trading Coach*, once wrote:

> "There is no question in my mind that, if I were to start trading full-time, knowing what I know now, I would either join a proprietary trading firm or would form my own "virtual trading group" by connecting online (and in real time) with a handful of like-minded traders."

You need to be part of a mastermind group that will add value to your trading career. To whom can you turn to ask trading questions? I encourage you to join a community of traders. Trading alone is very difficult and can be emotionally overwhelming. It is very helpful to join a community of traders so that you can ask them questions, talk to them, learn new methods and strategies, get some hints and alerts about the stock market, and make your own contributions. You will also notice that senior traders often lose money. It can be comforting to see that losing money is not limited to you, and that everyone, including experienced traders, has to take a loss. As I've said, it's all part of the process.

There are many chatrooms that you can join on the Internet. Some of them are free, but most of them charge a fee. In our chatroom, you can see my trading platform and stock screener in real time while I am trading and listen as I explain my strategy and thought process. You can also take your own trades while still being a part of our community.

You may also want to find a trading mentor. A good mentor can positively impact your trading career in so many different ways. Today, because of algorithmic programs and market volatility, it's much harder for new traders to survive the learning curve. A good mentor can make a huge difference. A mentor demonstrates the professionalism required to be successful. A mentor can lead you to discover the talent inside of you. Sometimes you just need to be told that you can do it. In online trading communities, experienced traders mentor new traders at times for a fee, but often for free. I personally mentor a few traders at a time, and of course, I myself did and still have a trading mentor. It is important to note though that mentorship does not work unless you are receptive, listen, and then put in the work necessary to adapt successfully.

You should find a mentor whose trading style fits with your personality. For example, if momentum trading is your favorite style, you're wasting your time talking to me. Although I trade them from time to time, my style is really only for those who have an intraday swing day mentality. I mostly focus on VWAP, Opening Range Breakouts and Support or Resistance trades.

Reflection and Review

By now, you may correctly think that trading psychology and self-discipline, a series of proven trading strategies, and excellent money and risk management are the essential elements of success in trading. But there is another element that ties all of your trading fundamentals together: record-keeping.

Keeping records of your trades will make you a better trader as it will enable you to learn from your past successes and failures. In fact, the most important and the most effective way to continuously improve as a trader is to keep a diary of your trades. There are many consistently profitable traders around the world, trading different markets with different methods, but they all have one thing in common: they keep excellent records of their trades. It is a very tedious and boring task; but it is also a very necessary task. Journal your trades daily. Make sure to include the following points in your trading journal:

1. Your physical well-being (lack of sleep, too much coffee, too much food the night before, etc.)

2. The time of the day you made the trade

3. The strategy you were anticipating

4. How you found the opportunity (from a scanner, a chatroom, etc.)

5. Quality of your entry (risk/reward)

6. Sizing/management of your trade (scaling in and out as planned)

7. Execution of exits (following profit targets or stop losses)

Using either *Screenshot Captor* or *Lightshot* (both of which are free software), I personally take a screenshot from my screen and journal my trades. Please visit our website for ideas from some experienced traders on how they journal their trades. Many of them have shared their Excel spreadsheet or other tools they are using in our publicly available forum at https://forums.bearbulltraders.com. You do not have to follow any of our styles, but you should find what works best for you because, in order to be successful, you must journal your trades daily.

Mike Bellafiore, co-founder of SMB Capital (a proprietary trading firm in New York City), writes in his book, *One Good Trade*, that the professional traders at his firm video record all of their trades during the day. In their afternoon session, they sit around their conference room tables, enjoy a lunch catered by the firm, review their trades and groupthink about better ways to take your money. Trading is a full-contact sport, and anything less than your complete focus is disrespectful to the game and will certainly knock you out of that game. Profitable traders constantly evaluate their trading system and are continually making adjustments.

New traders often ask me how to improve after a series of losses and a period of struggling. I recommend to them that they review their journal and look more specifically at what precisely they are doing poorly at in their trading. I am doing poorly doesn't mean anything. You cannot improve if you don't have a proper record of your daily trades.

- Is it your stock selection?
- Is it your entry points?
- Is it your discipline or psychology?
- Is it your platform or clearing firm (broker)?
- What about other traders, is it a bad month for everyone or just for you?

One time a trader complained about her order execution speed. I remotely connected to her PC (using TeamViewer, a remote control/remote access software) and evaluated the CPU performance. I had to remove many unnecessary programs and apps from her PC, run a malware scanner and remove a variety of intrusive software, computer viruses, spyware, adware, scareware, and other malicious programs. I freed up a lot of the PC's memory and CPU capacity and her trading execution speed increased significantly. Your PC, just like your body and mind, needs to be kept clean, lean and fast, all of which have a direct effect on your trading platform and eventually your trading results.

I personally live video record all of my trades during the morning session (as I rarely make any trades Mid-day or at the Close). I believe traders, like athletes, should watch their trading videos. The best athletes and teams watch films of themselves to see what they're doing right and wrong, and how best to improve. I will review my tapes during Mid-day and make sure to note important observations on my entry, exit, price action, Level 2 signals and so on. I try to learn as much as possible from my trades. Sometimes I look for new algorithmic programs that I must be aware of. I search for areas where I could have added more size. This is one of my trading weaknesses. I also do a poor job of holding for a longer time the stocks that are going in my favor. I therefore consider trades that I could have held longer. I make sure to find spots where I was too aggressive. I look for times where I took a trade even though it did not offer a good risk/reward opportunity. I review my position sizing and why and where I added more. That is *How to Day Trade for a Living.* There is no other way to get better. There are no excuses in trading.

Watching trading videos also shows me how easy trading is when there are no emotions attached to a trade. When I review my work, I am not invested in a trade in real time with real money. Trading live, the market seems fast and unpredictable. When you watch back your trading video, you see that the market is actually very slow. There are times when I see the pattern in a stock by watching my video and recognize how I traded the stock backward, and that is embarrassing for someone of my experience.

I later review my videos over the weekend to create educational series to use in teaching day trading. Over the weekend, after I celebrate the winning week on Friday night with my friends and family, I lock myself into my home office and cut tape after tape to develop and update my training programs.

Watching your videos is an exercise that can benefit all traders no matter their experience. New traders need to watch the markets trade. Watching your videos increases your trading experience and confidence and significantly shortens your learning curve. But I agree, it takes time and it is indeed boring.

DO NOT BE A GAMBLER. BE A TRADER.

On Thursday, April 23, 2020, at around 4:15 pm ET, my phone rang and I saw a California number on it. I picked up the phone, thinking that maybe one of my family members who lives in the state was calling me. No, it was the friend of a friend. My friend, who lives in L.A., had introduced us a few nights earlier because this person wanted to get some trade ideas from me. He had an account of around $400,000 USD and he'd been entering and exiting positions without much of a plan. He was doing some day trading, he was doing some swing trading, he was doing a little of this and a little of that. And all without a plan. Yikes!

In our first chat, I was terrified by what he told me and how uninformed he was. He showed a pure gambler's mentality with absolutely no trade plan or risk management in place. The platform of his broker, Ally Invest, is not a direct-access one, and his orders had been getting filled with a time delay and at random prices. I was concerned, but he did not seem to mind my concerns at all. He was primarily looking for the next big idea that would make him rich, and he was incorrectly thinking that I might have some hot bit of insider information on a stock!

As I answered his call, he anxiously asked me what I thought about Intel Corporation (ticker: INTC). I looked at my platform, and saw that INTC had reported earnings and was down, trading at $57, -7% after hours. He was desperate, he was long, and with the use of margin he was holding a position worth $1.2M. He asked me, *"Intel is a good company, yes? It will come back up, yes? I am down $80,000, what should I do?"* I asked him what his original game plan was. He advised me that he did not have one. He thought Intel must be a good company so he decided to gamble on it. That was his plan!

I did not know what to tell him. Everything looked bearish on INTC's chart. The market was weak. We were in a global pandemic bear market. I told him that I really did not know what was best for him to do. It was not that I did not want to help him, I honestly did not know how to help him get out of the mess. If I had told him to accept the $80,000 loss and come out post market, what if the next day the stock bounced? What if I had told him *"no"*, wait on it, and then INTC traded even lower the next day? I honestly didn't have any advice for him.

The next day, INTC's stock recovered some of those after-hours losses. I messaged him to ask how he was doing. He said that his broker liquidated half of his position, and he came out of the trade with a $20,000 loss. He blamed the broker! He did not realize that the problem was not the broker but his own mindless, "strategy-less" gamble.

These stories are quite common. I hear them all of the time, and every month at least three or four emails that I receive are about these types of situations. A good example is from March 27, 2020. A person in Singapore emailed me that day. She was short the market and had got stuck in a rally that had occurred around March 26, 2020. She was down $20,000 on a $57,000 account. She was planning to add another $50,000 to double her position. She had no idea what she was doing, and she was trading from a mobile app.

I did not know what to tell her about her specific predicament but there is one very important rule I always share: do not average down; do not send good money after bad.

Trading attracts people who are the most prone to gambling. That is why it has such a high failure rate. It is not that the game is rigged against you (which to be fair, perhaps there is some truth to that, just a bit though). Trading has such a high failure rate quite simply because people who should not trade, trade.

Gamblers are doomed to lose in the stock market; nothing will save them in this game. Aside from war, I sincerely believe that trading is the most dangerous human endeavor possible. It truly is the most self-destructive activity you will ever see.

To end this section on a much more positive note, being part of an accountability group is a great way to keep yourself accountable and in line. Even if you are not part of an online community, make sure to have a mastermind group of people supporting you. Talk with your mentors and be open to their ideas, especially when you find yourself doing things in the market that you know you shouldn't be. As I wrote in Chapter 9, self-confidence is great, but self-awareness is more important.

PLAN YOUR TRADING BUSINESS

An often neglected or disregarded aspect of trading is the development of a proper *"business plan"*. Do not get this confused though with your daily trading plan (the if-then statements you develop each trading day) and what I will soon be describing as your trading framework. Every business needs a business plan. In order to attract financing or investors, businesses ranging in size from major international corporations to local mom-and-pop shops have had to develop business plans illustrating how they will be successful in their respective ventures. Trading is a serious business and it is in no way a get-rich-quick scheme, so just like any other business, you also should develop a trading business plan that clearly outlines how you will be successful in your own venture. A trading business plan can be broken down into three main areas: the trading framework (summarized in the next paragraph), activities designed to improve upon or support the trading framework, and the tasks required to be attended to outside of actual trading.

Your trading framework is the core of your trading business plan. It is what you will execute during market hours. It consists of your money and risk management principles, the strategies and patterns you trade, your trade management rules, and an outline of how you are accountable for any actions which deviate from your framework. The money and risk management component consists of understanding and knowing what I will call your "numbers" so that you can apply the right amount of risk toward a trade in order to receive an acceptable return. You need to determine such things as what percentage of your account you will risk per trade (or a maximum dollar value you will risk per trade), when you will scale up, how much money you are aiming to make each day, the maximum amount of money you are prepared to lose each day, and the maximum number of trades per day you want to take. This part of your trading framework is extremely important because if your "numbers" are miscalculated, your winners could be smaller than your losers, and that will result in a declining net equity curve (your profit and loss after deducting your broker's commissions and fees).

In the next part of your trading framework, you want to determine what your strategies as well as your trade management rules are. This is where you define what type of stocks and price range you are good at trading as well as what part of the trading day (the hours) you do best in. This in most respects is how you will build your watchlist each morning. (Do notice that I wrote "good at trading", as this is very different from what you may like to trade or want to trade.) One of the most difficult aspects of trading is managing the trade once you are in the midst of it. Common questions new traders ask members of our community include when should a first partial be taken, what percentage of the position should the first partial be, should stop loss be moved to break-even after taking a partial, and should either mental or hard stops be used. (If you do not recall what the term "partial" means, an excellent example from my colleague John Hiltz is included in the commentary accompanying Figure 9.2 in the last chapter.). The truth is that the answers to these sort of questions can only be provided by the trader themself as each trader's winning percentage of trades, stop distance, account size, and trading goals are different.

The last component of your trading framework is accountability. This is vital because, as a retail trader, you are often trading alone and you can fairly easily rationalize to yourself, justify, or make excuses for your actions. This is where having a trading buddy or mentor is very important, as they can hold you accountable to your trading framework when you violate it or break one of your trading rules. In addition, since your buddy or mentor is also a trader, they understand what you are going though and they can encourage you when you feel everything is lost (and trust me, those days will come). So, you may be wondering, how are you expected to come up with all of the numbers and statistics that should be recorded in your trading framework. While your trading framework is targeted at what you should be doing during market hours (9:30 a.m. to 4 p.m. ET), there are many specific activities you can do either before 9:30 a.m. ET or after 4 p.m. ET which will serve to improve your trading, and ultimately your trading framework.

Of all the activities you should be doing outside of market hours, journaling each of your trades is by far the most important. This is because it allows you the ability to monitor your progress and analyze which strategies are working. It also assists you in determining what areas you need to improve in. Your journal does not have to be long and complicated, and it can include mostly images.

What follows is a brief description of other supportive activities that will help to improve your trading framework. Do remember that each of these activities should be utilized in a way that permits you to develop a trading framework consistent with your personal abilities. One size definitely does not fit all.

Education Plan – Creating an education plan gives you a visual picture of what you will need to accomplish over a period of time and provides you with an idea of how long it will take you to meet your trading goals. It is important to know what is required as you progress through the learning curve. Having a well-thought-out education plan allows you to manage expectations throughout your journey.

Goals – Setting daily, weekly, monthly, quarterly, and yearly goals (and making progress on them) assists in maintaining a positive emotional attitude toward the ups and downs of learning to day trade. You want to ensure you have SMART (specific, measurable, attainable, relevant, time–based) goals.

Trading Rules – Rules are meant to be developed outside of market hours when you have a clear head and are not under pressure or distress. These rules are made to safeguard you when your mind is clouded and your emotions are at their peak. Although it may not seem like it during market hours, rules are your friend and they will protect you from yourself.

Mission Statement – This is a key tool that can be as important as the actual trading business plan it is a part of. Your mission statement captures the essence of your trading goals and the philosophies which support them. Equally important, your mission statement signals what your business is all about to yourself. Answering these questions will help you create a verbal picture of your business plan:

- Who is going to be your support network?
- What are your long–term goals?
- When are you available to trade?
- Who are you going to learn from?
- Why do you want to day trade?
- What capital is available to you?

The last part of your trading business plan is all of the items that take up time but do not directly affect the performance of your trading framework. In business, this would be considered the administrative side of the house, the things that have to be done in order to successfully operate the business.

Action Plan – This explains how you will operate and manage your trading business. It addresses the back-office activities that do not relate directly to your trading framework. Some of these activities include setting up your trading station, deciding on a community of traders to join, retaining a tax planner, developing your daily routine, etc.

Vision – This is one part your dream for the trading business and another part the path you are laying out for your trading business in the future. The vision statement is generally written with long-term perspective in mind. The statement should be well-written and compacted into one or two descriptive and passionate sentences about your desires for pursuing trading as a career.

Trading Business Timeline – A timeline should be used to manage the progression from your initial decision to start trading, to your trading education and simulator training program, to meeting your end goal of live trading. This timeline is essential to tracking the various tasks that need to be completed in each step of your journey. It is continually updated as progress is made to ensure your trading business does not become stagnant. It uses benchmarks to evaluate progress and keep the focus on how much has been accomplished.

Tools and Services – This is the area of your business plan where you will consider such matters as what Internet service provider to have, who will be your broker, what trading platform you will use, whether you will purchase scanners (and if so, from which company), and which community of traders you would like to be a part of. With regard to this last point, it is important that the trading community you join fits with your own trading style.

As stated previously, it is very easy to confuse the trading business plan with your trading framework. Do remember that your trading framework is how you will execute your trades during market hours, and it is just one part of your overall trading business plan. Your business plan encompasses everything involved with trading and is designed to assist you through the learning curve to become a successful trader.

An excellent webinar on how to develop your business plan from the perspective of a new trader was hosted by one of our experienced traders and coaches, Mike Baehr, who served 23 years as a member of the U.S. Marine Corps. It is available for viewing by the public here:

www.bearbulltraders.com/businessplan

I hope you enjoy the webinar and use the accompanying notes provided in the link to begin the process of developing your own trading business plan.

JOURNALING YOUR TRADES

As mentioned earlier, I used to write a blog post about my trades and document my thoughts for each and every trade in the Bear Bull Traders forums (*https://forums.bearbulltraders.com*). Commencing in the summer of 2016, I would then upload a recap summary to YouTube. Although I have somewhat changed my practice, members of our community continue to make regular contributions to our YouTube channel. This blog helped me to maintain a good record of all of my trades, and also helped the members of our trading community (and others of course) to learn more by reading about my experiences.

Early in 2020, I decided to stop journaling as regularly as I used to in YouTube and writing my blog manually and instead use online services. The majority of traders in our community are also now using online services such as Tradervue (*www.tradervue.com*) or Chartlog (*www.Chartlog.com*). These online programs connect to your trading platform and extract all of the relevant information for you automatically and provide you with vital information about your trading. Regardless if you are trading live or practicing in a simulator, journaling must be a part of your trading journey. The end result and analysis derived from these online programs is amazing (as is the information you can glean from a more traditional journaling approach). This information can include:

- Your biggest loss
- Your biggest win
- Your ratio of losers to winners
- The commissions you are paying out
- The best time of the day for your trading
- The worst time of the day for your trading
- The average hold time for your trades

Learning the "facts" about your trading that I have listed above, and this is only a partial list, is extremely important in developing your trading skills.

As I noted earlier, I use a free software called *Screenshot Captor* (or sometimes *Lightshot*) to take a screenshot from my platform in real time right after I end a trade. I can see my entries and exits on the chart and I just add my thought process to the journal along with anything else I think I should note from that trading day. I often use these screenshots or videos for educational purposes such as our community's weekly Wednesday workshops as well as for updating our live and recorded course materials.

Often traders in our community will discuss my trades with me and I will learn something from them. You can never be too experienced to learn from someone else! Sometimes I edit videos of my daily trades and post them on my YouTube channel. I keep a library of all of my trading videos and cut and edit them for a trading course that I am currently preparing.

TRADING AND CLIMBING

I am often asked by both new traders and hopeful traders how they can become successful in the stock markets. My response almost always compares trading to climbing. I spent much of my youth in the mountains and I still thoroughly enjoy being able to explore the higher altitudes of our world. As I alluded to in the first chapter, mountains fascinate me! I began alpine climbing in college and then, later, I developed a passion for the financial markets. Mountaineering and trading are risky endeavors but, at the same time, they are incredibly rewarding, and I've found in my experiences that they appeal to a particular group of people. I want to share in what follows three traits inherent in both successful alpinists and successful traders.

1. They are process-oriented.

Achievement in any venture comes from being process-oriented, not result-oriented. Bernadette McDonald, a Canadian author and mountain climber, writes in *Freedom Climbers*, "*To be a climber, one has to accept that gratification is rarely immediate.*" You will invest time and energy and resources to climb a peak, only to have to turn back because of the wind, the weather or the unexpected. If the only aspect of the climb you look forward to is standing on the summit and taking photographs, you will soon find climbing to be the most boring of pursuits. For me, the beauty of climbing is found in every step, every move, every turn, and every new glimpse of scenery. It is the same with trading. New traders will usually lose money at the beginning, and some will become frustrated, curse the markets, and leave. Those who come to trading with the goal of learning the process of how to trade, and are not caught up in their first months with their P&L, are the ones who most likely will make it. This is true in every undertaking of life. Mark Zuckerberg, on the ten-year anniversary of Facebook in 2014, shared a post that hits me even to this day:

> *"People often ask if I always knew that Facebook would become what it is today. No way."*

Mark Zuckerberg believed that there was a better way for students to connect with each other and so, along with a few friends in college, he just "did it". He never dreamed that one day Facebook would be one of the largest companies in the world or that he would become one of the richest people on the planet. He instead concentrated on the process.

> *"When I reflect on the last 10 years, one question I ask myself is: why were we the ones to build this? We were just students. We had way fewer resources than big companies. If they had focused on this problem, they could have done it.*

> *"The only answer I can think of is: we just cared more. While some doubted that connecting the world was actually important, we were building.*

While others doubted that this would be sustain-
able, you [our users] were forming lasting
connections."

2. They take risks, but they also manage that risk.

In mountaineering, you literally take a risk with every single step. But that does not stop climbers from doing what they love to do. They manage and minimize their risk as much as possible. They define rules and build protocols on how to protect themselves so they can do what they are passionate about. There is **no gain without risk**. This is the same for traders. Since every trade puts your money in jeopardy, you need to learn to manage your risk. How? You in part set stop losses, you ensure you're diversified and that not all of your money is tied up in one losing trade, and you must always have a well-thought-out trading plan. Those who trade "big" and try to make a so-called home run trade, without any plan, are like those who jump out of a plane without a parachute. They are gamblers at best.

3. They have passion.

You can never truly become a climber if you do not have a passion for mountains. Besides all of the risks, it is common to experience moments of extreme temperatures, exhaustion, frostbite and such. But we climbers are a passionate people and we thrive on these things. There is truth in the saying, it does not have to be fun in order to be fun. Anatoli Boukreev, the late mountaineering legend, said, *"Mountains are not Stadiums where I satisfy my ambition to achieve, they are the cathedrals where I practice my religion."* The same is true with trading. If you sincerely want to become a trader, you must embrace every aspect of it including its losses, its unpleasant moments, and its complexity. That is the same for any endeavor in life. Accomplished entrepreneurs, politicians, professionals, virtually anyone who has found success in their field, are passionate about what they do. These are the people who we remember. As Stephen King wrote in *Pet Sematary*, *"There is **no gain** without risk, perhaps **no risk without love!**"*

My advice: choose to become what you love, not what you need or what you should be. Be brave enough to take the necessary controlled risks to get there. Be patient. Focus on the process. Learn from your experiences.

FINAL WORDS

You need to practice. You need experience deciphering market patterns and you need to be constantly tweaking your **if-then** statements for your trading setups. Every day is a new game and a new puzzle to solve. As I've mentioned, many people believe that trading can be reduced to a few rules that they can follow every morning. Always do this or always do that. In reality, trading isn't about "always" at all; it is about each situation and each trade. You must learn how to think in day trading, and this is no easy task.

You must start recognizing patterns and developing trading strategies. And these strategies must be practiced in real time and under stress. Trading in simulators can help and is absolutely necessary, but there is no substitute for trading with your real hard-earned cash where your results actually matter.

When you begin as a trader, you most likely will be horrible. Many times at the beginning of my career I came to the conclusion that day trading was not for me. As I wrote earlier in this chapter, even now that I am an experienced and profitable trader, there is at least one day almost every month that I wonder if I can trade in this market any longer. Of course, this feeling of disappointment goes away faster these days, usually after the next good trade. But for you, because you have not seen success yet, surviving the learning curve is very difficult. I know that. However, this does not mean you should lose a lot of money when you trade live at the beginning. Trading in the simulators will help to prepare you for real trading with real money.

If you are signing up for a training course or mentorship program, you should very carefully read about their plan. A good training program will only encourage you to trade the easiest setups when you start. For example, for the first month live, I believe new traders should only trade Opening Range Breakouts or ABCD Patterns. The next month, new traders can shift to reversal trades exclusively.

The following month, you could focus on Moving Average Trend trades. After that, you can focus on Bull Flag

Momentum plays (momentum trades are the hardest to execute and manage risk in). To me, it is important for a beginner trader to focus in on studying only one strategy at a time.

New traders often expect to make money immediately, and when they don't, they let this affect their work. When they do not see the results that they expected, they start to focus on the wrong things. Some increase their share size, hoping that this will help them make more money. Many will not prepare as hard as they should because they become discouraged. They ask themselves, *"What is the point of preparing hard if I cannot make money?"* They start to take chances that a successful and experienced trader would never take. They become gamblers. This leads to even more significant losses and only adds to their problems.

While there is no one right way to make money trading, there is only one right way to begin your trading career. When you first begin, you must focus on the process of trading, not on how to make money for a living. You must allow at least six to eight months before you will become consistently profitable. If you are not willing or are unable to do this, then you should find another career. Some are not able to either financially or psychologically commit this much time to this pursuit. If this is the case, then again, you should find another profession.

I cannot emphasize enough to you how unimportant the results are from your first six months of trading.

They do not matter. During these first months, you are building the foundation for a lifetime career. Do you think in year ten that your results in your first six months will be significant?

Becoming a consistently profitable trader could turn out to be the hardest thing you will ever do. The intensive training process that you must follow takes six to eight months and requires much hard work. It will enable you to find out how good you can be, but to do that you must genuinely believe that you will become great.

All of us have mental weaknesses that we must conquer. If we stubbornly insist on trying to prove to the market that we are right, we will pay a high price. Some traders cannot accept a loss and exit stocks that trade against them. Some take small profits prematurely instead of waiting for the final profit target. Some are afraid to make a decision to enter a trade with an excellent risk/reward that they recognize. The only way to get better is to work on your weaknesses.

There is no shame in failing as a trader. The real shame is in not pursuing your dreams. If you are passionate about trading and never try it, then you will live your life wondering what might have been. Life is too short not to embrace new challenges. To take on any challenge in life and fail is very honorable. If you have the courage to take a chance and day trade, that decision will serve you well later in life. The next career change or challenge you accept might be the one that works out for you, and what you learn about yourself in the process will be invaluable.

At the end of this book, I have summarized my ten rules of day trading. I have printed this page and posted it next to my trading station. I reread it often. I encourage you to do the same. I know these rules will help you to keep on track and to be successful.

Last but not least, if you enjoyed reading this book and found it useful, I would very much appreciate your taking a few minutes to write a review on the Amazon website. The success of a book like this is based on honest reviews, and I will consider your comments in making revisions. If you have any feedback, feel free to send me an email. Your review on Amazon will help other people to make informed decisions about my book. I purposely priced it low so more people would be able to purchase it and use it. Teaching people and helping them to start a new career fulfills something inside of me that motivates me every day, so I hope you can help me to accomplish this mission of promoting and encouraging ongoing learning.

If you're ever interested in connecting with me, check out our website at *www.BearBullTraders.com* or send me an email at *andrew@BearBullTraders.com*. I'd be happy to have a chat with you. When you review our website, you will find several free resources available for members of the public. I hope you will find them helpful in your own trading journey.

Thank you, and happy trading!

ANDREW'S 10 RULES OF DAY TRADING

RULE 1: Day trading is not a strategy to get rich quickly.

RULE 2: Day trading is not easy. It is a serious business, and you should treat it as such.

RULE 3: Day traders do not hold positions overnight. If necessary, you must sell with a loss to make sure you do not hold onto any stock overnight.

RULE 4: Always ask, "Is this stock moving because the overall market is moving, or is it moving because it has a unique fundamental catalyst?"

RULE 5: Success in day trading comes from risk management - finding low-risk entries with a high potential reward. The minimum win:lose ratio for me is 2:1.

RULE 6: Your broker will buy and sell stocks for you at the Exchange. Your only job as a day trader is to manage risk. You cannot be a successful day trader without excellent risk management skills, even if you are the master of many effective strategies.

RULE 7: Retail traders trade only Stocks in Play, high relative volume stocks that have fundamental catalysts and are being traded regardless of the overall market.

RULE 8: Experienced traders are like guerrilla soldiers. They jump out at just the right time, take their profit, and get out.

RULE 9: Hollow candlesticks, where the close is greater than the open, indicate buying pressure. Filled candlesticks, where the close is less than the open, indicate selling pressure.

RULE 10: Profitable trading does not involve emotion. If you are an emotional trader, you will lose your money.

GLOSSARY

ALPHA STOCK: a Stock in Play, a stock that is moving independently of both the overall market and its sector, the market is not able to control it, these are the stocks day traders look for.

ASK: the price sellers are demanding in order to sell their stock, it's always higher than the bid price.

AVERAGE DAILY VOLUME: the average number of shares traded each day in a particular stock, I don't trade stocks with an average daily volume of less than 500,000 shares, as a day trader you need sufficient liquidity to be able to get in and out of the stock without difficulty.

AVERAGE RELATIVE VOLUME: how much of the stock is trading compared to its normal volume, I don't trade in stocks with an average relative volume of less than 1.5, which means the stock is trading at least 1.5 times its normal daily volume.

AVERAGE TRUE RANGE/ATR: how large of a range in price a particular stock has on average each day, I look for an ATR of at least 50 cents, which means the price of the stock will move at least 50 cents most days.

AVERAGING DOWN: adding more shares to your losing position in order to lower the average cost of your position, with the hope of selling it at break-even in the next rally in your favor, as a day trader, don't do it, do not average down, ever, a full explanation is provided in this book, to be a successful day trader you must avoid the urge to average down.

BEAR: a seller or short seller of stock, if you hear the market is bear it means the entire stock market is losing value because the sellers or short sellers are selling their stocks, in other words, the sellers are in control.

BEARISH CANDLESTICK: a candlestick with a big filled body demonstrating that the open was at a high and the close was at a low, it tells you that the sellers are in control of the price and it is not a good time to buy, Figure 6.1 includes an image of a bearish candlestick.

BID: the price people are willing to pay to purchase a stock at a particular time, it's always lower than the ask price.

BID-ASK SPREAD: the difference between what people are willing to pay to purchase a particular stock and what other people are demanding in order to sell that stock at any given moment, it can change throughout the trading day.

"BLACK BOX": the top secret hidden computer programs, formulas and systems that large Wall Street firms use to manipulate the stock market.

BROKER: the company who buys and sells stocks for you at the Exchange, because day trading requires fast order execution, you really must use what is called a direct-access broker, conventional online brokers (also known as full-service brokers) provide considerably more investment advice, tax tips, retirement planning and such, but generally do not offer the necessary fast order execution, and are therefore more suited for investors and retail swing traders.

BULL: a buyer of stock, if you hear the market is bull it means the entire stock market is gaining value because the buyers are purchasing stocks, in other words, the buyers are in control.

BULL FLAG: a type of candlestick pattern that resembles a flag on a pole, you will see several large candles going up (like a pole) and a series of small candles moving sideways (like a flag), which day traders call consolidating, you will usually miss the first Bull Flag but your scanner will alert you to it and you can then be ready for the second Bull Flag, you can see an example of a Bull Flag formation in Figure 7.5.

BULLISH CANDLESTICK: a candlestick with a large body toward the upside, it tells you that the buyers are in control of the price and will likely keep pushing the price up, Figure 6.1 includes an image of a bullish candlestick.

BUYING LONG: buying a stock in the hope that its price will go higher.

BUYING POWER: the capital (money) in your account with your broker plus the leverage they provide you, for example, if your broker gives you a leverage of 4:1 and you have $25,000 in your account, you can actually trade up to $100,000.

CANDLESTICK: a very common way to chart the price of stocks, it allows you to easily see the opening price, the highest price in a given time period, the lowest price in that time period and the closing price value for each time period you wish to display, some people prefer using other methods of charting, I quite like candlesticks because they are an easy-to-decipher picture of the price action, you can easily compare the relationship between the open and close as well as the high and the low price, you can see examples of bearish and bullish candlesticks in Figure 6.1.

CHASING THE STOCK: wise day traders never chase stocks, you chase a stock when you try to purchase shares while the price is increasing significantly, successful day traders aim to enter trades during the quiet times and take their profits during the wild times, when you see a stock surging up, you patiently wait for the consolidation period, patience truly is a virtue!

CHATROOM: a community of traders, many of which can be found on the Internet.

CHOPPY PRICE ACTION: stocks trading with very high frequency and small movements of price, day traders avoid stocks with choppy price action, they are being controlled by the institutional traders of Wall Street.

CLOSE: the last hour the stock market is open, 3 p.m. to 4 p.m. New York time, the daily closing prices tend to reflect the opinion of Wall Street traders on the value of stocks.

COMMISSION-FREE BROKER: a relatively new type of broker which does not charge a commission for each trade you make, they are not suitable for day trading as they generally do not provide the fast execution of trades that day traders need, with that said, they have revolutionized the trading industry by forcing established players to either abolish or significantly reduce their commissions.

Consolidation period: this happens when the traders who bought stocks at a lower price are selling and taking their profits while at the same time the price of the stock is not sharply decreasing because buyers are still entering into trades and the sellers are not yet in control of the price.

DAY TRADING: the serious business of trading stocks that are moving in a relatively predictable manner, all of your trading is done during one trading day, you do not hold any stocks overnight, any stocks you purchase during the day must be sold by the end of the trading day.

DOJI: an important candlestick pattern that comes in various shapes or forms but are all characterized by having either no body or a very small body, a Doji indicates indecision and means that a fight is underway between the buyers and the sellers, you can see examples of Doji candlesticks in Figure 6.8.

ENTRY POINT: when you recognize a pattern developing on your charts, your entry point is where you enter the trade.

EXCHANGE-TRADED FUND/ETF: an investment fund traded on the Exchange and composed of assets such as stocks or bonds.

EXIT POINT: as you plan your trade, you decide your entry point, where you will enter the trade, and where you will exit the trade, if you do not exit properly you will turn a winning trade into a losing trade, whatever you do, don't be stubborn, if a trade goes against you, exit gracefully and accept a loss, don't risk even more money just to prove a point, the markets can be unpredictable.

EXPONENTIAL MOVING AVERAGE/EMA: a form of moving average where more weight is given to the most currently available data, it accordingly reflects the latest fluctuations in the price of a stock more than the other moving averages do.

FLOAT: the number of shares in a particular company available for trading, for example, in June 2020, Apple Inc. had 4.33 billion shares available.

FOREX: the global Foreign Exchange Market where traders – but not day traders – trade currencies.

FUNDAMENTAL CATALYST: this is what you as a day trader are looking for, some positive or negative news associated with a stock such as an FDA approval or disapproval, a restructuring, a merger or an acquisition, something significant that will impact its price during the trading day.

FUTURES: Futures trading is when you trade a contract for an asset or a commodity (such as oil, lumber, wheat, currencies, interest rates) with a price set today but for the product to not be delivered and purchased until a future date, you can earn a profit if you can correctly predict the direction the price of a certain item will be at on a future date, day traders do not trade in Futures.

GAPPERS WATCHLIST: before the market opens, you can tell which stocks are gapping up or down in price, you then search for the fundamental catalysts that explain these price swings, and you build a list of stocks that you will monitor that day for specific day trading opportunities, the final version of your watchlist generally has only two, three or four stocks on it that you will be carefully monitoring when the market opens, also called simply your watchlist.

GUERRILLA TRADING: what day traders do, it's like guerrilla warfare, you wait for an opportunity to move in and out of the financial battlefield in a short period of time to generate quick profits while keeping your risk to a minimum.

HIGH FREQUENCY TRADING/HFT: the type of trading the computer programmers on Wall Street work away at, creating algorithms and secret formulas to try to manipulate the market, although HFT should be respected, there's no need for day traders to fear it.

HIGH RELATIVE VOLUME: what day traders look for in Stocks in Play, stocks that are trading at a volume above their average and above their sector, they are acting independently of their sector and the overall market.

HOTKEY: a virtual necessity for day traders, key commands that you program to automatically send instructions to your broker by touching a combination of keys on your keyboard, they eliminate the need for a mouse or any sort of manual entry, high-speed trading requires Hotkeys and you should practice using them in real time in a simulator before risking your real money, for your reference I've included as Figure 5.4 a listing of my own Hotkeys.

IF-THEN STATEMENT/SCENARIO: before the market opens and before you do an actual trade, you should create a series of if-then statements (or if-then scenarios) to guide you in your trade, for example, if the price does not go higher than ABC, then I will do DEF, Figure 10.2 is an example of some if-then statements/scenarios that I have marked on a chart.

ILLIQUID STOCK: a stock that does not have sufficient volume traded during the day, these stocks are hard to sell and buy without a significant slippage in price.

INDECISION CANDLESTICK: a type of candlestick that has similarly sized high wicks and low wicks that are usually larger than the body, they can also be called spinning tops or Dojis and they indicate that the buyers and sellers have equal power and are fighting between themselves, it's important to recognize an indecision candlestick because it may very well indicate a pending price change, you can see examples of indecision candlesticks in Figures 6.6 through 6.8.

INDICATOR: an indicator is a mathematical calculation based on a stock's price or volume or both, you do not want your charts too cluttered with too many different indicators, keep your charts clean so you can process the information quickly and make decisions very quickly, almost all of the indicators you choose to track will be automatically calculated and plotted by your trading platform, always remember that indicators indicate but do not dictate, Figure 5.2 is a screenshot of the type of chart I use with my indicators marked on it.

INSTITUTIONAL TRADER: the Wall Street investment banks, mutual and hedge fund companies and such, day traders stay away from the stocks that institutional traders are manipulating and dominating (I'll politely call that 'trading' too!).

INTRADAY: trading all within the same day, between 9:30 a.m. and 4 p.m. New York time.

INVESTING: although some people believe investing and trading are similar, investing is in fact very different from trading, investing is taking your money, placing it somewhere, and hoping to grow it in the short term or the long term.

LAGGING INDICATOR: these are indicators that provide you with information on the activity taking place on a stock *after* the trade happens.

LATE-MORNING: 10:30 a.m. to 12 p.m. New York time, the market is slower but there is still good volatility in the Stocks in Play, this is one of the easiest times of the day for new traders, there is less volume compared to the Open but also less unexpected volatility, a review of our new traders' trades indicates that they do the best during the Late-Morning session.

LEADING INDICATOR: a feature of Nasdaq Level 2, it provides you with information on the activity taking place on a stock *before* the trade happens.

LEVEL 2: successful day trading requires access to the real time Nasdaq TotalView Level 2 data feed, it provides you with the leading indicators and information on the activity taking place on a stock before the trade happens as well as important insight into a stock's price action, what type of traders are buying or selling the stock and where the stock is likely to head in the near term, Figure 5.1 is an image of a Level 2 quote.

LEVERAGE: the margin your broker provides you on the money in your account, most brokers provide a leverage of between 3:1 and 6:1, a leverage of 4:1, for example, means if you have $25,000 in your account, you have $100,000 of buying power available to trade with.

LIMIT ORDER: an instruction you give to your broker to buy or sell a specific stock at or better than a set price specified by you, there is a chance the limit order will never be filled if the price moves too quickly after you send your instructions.

LIQUIDITY: successful day traders need liquidity, there must be both a sufficient volume of stock being traded in a particular company and a sufficient number of orders being sent to the Exchanges for filling to ensure you can easily get in and out of a trade, you want plenty of buyers and plenty of sellers all eyeing the same stock.

LONG: an abbreviated form of "buying long", you buy stock in the hope that it will increase in price, to be "*long 100 shares AAPL*" for example is to have bought 100 shares of Apple Inc. in anticipation of their price increasing.

LOW FLOAT STOCK: a stock with a low supply of shares which means that a large demand for shares will easily move the stock's price, the stock's price is very volatile and can move fast, most low float stocks are under $10, day traders love low float stocks, they can also be called micro-cap stocks or small cap stocks.

MARGIN: the leverage your broker gives you to trade with, for example, if your leverage is 4:1 and you have $25,000 in your account, your margin to trade with is $100,000, margin is like a double-edged sword, it allows you to buy more but it also exposes you to more risk.

MARGIN CALL: a serious warning from your broker that you must avoid getting, your broker will issue you a margin call if you are using leverage and losing money, it means your loss is equal to the original amount of money in your account, you must either add more money to your account or your broker will freeze it.

MARKETABLE LIMIT ORDER: an instruction you give to your broker to immediately buy or sell a specific stock within a range of prices that you specify, I use marketable limit orders when day trading, I generally buy at "ask+5 cents" and I sell at "bid-5 cents".

MARKET CAP/MARKET CAPITALIZATION: a company's market cap is the total dollar value of its float (all of their shares available for trading on the stock market), for example, if a company's shares are worth $10 each and there are 3 million shares available for trading (a 3 million share float), that company's market cap is $30 million.

MARKET MAKER: a broker-dealer that offers shares for sale or purchase on the Exchange, the firm holds a certain number of shares of a particular stock in order to facilitate the trading of that stock at the Exchange.

MARKET ORDER: an instruction you give to your broker to immediately buy or sell a specific stock at whatever the current price is at that very moment, I'll emphasize the phrase "whatever the current price is", the price might be to your benefit, it very well might not be though if it has suddenly changed in the time since you gave your instructions to your broker.

MEDIUM FLOAT STOCK: a stock with a medium float of between 20 million and 500 million shares, I mostly look for medium float stocks in the range of $10 to $100 to trade, many of the strategies explained in this book work well with medium float stocks.

MEGA CAP STOCK: a stock with a huge supply of shares, for example, Apple Inc. had 4.33 billion shares available for trading in June 2020, their stock prices are generally not volatile because they require significant volume and money to be traded, day traders avoid these types of stocks.

MICRO-CAP STOCK: a stock with a low supply of shares which means that a large demand for shares will easily move the stock's price, the stock's price is very volatile and can move fast, most micro-cap stocks are under $10, day traders love micro-cap stocks, they can also be called low float stocks or small cap stocks.

MID-DAY: 12 p.m. to 3 p.m. New York time, the market is generally slow at this time with less volume and liquidity, it's the most dangerous time of the day to be trading.

MOVING AVERAGE/MA: a widely used indicator in trading that smooths the price of a stock by averaging its past prices, the two basic and most commonly used MAs are the Simple Moving Average (SMA), which is the simple average of a stock over a defined number of time periods, for example 1-minute, 5-minute, or daily charts, and the Exponential Moving Average (EMA), which gives more weight to more recent prices, the most common applications of MAs are to identify the trend direction and to determine support and resistance levels, I use 9 EMA, 20 EMA, 50 SMA and 200 SMA on all of my charts, your charting software will have most of the types of MAs already built into it.

NET EQUITY CURVE: your profit and loss after deducting your broker's commissions and fees.

OPEN: the first thirty to sixty minutes the stock market is open, from 9:30 a.m. up to 10:30 a.m. New York time.

OPENING RANGE: when the market opens, Stocks in Play will often experience what I call violent price action, heavy trading will impact the price of the stock and you should be able to determine what direction the price is heading toward and whether the buyers or sellers are winning, now that I am a more seasoned trader, I often trade a 1-minute Opening Range Breakout, until you do have that experience and confidence though, it is best to trade Opening Range Breakouts at a longer time frame where there is less volatility.

OPTIONS: a different type of trading, it's trading in contracts that give a person a right, but not a duty or requirement, to buy or sell a stock at a certain price by a specific date.

OVER-THE-COUNTER (OTC) MARKET: most day traders do not trade in the OTC market, it's a specific market used to trade in such items as currencies, bonds and interest rates.

PATTERN DAY TRADE RULE: a regulation in the United States that requires day traders in the United States to have at least $25,000 in their account unless they use a non–U.S.-based broker, it does not impact day traders who live in Canada, England, or any other country other than the United States, with that said, other countries might very well enforce similar rules and regulations, before commencing day trading you should contact your local brokers and ask about the minimum requirements for day trading in your jurisdiction.

PENNY STOCK: the shares of small companies that can trade at very low prices, the prices can be very easily manipulated and follow no pattern or rule whatsoever, fraud is rampant in penny stock trading, day traders do not trade penny stocks.

PLAYBOOK: my friend, Mike Bellafiore, in his book, *The PlayBook*, explains how a serious trader can build their trading business, he rightly recommends you build a PlayBook of very specific trades that you trade best, and you then just trade that PlayBook.

POSITION SIZING: refers to how large of a position you can take per trade, it's a technique and skill that new traders must develop but, please remember one of my rules, you must never risk more than 2% of your account in any one trade.

PRE-MARKET TRADING: trading that takes place before the market officially opens at 9:30 a.m. New York time, I personally avoid pre-market trading because since so few traders are trading, you have to trade in very small share sizes, if you are considering pre-market trading, you should check with your broker to see if they permit it, with all of that said though, it's useful to keep an eye on pre-market trading, a stock that is gapping up or down by 2% or more in the pre-market definitely gets my attention and may make my watchlist for the day.

PREVIOUS DAY CLOSE: the price of a stock when the market closes on the previous day, knowing the previous day close of a stock is a useful tool for gauging if a stock may come into play the following day and it is a figure used in a number of strategies and patterns explained in this book.

PRICE ACTION: the movement in price of a stock, I prefer using candlesticks to chart the price action of a stock, capturing its highs and lows and the relationship between the open and close.

PROFIT TARGET: as a day trader, you should have a daily profit target and once you reach it, don't be greedy and risk it, you can turn off your computer and enjoy the rest of your day, in addition, for each trade you set up, you should have a specific profit target that your strategy is based upon.

PROFIT-TO-LOSS RATIO: the key to successful day trading is finding stocks that have excellent prof-it-to-loss ratios, these are the stocks with a low-risk entry and a high reward potential, for example, a 3:1 ratio means you will risk $100 but have the potential to earn $300, a 2:1 ratio is the minimum I will ever trade, also called risk/reward ratio or win:lose ratio.

R: traders often refer to the amount of money risked in a trade as "R", a trade where you lose this risked money is called a -1R trade, a trade where you make twice as much as you risk would be a 2R trade.

REAL TIME MARKET DATA: to be a successful day trader, you need access to real time market data (that you usually must pay for), without any delay, as you will be making decisions and entering and exiting trades literally in minutes, swing traders on the other hand, who enter and exit trades within days or weeks, need only have access to end-of-day data, and that data is available for free on the Internet.

RELATIVE STRENGTH INDEX/RSI: a technical indicator that compares the magnitude of recent gains and losses in the price of stocks over a period of time to measure the speed and change of price movement, your scanner software or platform will automatically calculate the RSI for you, RSI values range from 0 to 100, an extreme RSI below 10 or above 90 will definitely catch my interest.

RETAIL TRADER: individual traders like you and I, we do not work for a firm and we do not manage other people's money.

RISK MANAGEMENT: one of the most important skills that a successful day trader must master, you must find low-risk trading setups with a high reward potential, each trading day you are managing your risk.

RISK/REWARD RATIO: the key to successful day trading is finding trading setups that have excellent risk/reward ratios, these are the trading opportunities with a low-risk entry and a high reward potential, for example, a 3:1 ratio means you will risk $100 but have the potential to earn $300, a 2:1 ratio is the minimum I will ever trade, also called profit-to-loss ratio or win:lose ratio.

S

SCANNER: the software you program with various criteria to find specific stocks to day trade in, Figures 4.2 to 4.5 are screenshots of the scanners I often use.

SHORT: an abbreviated form of "short selling", you borrow shares from your broker, sell them, and hope that the price goes even lower so you can buy them back at a lower price, return the shares to your broker and keep the profit for yourself, to say "*I am short AAPL*" for example means you have borrowed and then sold shares in Apple Inc. and are hoping their price goes even lower.

SHORT INTEREST: the quantity of shares in a stock that have been sold short but not yet covered, it is usually reported at the end of the day, I generally do not trade stocks with a short interest higher than 30%, a high short interest means that traders and investors believe a stock's price will fall.

SHORT SELLING: you borrow shares from your broker and sell them, and then hope the price goes even lower so you can buy them back at the lower price, return the shares to your broker and keep the profit for yourself.

SHORT SELLING RESTRICTION/SSR: a restriction placed on a stock when it is down 10% or more from the previous day's closing price, regulators and the Exchanges place restrictions on the short selling of a stock when its price is dropping, when a stock is in SSR mode, you are still allowed to sell short the stock, but you can only short when the price is going higher, not lower, intraday.

SHORT SQUEEZE: occurs when the short sellers panic and are scrambling to return their borrowed shares to their brokers, their actions cause prices to increase quickly and dangerously, you want to avoid being stuck short in a short squeeze, what you do want to do is ride the squeeze when the price quickly reverses.

SIMPLE MOVING AVERAGE/SMA: a form of moving average that is calculated by adding up the closing price of a stock for a number of time periods and then dividing that figure by the actual number of time periods.

SIMULATOR: it's mandatory for new day traders who wish a successful career to trade in a simulator for several months, you should purchase a simulated account that provides you with real time market data and you should only trade in the share volume and with the amounts of money you will actually be trading with when you go live, simulators are an excellent way to practice using your Hotkeys, to practice creating if-then statements and to practice (and practice some more) your strategies.

SIZE: the "size" column on your Level 2 will indicate how many standard lots of shares (100 shares = 1 standard lot) are being offered for sale or purchase, a "4" for example means 400 shares.

SMALL CAP STOCK: a stock with a low supply of shares which means that a large demand for shares will easily move the stock's price, the stock's price is very volatile and can move fast, most small cap stocks are under $10, some day traders love small cap stocks but do note that they can be really risky, they can also be called low float stocks or micro-cap stocks.

SOCIAL DISTANCING: for traders, social distancing means staying very far away from anyone who thinks the stock market is a get-rich-quick scheme, in light of the 2020 COVID-19 pandemic and social distancing guidelines, protect your wealth by staying away from anyone who think stocks are designed to help you get rich overnight.

SPINNING TOP: a type of candlestick that has similarly sized high wicks and low wicks that are usually larger than the body, they can be called indecision candlesticks and they indicate that the buyers and sellers have equal power and are fighting between themselves, it's important to recognize a spinning top because it may very well indicate a pending price change, Figures 6.6 and 6.7 are examples of spinning tops.

STANDARD LOT: 100 shares, the "size" column on your Level 2 will indicate how many standard lots of shares are being offered for sale or purchase, a "4" for example means 400 shares.

STOCK IN PLAY: this is what you as a day trader are looking for, a Stock in Play is a stock that offers excellent risk/reward opportunities, it will move higher or lower in price during the course of the trading day and it will move in a way that is predictable, stocks with fundamental catalysts (some positive or negative news associated with them such as an FDA approval or disapproval, a restructuring, a merger or an acquisition) are often Stocks in Play.

STOP LOSS: the price level when you must accept a loss and get out of the trade, the maximum amount you should ever risk on a trade is 2% of your account, for example, if your account has $20,000 in it, then you should never risk more than $400 on a single trade, once you calculate the maximum amount of money you can risk on a trade, you can then calculate your maximum risk per share, in dollars, from your entry point, this is your stop loss, your stop loss should always be at a reasonable technical level, in addition, you must honor your stop loss, do not change it in the middle of a trade because you hope something will happen, gracefully exit your trade and accept the loss, do not be stubborn and risk your account.

SUPPORT OR RESISTANCE LEVEL: this is the level that the price of a specific stock usually does not go higher than (resistance level) or lower than (support level), stocks often bounce and change the direction of their price when they reach a support or resistance level, as a day trader you want to monitor these levels because if your timing is correct you can profit from that rapid change in price direction, I provide some detailed commentary in this book on how to find support and resistance levels, the previous day close is one of the most powerful levels of support or resistance, Figure 7.26 is an example of a chart that I have drawn support and resistance lines on.

SWING TRADING: the serious business of trading stocks that you hold for a period of time, generally from one day to a few weeks, swing trading is a completely different business than day trading is.

TICKER: short abbreviations of usually one to five letters that represent the stock at the Exchange, all stocks have ticker symbols, Apple Inc.'s ticker for example is AAPL.

TRADE MANAGEMENT: what you do with your position when you enter a trade and before you exit it, you don't just sit patiently in front of your computer screen with your fingers crossed for good luck and watch what happens, as you monitor and process the information that is changing in front of you, you must adjust and fine-tune the trade you are in, you must be actively engaged in your trade, the only practical way to gain experience in trade management is in a simulator, using the share volume and actual amounts of money you will one day be trading with live.

TRADE PLAN/TRADING PLAN: the plan you develop before you actually enter a trade, it takes hard work to develop a solid trade plan and to then practice sufficient self-discipline to stick with the plan, see also the definition for if-then statement/scenario, be careful to not confuse your trade plan/trading plan with your trading business plan.

TRADING BUSINESS PLAN: trading is a serious business and it is in no way a get-rich-quick scheme, so just like any other business, you should develop a business plan that clearly outlines how you will be successful in your own venture, a trading business plan can be broken down into three main areas: the trading framework, activities designed to improve upon or support the trading framework, and the tasks required to be attended to outside of actual trading, detailed commentary on creating your trading business plan is included in Chapter 10, be careful to not confuse your trading business plan with your trade plan/trading plan.

TRADING FRAMEWORK: the core of your trading business plan, it is what you will execute during market hours, it consists of your money and risk management principles, the strategies and patterns you trade, your trade management rules, and an outline of how you are accountable for any actions which deviate from your framework, detailed commentary on creating your trading framework is included in Chapter 10.

TRADING PLATFORM: a software that traders use for sending orders to the Exchange, brokers will offer you a trading platform that is sometimes for free but often for a fee, platforms are either web-based or as a software that needs to be installed on your computer, your trading platform provides your charting and order execution platform, having a good trading platform is extremely important as it needs to be fast and able to support Hotkeys and excellent charting capabilities, I myself use and recommend DAS Trader, I pay a monthly fee to access their platform and real time data.

VOLUME WEIGHTED AVERAGE PRICE/VWAP: the most important technical indicator for day traders, your trading platform should have VWAP built right into it, VWAP is a moving average that takes into account the volume of the shares being traded at any given price, while other moving averages are calculated based only on the price of the stock on the chart, VWAP considers the number of shares in the stock being traded at each price, VWAP lets you know if the buyers or the sellers are in control of the price action.

WARRANT: a tool used to purchase shares in the future at a set price.

WATCHLIST: before the market opens, you can tell which stocks are gapping up or down in price, you then search for the fundamental catalysts that explain these price swings, and you build a list of stocks that you will monitor that day for specific day trading opportunities, the final version of your watchlist generally has only two, three or four stocks on it that you will be carefully monitoring when the market opens, also called your Gappers watchlist.

WIN:LOSE RATIO: the key to successful day trading is finding stocks that have excellent win:lose ratios, these are the stocks with a low-risk entry and a high reward potential, for example, a 3:1 ratio means you will risk $100 but have the potential to earn $300, a 2:1 ratio is the minimum I will ever trade, also called profit-to-loss ratio or risk/reward ratio.

Printed in Poland
by Amazon Fulfillment
Poland Sp. z o.o., Wrocław
05 March 2022

7220c68a-bdb0-4f3f-9352-7e0a3ce9c9afR01